D1569479

DOES GOVERNMENT NEED TO BE INVOLVED IN PRIMARY AND SECONDARY EDUCATION

NEW DIRECTIONS IN PUBLIC ADMINISTRATION
VOLUME 1
GARLAND REFERENCE LIBRARY
VOLUME 1138

NEW DIRECTIONS IN PUBLIC ADMINISTRATION

CLAIRE L. FELBINGER AND SYLVESTER MURRAY, *Series Editors*
CAROLYN BAN, *Senior Advisor*

DOES GOVERNMENT NEED
TO BE INVOLVED IN PRIMARY
AND SECONDARY EDUCATION
Evaluating Policy Options Using
Market Role Assessment
by Michael T. Peddle

ENVIRONMENTAL JUSTICE
THROUGH RESEARCH-BASED
DECISION-MAKING
by William M. Bowen

DOES GOVERNMENT NEED TO BE INVOLVED IN PRIMARY AND SECONDARY EDUCATION
EVALUATING POLICY OPTIONS USING MARKET ROLE ASSESSMENT

MICHAEL T. PEDDLE

GARLAND PUBLISHING, INC.
NEW YORK & LONDON
2000

Published in 2000 by
Garland Publishing, Inc.
29 West 35th Street
New York, NY 10001

Garland is an imprint of the Taylor & Francis Group

10 9 8 7 6 5 4 3 2 1

Library of Congress Cataloging-in-Publication Data

Peddle, Michael T.
    Does government need to be involved in primary and secondary education :
    evaluating policy options using market role assessment / Michael T. Peddle.
        p. cm. — (Garland reference library of social science ; v. 1138. New
    directions in public administration ; v. 1)
      ISBN 0-8153-2572-X (alk. paper)
        1. Education, Elementary—Government policy—United States—Evaluation.
    2. Education, Secondary—Government policy—United States—Evaluation.
    3. Educational change—Government policy—United States—Evaluation.   I. Title.
    II. Garland reference library of social science ; v. 1138.   III. Garland reference
    library of social science. New directions in public administration ; v. 1.

LC89 .P32 2000
379.1'5'0973—dc21   00-034084

Between the time Website information is gathered and the date of publication,
individual sites may have moved or may no longer be active. Therefore, the
publisher cannot guarantee that the Websites listed herein are accessible at the
URL provided.

Printed on acid-free, 250-year-life paper.
Manufactured in the United States of America

This book is dedicated to all of the teachers who have influenced my life, especially Henry, Jo, and Chris

Contents

Series Editors' Foreword

Welcome to New Directions in Public Administration, a series by Garland Publishing designed to present the exciting work in public administration and to explore cross-cutting issues in public sector management.

It is a time of transition and reform for public administration in practice. Calls for performance-based management at all levels of government require managers to employ new constellations of tools, approaches, and techniques to deal effectively with an increasingly complex environment—one with global implications. Policy makers also require guidance on innovative approaches to addressing policy issues, the solutions to which seldom gain instant consensus.

It is also a time of transition and creativity in public administration theory. New Directions in Public Administration is an outlet for scholars who are pushing the theoretical envelope, exploring new techniques, investigating new issues, and building critical theory which explains and predicts political and managerial phenomena.

The first book in this series, *Does Government Need to Be Involved in Primary and Secondary Education: Evaluating Policy Options Using Market Role Assessment,* is by Michael T. Peddle of Northern Illinois University. Peddle operates under the assumption that primary and secondary education reform is an "ill-structured problem" which, until there is consensus on the definition of the problem, will continue to defy solution. He offers a problem-solving technique, market role assessment, to determine the role of the government in the reform process. He argues that this analytic framework has general application to a wide variety of public policy questions for which there is no consensus on the problem and for which there are multiple solutions. Peddle's work demonstrates a new approach to perennial policy problems.

The second book in the series, *Environmental Justice through Research-Based Decision-Making* by William M. Bowen, will continue this cutting-edge analytic approach to examining this growing policy concern.

Future contributions will focus on administrative reform, race and gender, regionalism, globalization, ethics, and other facets of public administration which provide new directions for the profession. We look forward to providing you the best in public administration scholarship through this series.

Claire L. Felbinger   Sylvester Murray
Washington, D.C.   *Cleveland, OH*

Acknowledgments

This book could not have been written and published without the support and assistance of many individuals. Before expressing my gratitude to some of these people, I must first acknowledge my debt to Northern Illinois University (NIU). The first draft of the manuscript was written while I was on a sabbatical leave granted and funded by the university. My thanks to the university, my colleagues in the College of Liberal Arts and Sciences, Department of Political Science, and Division of Public Administration for the faith they expressed in me and in this book by supporting my request for a sabbatical leave.

I would also like to express my sincere thanks to Pete Trott, director of the Center for Governmental Studies at NIU, and John Lewis, associate director of the center. Pete and John not only made the resources of the center available to support the project but also were respectful of those long periods of time when I needed to disappear in order to complete the manuscript. In some cases, this meant that they needed to take more responsibility for our joint projects. Their support was invaluable. Thank you also to Pat Barger, Paulette Bowman, and Chris Welch, who ably managed my life and kept my distractions to a minimum while I worked on the manuscript.

Thank you to the members of my "education brain trust" who helped to keep me focused, interested, and energized about issues relating to primary and secondary education. Bob Hammon, John Lewis, Suzanne Juday, Dave Wirsing, Bill Stepien, Pete Trott, Carol Zar, Judy Temple, and many others contributed greatly to the book through their thoughtful and insightful conversations with me during the writing process. I thank them for their intellectual stimulation.

I would also like to thank Dick Bingham and David Estrin for their faith early in the project; Carolyn Ban for guiding the manuscript through its beginning, tumultuous phase; Claire Felbinger for caring about the project more than any author could ever expect or deserve; Amy Shipper for kick-starting the final phase of the project; and Mia Zamora for her patient answers to my numerous questions.

My colleagues in the Division of Public Administration at NIU must be acknowledged for their unconditional support of the project. In particular, I thank Jim Banovetz for his encouraging words; Irene Rubin for her patient and willing counsel on publishing books and managing the anxieties of the process; and Heidi Koenig for always being willing to listen, even when she did not have the time.

Finally, I must thank the most important people in my life: my family. Since this project began, my family has expanded as a result of the marriage of my youngest sister, the birth of my two nephews and my niece, and my own marriage to my wife, Chris, that included becoming the proud stepdad to an energetic 10-year-old named Brittany. My family has endured several holidays that included my laptop computer and bulging files as stowaways. The last few months of the project involved many hundreds of hours of work that meant little or no time for my wife and stepdaughter. Nevertheless, they were extremely supportive and understanding. Indeed, Chris helped type the numerous revisions in the final manuscript, a nearly impossible task given the scribblings she had to decipher. Her care and accuracy in helping with the revisions saved me much time and effort, making all the difference in meeting my deadlines and maintaining my sanity. I will never be able to fully express my gratitude to Chris and Brittany for their support. However, it is only fitting that when someone asks me, "Now that you have finished the book, what are you going to do?" I can truthfully and ecstatically answer, "We're going to Disney World!"

DOES GOVERNMENT NEED TO BE INVOLVED IN PRIMARY AND SECONDARY EDUCATION

Prologue

According to a familiar adage, "Give a person a fish and feed her for a day; teach her to fish and feed her forever." Similarly, teachers of analytical subjects such as math, chemistry, and statistics recognize the importance of (1) teaching students problem-solving skills that enable their students to recognize the type of problem with which they are faced, and (2) teaching the requisite analytical tools necessary to produce a well-reasoned answer.[1] In this book, a problem-solving framework is introduced that can be used to analyze a wide variety of public policy problems. This framework is demonstrated through an analysis of some of the policy issues related to government's role in the reform of primary and secondary education in the United States.

This book represents the product of several years of personal frustration with the public policymaking process in general, as well as the lack of progress toward meaningful reform in primary and secondary education in my home state of Illinois in particular. This frustration has become more focused as a result of numerous discussions I have had with policymakers and policy observers that have convinced me that primary and secondary education reform remains an "ill-structured problem."[2] Recognizing the ill-structured nature of the problem offers an explanation as to why issues regarding primary and secondary education generally have defied solution, at least through application of one of the set of familiar policy remedies comfortably applied to more well-structured problems. It also suggests a reason why primary and secondary education reform has at best been addressed in a limited manner and by a limited number of jurisdictions or communities.

Despite the importance and pressing societal implications of school reform, in most jurisdictions such reform has not been addressed in a coordinated and comprehensive manner. Yet, judging by the attention given to primary and secondary education in the popular press, in election campaigns, in legislative debates, and in academic journals, lack of interest does not appear to be the major factor explaining the singular lack of success in making substantive progress on primary and secondary school reform. Such is usually the fate of ill-structured problems.

Ill-structured problems tend to be particularly difficult for the average person to solve. Unfortunately, many if not most public policy issues represent ill-structured problems (Voss, Greene, Post, and Penner 1983). Thus, it is important for the contemporary public administrator to understand the basic nature of such problems in order to be a more effective participant in the public policy process. Support for this notion can be discerned in the public policy literature.

The importance of problem definition in public policy is an issue that has been addressed by a number of authors in recent years.[3] In particular, "much research has catalogued the wide disparity in problem definition by relevant stakeholders and the damage that this lack of consensus contributes to the failure of problem solving" (Scavo, Simon, and Siemienska 1999, p. 3). The authors go on: "Such disparities in the definition of these major societal problems make solutions to these problems much less likely since those who are responsible for solving the problems look to completely different factors for solutions." A primary goal of this book is to offer an analytical framework that will assist diverse stakeholders in coming to agreement about problem definition. With this assistance, stakeholders will greatly increase their chances of formulating a set of possible solutions that can be evaluated for feasibility and relative strength. Developing an analytical framework for public policy problem definition in no way ensures formulation of a politically desirable solution or solution set that diverse groups can support. However, few if any solutions can even be identified in the absence of an agreed-upon framework within which the problem can be defined.

Primary and secondary education reform is used as the public policy issue within which the problem definition framework is explained. However, it should be noted that the framework developed in the book and used to analyze government's role in school reform is one that has general applications to a wide variety of public policy problems. The framework is designed to be easy to use. In particular, it should be of benefit to public administrators as they formulate reports for their legislative bodies and as they seek to be responsive, accountable, and informative to their government's constituents.

The reform of primary and secondary education represents the type of ill-structured public policy problem that is often very difficult to solve. In particular, such reform represents an issue whose boundaries are not clearly defined, and as a result the menu of possible reform strategies is even less clearly understood or defined. These traits alone are sufficient to classify primary and secondary education reform as an ill-structured problem (Simon 1973). "Mason and Mitroff . . . describe ill-structured problems as being difficult to define, often allowing more than a single path to solution, and requiring action steps in spite of ambiguities" (Stepien and Pyke 1997, p. 384). But why does this observation matter for the teaching and learning of public policy analysis, for education policy in particular, or for the analysis presented in this book? Interest in ill-structured problems and their solution is driven by several factors.

First, problem definition is intimately related to one's ability to solve a problem. For example, statistics students are able to solve even the most complex problems once the class or category (e.g., hypergeometric, binomial, Poisson) of problem has been identified for them. Similarly, math students working on story problems know they need to define each problem before working on its solution.[4]

The link between difficulty in problem definition and difficulty in problem solution exists for a variety of reasons. Uncertainty seems to wreak havoc with the human psyche—even when the underlying problem is well structured, as is the case with many story problems. Few people are comfortable trying to solve ill-structured problems, mainly because of lack of training and experience. Part of this is owing to the problem definition that is required to solve an ill-structured problem. "One reason for the lack of fit between problem solving for well-structured and ill-structured problems is that well-structured problems do not require that students engage in *problem finding* as part of the overall process of finding a solution" (Gallagher, Stepien, and Rosenthal 1992, p. 195). Ironically, many of the most interesting and pervasive problems faced in society are ill structured, and most Nobel prizes are won for solutions to ill-structured problems. The contemporary public administrator deals with such problems on a day-to-day basis. Indeed, much of the seminal work on ill-structured problems themselves was done by Nobel laureate Herbert A. Simon, a name familiar to all students of public administration, though few are likely to have been introduced to this area of his work or to ill-structured problem solution *per se*.

Yet, methods for approaching and producing solutions or solution sets to ill-structured problems are not terribly hard or intimidating to learn. Indeed, creative problem-solving is being taught and encouraged in many elementary schools (Gallagher 1997). Disciplines such as economics and chemistry have been built on the analysis of ill-structured problems. The practice of forensic medicine involves the repetitive solution of problems that are often ill structured, and diagnoses in medicine are obtained through the solution of ill-structured problems (Brandon and Majumdar 1997; Mandin, Jones, Woloschuk, and Harasym 1997). Books have been written extolling the virtues of problem-based learning for administrators (Bridges 1992). Thus, the solution of ill-structured problems has broad applicability in numerous disciplinary frameworks.[5]

Second, ill-structured problems are usually characterized by multiple solutions, more than one of which may be viewed as correct or acceptable at a given point in time or under a given set of circumstances. Public administrators will recognize this characteristic in many policy decisions they are asked to make. Learning to evaluate multiple solutions is an important life skill, one that is especially crucial in solving those problems that may be characterized as ill structured. Cost-benefit analysis is generally based on the analysis of an ill-structured problem, and algorithms such as the cost-benefit ratio, net present value, and internal rate of return of projects provide alternative methods of choosing between the multiple solutions often presented in cost-benefit problems.

Third, most substantial public policy issues can be viewed as ill-structured problems, and the study of solving such problems has received very little attention (e.g., see Voss, Greene, Post, and Penner 1983). Gun control, abortion rights, welfare, and tax preferences are examples of current policy issues that fit the definition of ill-structured problems. Understanding the nature of these problems and their solution greatly assists in understanding and making progress in many contentious public policy debates.

Fourth, and perhaps most important, the application of conventional problem solution techniques to ill-structured problems by "novice" problem solvers generally results in outcomes that are hastily arrived at, incomplete, and costly in terms of wasted time and effort, including undoing the consequences of the inappropriate decision. Thus, policy outcomes can be improved through increased awareness of the notion of ill-structured problems and their solution. Moreover, solution of ill-structured problems in the social sciences is further complicated by two factors that Voss et al. (1983 p. 169) identify as the *lack of agreed upon solutions* and the *delay of implementation.* These factors have implications for the range of solutions that can be considered in addressing social science problems.

This book seeks to provide a thorough discussion and evaluation of government's role in primary and secondary school reform in the context of a problem structuring technique that is applicable to a wide variety of public policy issues. The analysis is firmly grounded in the conception of primary and secondary school reform as an ill-structured problem. Although the primary focus of the book is on explanation and application of the problem structuring technique, it is hoped that some insight into appropriate paths for primary and secondary school reform will be a secondary benefit. However, one should not be deluded into thinking that this book will provide magical reform ideas for immediate application in the schools. Indeed, the intent of the book's substantive analysis of primary and secondary education is to provide perspective related to *government's role* in school reform rather than the merits of specific reform ideas such as classroom innovations and changes in the structure of educational physical plants.[6] Retaining this focus is important, given the immense and ill-structured nature of primary and secondary school reform as a public policy issue. Conventional problem solution methods generally do little to prevent diversions that may ultimately hinder resolution of the problem.

The problem structuring technique around which this book is organized is straightforward and broad in its application to a variety of public policy problems. It is grounded in (1) the identification of various roles that can be played by economic actors in a market for any good or service, and (2) the assessment of the appropriate division of role responsibilities among the candidate actors. For this reason, the technique can be called *market role assessment.*

Market role assessment makes use of many concepts and tools familiar to public finance economists. Even though effective use of market role assessment as a tool for problem definition and analysis of ill-structured public policy problems does not require one to be an economist, it does require some appreciation for the economic framework that provides the skeleton upon which we can build our public policy tool.[7]

The book begins with a brief but thorough discussion of government's role in a mixed economy[8] as generally defined by economists. The primary goal of this discussion is to develop an understanding of the general boundaries of public sector and private sector action.[9] Progress toward solution of an ill-structured problem requires an attempt to circumscribe the problem through application of a boundary framework that enables the issue to be considered in a more static decision environment. One seeks to place finite boundaries on the problem so as to make its conception and solution more conceivable and tractable.

Ted Gaebler, co-author of *Reinventing Government* (Osborne and Gaebler 1992), teaches a variant of this circumscription technique in his entrepreneurial government workshops. He suggests an eight-step method for conducting a rigorous reappraisal of functions, policies, or projects. Such a reappraisal is analogous to the mission of this book with respect to market role assessment and its application to primary and secondary school reform. Gaebler (1996) outlines eight questions to be answered as part of a critical reappraisal, all of which will be addressed at some level in this book in subsequent discussions using market role assessment. Gaebler states his questions as follows:

- Should the activity continue to be done by government?
- Should the activity continue to be done by this level of government?
- Should government be doing this with partners or with alternative funding sources such as grants?
- Should a government corporation (enterprise funds, franchise, or privatization) be considered?
- Is the activity critical to the organizational mission *based on customer input?*
- Is it time to terminate or obliterate the program, function, or rules?
- Can ways be found to cut costs or improve performance by introducing competition?

- Can service be improved by putting customers first, empowering employees, and eliminating red tape?

It should be noted that such circumscribing assumptions or questions, when correctly formulated, represent simplifications of reality rather than distortions of reality. Furthermore, the failure to impose such a boundary framework generally renders solution, or progress toward solution, of an ill-structured problem nearly impossible. With respect to the issue of primary and secondary school reform, a beginning point in defining school reform is provided by a recent monograph from the National Conference of State Legislatures. "Reforms include changes in how schools are run, how teachers teach and how they learn to teach, and how students learn. There is a new emphasis on integrated services and partnerships with businesses and the community" (Zinser 1994, back cover). Even in the context of this useful contribution to setting reform boundaries, government's role remains ambiguously defined at best. We now begin our effort to understand market role assessment and to use it to define and analyze the issue of government's role in school reform.

NOTES

[1]For example, see Charles and Silver (1988).

[2]Ill-structured problems exhibit the following characteristics: (1) in order to be understood, more information than is initially available is needed; (2) the problem definition changes as new information is added; (3) many perspectives can be used to interpret information; and (4) no absolutely "right" answer exists (Barrows 1990).

[3]For example, Kingdon (1995) presents an entire section on the importance of problem definition in public policy.

[4]It should be noted that mathematicians who advocate greater use of problem-based learning often do not consider traditional story problems to be either ill-structured problems or good teaching tools (Charles and Silver, 1988).

[5]Boud and Feletti (1991) present problem-based learning applications from at least fifteen disciplines, including social work, law, management, and economics.

[6]However, many reform ideas relate fundamentally to the appropriate role of government in the market for primary and secondary education. As such, some discussion of the relative merits of certain reforms will be appropriate and inevitable.

[7]The National Association of Schools of Public Affairs and Administration (NASPAA) accreditation standards for Master of Public Administration (MPA) programs encourage this kind of appreciation through a standard that requires institutions to use their curriculum to expose students to economics and economic institutions.

[8]A mixed economy is one that has both a private and a public sector.

[9]Although the appropriate role for government in the economy remains very controversial, the boundaries discussed in Chapter 1 generally are not the source of controversy. Rather, it is the determination of whether given situations are inside or outside the boundaries that creates disagreement.

An Introduction to Market Role Assessment
Government's Functions in a Mixed Economy

As mentioned in the Prologue, market role assessment can be a particularly useful part of the tool kit of contemporary public administrators. With government coming under increasing fiscal stress; debate regarding privatization of certain governmental activities; calls for improved accountability; and more emphasis on responsiveness and accountability to constituents, it is essential to understand the foundations for government involvement in the economy; this is an important ingredient in making good public policy decisions. The contemporary public administrator can benefit from being well versed in the application and use of market role assessment.

Market role assessment can be put to use directly as part of the public policy decisionmaking process and in the analysis of public policy proposals, including those brought forth by elected officials, interest groups, and citizens in general. At the most basic level, the framework provided by market role assessment enables the contemporary public administrator to evaluate his or her institution's relationship to its environment, as well as to assess the appropriateness of changes in that relationship or role.

Our introduction to market role assessment will proceed in two steps. First, government's functions in a mixed economy will be discussed and explored in this chapter. Then, market roles and their use as an analytical tool will be developed in Chapter 2.

Exploration of the use of market role assessment for analysis requires a clear understanding of how government's functions can be defined in a mixed economy. The framework outlined in this chapter represents a description of a mainstream formulation of government's economic role.[1] This formulation is not only the general foundation on which government provision of goods and services to constituents is justified and built, but it is also the foundation on which general boundaries are constructed between public sector and private sector activities. It is from this foundation that an understanding of market role assessment and its use as an analytical tool will be built.

A modern economy would have great difficulty surviving in the absence of a government. Even the most ardent libertarians and modern conservatives acknowledge that (at least conceptually) government is necessary, although many might say it is a *necessary evil*. At the same time, one might note that events of the past decade or so in Eastern Europe, the former Soviet Union, and China have reinforced the importance of *markets* to the sustainability and vitality of an economy.

An economy with both a private sector and a public sector, linked through the operation of markets, can be referred to as a mixed economy. The notion of a mixed economy describes the economic structure of nearly every country in the world, which speaks to the general applicability of the following analysis.

The characteristics and typical operation of a mixed economy leave several important functions for government. Among these functions are the following:

- establishment and enforcement of a legal framework that makes voluntary economic transactions within a price system[2] a viable means of economic interaction;
- adjusting market outcomes to aid in more closely conforming to collective notions of fairness or equity; and
- interventions designed to mitigate private market failures.

Stated in another way, government is asked to provide a framework that allows for the smooth operation of the price system, a framework for adjusting "undesirable" market outcomes that may result even when the market system performs as expected or designed, and a framework for adjusting "undesirable" market outcomes produced as a result of the assumptions of a perfectly competitive market system being violated.[3] These three generic roles for government are instructive of the broad expectations often placed on government[4] with respect to economic performance. This point becomes even clearer when we examine each role in more depth.

A FRAMEWORK FOR OPERATION OF THE PRICE SYSTEM

The smooth operation of a private market system requires much more than the application of simple assumptions like those underlying the circular flow model[5] presented at the beginning of a Principles of Economics course. For example, as students of comparative economic systems know, the circular flow assumption of a basic attribute such as private ownership of resources is not met in all economies. Furthermore, notions of private property and property rights do not appear to have a natural existence apart from explicit efforts to define and enforce the concepts. Yet, notions of private property and property rights are fundamental to the operation of a market system based upon voluntary economic transactions. Government plays an integral role in helping to define and enforce a legal framework within which a market system can operate more smoothly. This fundamental and overarching government function manifests itself in several ways.

Government generally is the institution through which property rights are defined and enforced.[6] Voluntary economic exchange is also fostered through the establishment and enforcement of contract law. The police powers granted to governments by constitution or statute help ensure orderly structure and reliable law enforcement or other types of intervention in the name of general welfare.[7] It should be noted that the nature of property rights and protection of the process and outcomes of voluntary economic transactions vary from nation to nation and government to government.

In the United States, the primary definition and enforcement of property rights occur through federal law (which may be administered through state and local judicial systems), whereas police powers are retained and exercised by all general purpose governments.[8] Furthermore, the definition of intellectual property rights in the United States is broader and these rights are more aggressively enforced than in most other countries. As an aside, this has created significant international relations issues as the U.S. government actively assists businesses and individuals in protecting their intellectual property from foreign piracy, counterfeiting, and patent infringement. Indeed, this has been a barrier in numerous recent trade negotiations, because many nations do not view intellectual property protection with the same priority that the United States does. This suggests that different market roles for government may be observed across nations with respect to intellectual property rights.

We now turn to other government functions in a mixed economy.

INTERVENTION TO IMPROVE MARKET OUTCOMES

The unfettered operation of a system of perfectly competitive markets[9] results in an economically efficient outcome, also referred to as a Pareto efficient outcome.[10] Pareto efficiency refers to a condition in which no person can be made better off without making at least one other person worse off. This said, it should be noted that the notion of economic efficiency is a distinctly positive, not normative, criterion. The criterion effectively differentiates between inefficient and efficient outcomes, but it offers no assistance in choosing between efficient outcomes or between inefficient outcomes. Thus, although an economic outcome may be produced by an unfettered system of perfectly competitive markets, and therefore be efficient in the economic sense, this same outcome may not be deemed a "good" outcome or a preferred outcome when evaluated on other criteria besides efficiency.

It is quite easy to develop scenarios in which an inefficient outcome would generally[11] be preferred to an efficient one, *but this preference will be grounded in criteria other than that of efficiency.* Thus, circumstances may be identified in which the market "works" in the sense of an economically efficient outcome but produces an undesirable outcome. In particular, market outcomes that are otherwise efficient are often criticized for being unfair or unjust.

One should note that when economists go about analyzing the gains from trade or the results of the operation of the free market from the perspective of economic efficiency, they typically assume that the initial endowments or shares of resources are fixed. An extreme but illuminating example of this analysis can be seen in an exercise known as the "divide a dollar" game.

The rules of this game are quite simple: two participants are asked to divide up one dollar in any way they choose. In the absence of (1) unequal power between the two individuals, or (2) an initial division of the dollar by the arbiter of the game, one might expect an equal division of the dollar. Not only would this division seem "fair" to most people, but it is evident that any other division would make one of the participants worse off, thereby qualifying the solution as a Pareto efficient outcome.[12] What is often less clear to observers of the game is that *any* division of the dollar would be Pareto efficient. Furthermore, *on the basis of efficiency,* one cannot choose one outcome over another, even if the division were to leave one person with the entire dollar and the other person with nothing.

Carrying the "divide a dollar" example just a bit further, imagine that the game began with the dollar divided in some fashion between the two participants by the game arbiter. Again, any such division would represent a Pareto efficient outcome, and there would be no reason to expect any trade or redivision of the dollar to result from voluntary action of the participants, because one of the participants would by necessity be made worse off by any exchange between the parties. However, it should be noted that the outcome of the game under these circumstances is determined by the initial division of the dollar by the arbiter.[13]

The initial division of the dollar is analogous to the endowment of resources with which one enters a market system. The efficient workings of the market system cannot overcome inequities in initial resource endowments, nor can it ensure that any market outcome meets any normative equity standard. To the extent that one values equity in economic outcomes and that the equity notion is not fulfilled by the operation of the unfettered market, one might look to outside intervention for improvement of market outcomes. The most common source of such outside intervention is government.

There are numerous examples of government intervening in markets to make outcomes more just or equitable, but it is once again important to distinguish between two distinct situations in which such intervention might take place: situations in which the market has operated soundly from the point of view of economic theory, and situations in which the market has failed to operate appropriately owing to a violation of one or more of the perfect competition assumptions. Our current discussion focuses on government interventions of the first type, whereas the next section of the chapter focuses on interventions that address the other set of situations, those economists generally call market failures.

As one example of an unpleasant market outcome, a worker may lose his or her job as a result of economic restructuring like that which has occurred in the U.S. steel industry and the U.S. textile industry. In such a case, one could argue that the market system has worked, through the reallocation of resources and job opportunities to industries and areas of the world where those resources find their greatest economic returns. Furthermore, the U.S. experience has indicated that many workers who are displaced by economic restructuring often remain unemployed or under employed as a result of lacking skills that are in high demand in the labor market (Reich 1991; Carnevale 1991; Krugman 1994; Barlett and Steele 1996).

Government intervention has often taken place in such situations. This intervention has ranged from subsidies to industries adversely affected by economic restructuring, to unemployment payments to displaced workers, to retraining programs targeted at displaced workers.[14] Indeed, one of the very significant issues in local economic development and higher education is the appropriate delivery of education and training programs to assist workers who are displaced or placebound, or whose skills are mismatched with the needs of local employers. Although primary and secondary education constitute an integral part of many of these solutions (e.g., school-to-work, cooperative education, English as a Second Language), the relationship among education, training, economic competitiveness, and government action is much richer and more controversial.[15]

Similarly, the government has intervened on behalf of other labor market participants who have had trouble finding employment as a result of skill deficiencies and other market-based barriers. Programs such the Comprehensive Employment and Training Act (CETA) and the Job Training Partnership Act (JTPA) were designed to help overcome barriers to employment that were grounded in the workings of the market. Pell Grants were designed to help fund education for those who would be precluded from purchasing higher education services at a market-driven price. School lunch programs are designed to improve nutrition among children whose families may not be able to regularly purchase the ingredients for nutritious meals or who may not understand the components of such meals. Thus, one need not look far to find examples of a wide variety of government interventions designed to improve market outcomes—including many that apply to education in general, and to the market for primary and secondary education in particular.

We now turn our attention to government interventions designed to improve outcomes in cases where the market has failed, (i.e., not produced a Pareto efficient outcome.)

INTERVENTION TO MITIGATE PRIVATE MARKET FAILURES

The conditions that must be met by a system of markets in order to ensure a Pareto efficient outcome are numerous and difficult to fulfill. The violation of any one of the assumptions of perfect competition may lead to undesirable market outcomes. Unlike the undesirable outcomes discussed in the previous section, this category of deficient outcomes is produced by a failure of the market system to achieve an efficient outcome owing to violation of one or more of the conditions required of a system of perfectly competitive markets. Such outcomes are called market failures.

Economic efficiency is a crucial condition in terms of resource allocation and consumer choice. When the conditions of perfectly competitive markets are met, market prices are accurate reflections of the valuation of goods and services by buyers and sellers, and the prices serve a rationing function. That is, the price a buyer is willing to pay under perfectly competitive circumstances is an accurate reflection of the value that buyer places on that unit of the product. Similarly, the price a seller is willing to accept for a unit of a product is an accurate reflection of the price required to compensate the seller for the costs of production, including a market-determined profit that serves as the return to entrepreneurial services. The effective operation of a perfectly competitive market system means that resources will be allocated to their highest value uses, the goods and services produced in the market will be those most desired by consumers, and products will be produced by the most efficient producers and purchased by those consumers who place the highest value on consumption of that good or service.

Unfortunately, the conditions required for such desirable allocative outcomes are rarely met in unfettered markets. Because government provides the major alternative to the market system in allocating resources, government is often looked to first as a mechanism for mitigating the deficiencies present in the unfettered operation of the market system. Fundamentally, the "government option" substitutes a system of political institutions, through which collective choice decisions are made and implemented, for a set of private institutions grounded in voluntary economic transactions between individuals that are based on rational, self-interested behavior. Some examples will help to illuminate the possible types of market failure and the generic function of government in helping to overcome these deficiencies.

Violations of the assumptions of perfect competition are common. They include such things as: market power, asymmetric information (including product safety issues), externalities,[16] discrimination, incomplete markets, unemployment, and inflation.[17] Each of these violations creates a disparity between the price upon which buyers make their purchase decisions and the price upon which sellers base their production and sales decisions. This disparity results in inefficiencies in the allocation of both resources and goods and services. Prices no longer serve a rationing function.

Government's role varies in helping to alleviate the effects of these deficiencies in market operations, but generally government intervention is designed to compensate in some way for the particular deficiencies in unfettered market operations. Some interventions, such as taxes and/or subsidies designed to offset the effects of externalities, are intended to make external adjustments to market conditions, which will then allow the market to achieve an efficient outcome without further intervention.

Government-based product testing and health/safety regulations are intended to help overcome asymmetric information problems that may exist in the market. That is, these measures are designed to help address deficiencies in the information available to consumers regarding the risks associated with products they wish to purchase, especially risks that are known (or could reasonably be expected to be known) by the seller.

In the case of market-based monopolies (i.e., monopolies based upon the ability of a given market to support the output of only one firm), the government may regulate the firm to approximate the outcome that might be expected from a competitive market. In the case of market power grounded in other barriers to entry, government intervention often takes the form of statutes outlawing collusive and predatory behavior. These statutes once again represent attempts to externally encourage behavior that more closely approximates that which would be expected in a perfectly competitive market.

Even though government interventions are often successful in improving the outcome produced by unfettered markets, rarely is a government intervention sufficient to restore perfectly competitive conditions or to produce an economically efficient outcome (especially when one notes that there is generally some cost associated with the government intervention). Indeed, economists define government failure as the failure to reach an efficient outcome through the use of politically based or collective choice tools such as those used in the public sector. Nevertheless, even in cases properly characterized as government failure, in many situations government intervention provides outcomes that are preferred by society to those of the unfettered market system. However, it should be noted that there is no theoretical reason that a government intervention will necessarily improve a market outcome; indeed, many successful government interventions involve introducing distortions into the economy to counteract the distortions present in the unfettered market system.[18] Furthermore, in some cases private alternatives to government intervention are possible and have worked.

Two familiar examples are Underwriters Laboratories and Consumers Union, organizations that provide information to consumers that helps offset otherwise asymmetric market information. College ratings by *U.S. News, Barron's,* the *Yale Daily News,* and others are all designed to help fill the information void for prospective college students. Unfortunately, the choices of educational institutions are much narrower for the average primary and secondary student, private education institutions generally do not compete as directly in primary and secondary education as they do in higher education, and the cost/benefit equation seems to make asymmetric market information about primary and secondary education a difficult, if not impossible, problem to overcome at present. However, a number of the reform efforts discussed later in the book may go a long way toward overcoming some of the serious market failures identified by critics of the current primary and secondary education system in the United States.

CONCLUSION

Understanding the generic functions that government plays in mixed economies allows us to more intelligently explore through market role assessment the role of government in the market for a particular good or service. Having explored the general functions of government in a mixed economy in this chapter, in Chapter 2 we turn our attention first to the importance of defining the characteristics of a good or service as an important part of the market role assessment process. The concept of market roles is then developed, and a framework for utilizing market role assessment as an analytical tool is explained.

NOTES

[1]For example, see Hyman (1996) for a discussion of government's role in the economy.

[2]A price system is an exchange system that is based upon the transactions that occur as a result of buyers and sellers finding trading partners by signaling through prices their willingness to buy or sell.

[3]When the assumptions underlying a system of perfectly competitive markets are violated, the allocation of resources, resource uses, and output is no longer guaranteed to be economically efficient (as it is in a system of perfectly competitive markets). In simple terms, this inefficiency means that (1) resources are not necessarily being put to their highest and best use, and (2) goods and services are not necessarily being allocated to those individuals and organizations that most highly value them.

[4]In a federal system of government, the roles of government are played with different intensity by the different levels of government. For example, the federal government in the United States has primary responsibility for the property rights framework and enforcement structure that provides the foundation for the smooth

operation of the price system. On the other hand, local governments generally have the greatest responsibility for the provision of everyday goods and services to the average citizen.

[5]The circular flow model provides an extremely simple representation of an economy. In its most basic form, the model describes an economy in which all resources are privately owned, all production is done by businesses, and all transactions take place in two sets of markets—one for resources or inputs, and one for finished goods and services. The model describes the movement of resources and products in an economy through two "circular flows" that link households and businesses through the markets. The basic form of the model has no government. An enhanced version of the circular flow model includes a government sector and provides an excellent, easily understandable, and visual depiction of the complications that result when government is introduced into a previously unfettered market system. In particular, the introduction of government means that there is an additional resource-using body in the economy, as well as another economic institution competing for goods and services. Hyman (1996) provides an excellent discussion and illustration of this model.

[6]It is often argued by legal scholars that property rights do not exist in the absence of government and that they are the result of collective choices made through government. See Cordes (1996) for a more thorough discussion of this point.

[7]It should be noted that government definition and enforcement of property rights, as well as the exercise of police powers, can have perverse and adverse consequences, especially when government action takes place outside of representative democracy. The confiscation of property from large groups such as the Jews during World War II was done through the exercise of police powers and property rights definitions. Retrospective application of more democratically rooted property rights are at the heart of recent efforts to recover the proceeds of Jews' Swiss bank accounts and other property that was unlawfully seized or lawfully hidden during this period.

[8]That is, federal, state, county, and municipal governments in most situations.

[9]A system of perfectly competitive markets, by definition, satisfies the following assumptions: There are numerous buyers and sellers in each market (i.e., diffuse economic power); there is full and free information; there is free entry and exit in all periods longer than the short run; all transactions take place in markets; and markets exist for all goods and services. When all these assumptions are simultaneously satisfied, the system of markets will produce economically efficient (i.e., Pareto efficient) outcomes.

[10]Economic efficiency is generally defined in terms of the notion of Pareto efficiency.

[11]Recalling that normative criteria are built upon value systems, one can only speculate about the likelihood of a given situation being judged as good or preferred. Nevertheless, in a society like ours, certain values are held widely enough so as to make such assertions about probable outcomes more than mere idle speculation.

[12]Recall that a Pareto efficient outcome is a state in which it is not possible to improve the well-being of any individual without making at least one other individual worse off.

[13]Without loss of generality, the same division also could have been performed in a random fashion.

[14]Numerous books have been written about government interventions related to economic restructuring. These include Reich (1987, 1991); Barlett and Steele (1996).

[15]See Reich (1991) and Peddle (1999) for further discussion of the links among education and training, economic development, and government's role in the economy.

[16]Externalities are costs or benefits from economic behavior that flow to third parties not directly involved in the behavior or transaction. For example, the loud playing of a stereo in a university residence hall room imposes a cost (i.e., a negative externality) on individuals who are trying to study in other rooms. Alternatively, passersby enjoy the beauty and fragrance of a flower garden as a positive externality of the care and attention given by the gardener. Third parties typically would not be compensated for negative externalities or charged for positive externalities in an unfettered market system, nor would the producers of negative externalities be charged or the producers of positive externalities be subsidized.

[17]For further information, see any introductory public finance text (e.g., Hyman 1996).

[18]For example, taxes and subsidies designed to internalize externalities.

CHAPTER 2

Market Role Assessment
Economic Goods and Market Roles

A role played by government in a mixed economy involves providing an alternative to the market allocation mechanism.[1] As explained in Chapter 1, government provides a desirable alternative to the unfettered market in two circumstances: cases in which the market works properly but produces an efficient outcome that is in some way not desirable, and cases in which the market does not work properly owing to a violation of one or more of the assumptions of perfect competition. Situations in the latter category are often referred to as market failures. Market failure is a common justification for government intervention in the market system. Among the general types of market failures are: market power, asymmetric information, externalities, discrimination, incomplete markets, unemployment, and inflation. Several of these forms of market failure are intimately linked to the characteristics of the good or service of interest. Therefore, it is important to understand the linkage between the characteristics of goods and services and the potential for market failure.[2]

Everyday life, even in the simplest of societies, involves the production and consumption of a wide variety of goods and services. Each of these goods and services is used to satisfy some human need or preference, and each item embodies a variety of attributes that help to define its ability to satisfy some human need or preference either directly or indirectly. The attributes of goods and services help to categorize these items into meaningful groupings that assist in differentiating commodities. For example, one can categorize a group of edible items as food, another group of items as shelter, and still another group of items as clothing on the basis of their shared characteristics and use.

Although such distinctions are very useful, one can distinguish between types of goods in a less familiar manner, one that assists in evaluating the relative attractiveness of using the market or using government as the primary means of allocating and distributing a given good or service. Economists generally define four categories of goods as differentiated by the characteristics of *rivalry* and *excludability*. Rivalry and excludability are useful in categorizing goods and services; they also represent crucial characteristics that can assist in analyzing the respective roles of the public sector and the private sector in the "market" for a particular good or service. The rivalry and excludability characteristics of goods and services provide a means of making preliminary judgments regarding the potential need for some type of public sector involvement in the market for a particular good or service.

In the simplest terms, the more excludable and rivalrous a good is, the more likely that the private sector should be primarily and exclusively involved in its market.[3] On the other hand, the more nonrivalrous and nonexcludable a good proves to be, the more likely that there is a significant role for the public sector to play in the market for the good.[4] Exploring these characteristics in more detail will help clarify these important concepts.

CLASSIFYING GOODS AND SERVICES BY RIVALRY AND EXCLUDABILITY

Rivalry in consumption is similar to the notion of a zero-sum game.[5] Consumption of a good is rivalrous if one consumer's consumption of the good or service precludes another consumer from consuming the same unit of the good or service. For example, an apple is rivalrous in consumption because if person A eats the apple, then that apple is no longer available for person B to eat. That is, any person's consumption of a rivalrous commodity reduces the amount available for consumption by other people. Alternatively, at least at some level, solar energy consumption is nonrivalrous. One person's use of solar panels to capture solar energy does not generally reduce the amount of solar energy available for other persons to consume.[6]

Excludability involves the ability to prevent persons who do not pay for a good or service from consuming that good or service. With substantial effort and the design of elaborate exclusion mechanisms, one can typically find a means of excluding nonpayers for almost any good or service. However, such exclusion efforts tend to be costly and may exceed the value of the good or service that is produced. Thus, excludability is defined somewhat more restrictively for reasons of practicality and application. That is, for a good to satisfy the exclusion principle and have the property of excludability, it must be *feasible* (i.e., practical) to exclude nonpayers from consuming units of the good or service. If a good or service does not satisfy the exclusion principle, theoretically its units cannot be priced in the market, because consumers who do not pay cannot be prevented from consuming the product, and sellers/producers could not be compensated for their costs or efforts.

Goods and services can be divided into four categories on the basis of rivalry and excludability. *(Pure) private goods* are those that are both rivalrous in consumption and excludable. Examples of such goods are easy to formulate. Processed food items are rivalrous in consumption, and units can be withheld from individuals who do not pay, whereas the good can be provided on a unit-by-unit basis to paying consumers. Traditional durable goods such as refrigerators and stoves would also fit into the category of private goods. Personal services such as hairstyling and massage therapy would also be examples of private goods because they are rivalrous in consumption and excludable. As one can see, a wide variety of goods and services can satisfy the conditions necessary to be classified as private goods. Within the realm of the primary and secondary education system, at some level many of the goods and services that are provided as a part of a primary and secondary education system and its operations fit this definition of a pure, private good. For example, a school lunch prepared in a school cafeteria would be both rivalrous and excludable,[7] as would consumable school supplies such as pencils, paper, and crayons.

The other extreme of the spectrum of classification consists of goods and services that are nonrivalrous in consumption and for which exclusion is not feasible. These goods and services are classified as *(pure) public goods.* In terms of rivalry, the characteristics of pure public goods are such that one individual's consumption of a given unit of the good or service does not preclude another individual from simultaneously obtaining the benefits from that same unit of the good or service. Alternatively, one person's consumption of the good or service does not reduce the amount of the good or service that is available for other persons to consume. With respect to excludability, pure public goods are such that it is not feasible to exclude persons who do not pay for the good or service from consuming units of that good or service. That is, once the good or service is produced and provided to one individual, the good or service is made available to other individuals with no feasible possibility of preventing these or other individuals from consuming the good or service, whether or not they pay for their consumption.[8] The classic example of a pure public good is national defense. A certain level of defense is provided to a given geographic area, and no individual's consumption of defense services within this area reduces the amount of defense available to other individuals in the area. Similarly, all individuals in the geographic area are protected equally whether they pay for the services or not, because defense cannot feasibly be withheld from a subset of individuals living in the area being protected. For example, if there were an antiaircraft gun in person A's backyard, next door neighbor person B's life and property would be protected by the gun regardless of his or her contribution to the cost of maintaining or operating the gun.

Although pure public goods and pure private goods are relatively easy to talk about from a theoretical point of view, careful analysis and thought often lead one to waver in classifying goods into these extreme categories. Indeed, the richness and utility of the classification system and its applicability to market role assessment is revealed through consideration of the intermediate classifications of goods and services along the dimensions of rivalry and excludability. These intermediate classifications consist of goods that are (1) rivalrous in consumption but for which exclusion of nonpayers is not feasible, or (2) nonrivalrous in consumption but for which exclusion of nonpayers remains feasible. Even though economists readily talk about these important categories of goods, no universal nomenclature has been attached to these types of goods and services. Owing to the importance of these categories of goods in ensuing discussions, the first category of goods or services will be identified as *nonexcludable private goods* and the second category as *excludable public goods*. Examples of goods in each of these categories will help to illuminate the kinds of goods and services represented.

Deep sea fishing is an example of a good that is rivalrous in consumption but for which exclusion of nonpayers is not feasible, that is, a nonexcludable private good. Each fish that is caught and kept represents a fish that is no longer available to be caught and kept by another person. Furthermore, each boat fishing at a given spot means that another boat cannot be fishing at exactly the same spot. Thus, deep sea fishing satisfies the basic conditions of being rivalrous in consumption.

On the other hand, excluding nonpayers is sufficiently difficult with respect to deep sea fishing that the feasibility of exclusion is questionable. Obviously, deep sea fishing is not unregulated, but such regulations tend to be geographically constrained and generally are not based upon the individual's unit consumption of deep sea fishing. Thus, as a general notion, deep sea fishing does not satisfy the exclusion principle and therefore cannot be priced in any meaningful sense. It should be noted, however, that the *products* of deep sea fishing (i.e., fish and seafood) can be classified as private goods that are subject to the exclusion principle and are priced through competitive market forces.

Art exhibitions in galleries and indoor concerts are examples of goods that are not rivalrous in consumption but for which exclusion of nonpayers is possible, that is, an excludable public good. One individual's consumption (i.e., viewing) of an art exhibit does not reduce the amount of art available for the next person to consume. Similarly, one person's consumption (i.e., listening) at a concert does not reduce the ability of other people to consume the same music at the same time. However, unlike pure public goods, it is feasible to exclude nonpayers from viewing a gallery exhibition or listening to a concert in an arena or hall. An admission charge enforced by limited, secured entrances and exits can be implemented easily. Nevertheless, it should be noted that the nonrivalrous characteristic of these goods means that measuring an individual's consumption of the good or service is difficult, if not impossible, in the absence of an individual's ability to measure his or her consumption and truthfully report this quantity for payment purposes. Thus, although nonpayers can be excluded feasibly, the relevance or appropriateness of the fee charged lacks the efficiency characteristics of market-determined prices for private goods. In primary and secondary education, simple examples of nonrivalrous but price excludable goods and services are actually fairly plentiful.

Popular classes in institutions of higher education are typically subjected to some form of allocation system based on permitting or priority. In the absence of permission to register for the course (the "price"), the student may be excluded. However, once the student is in the course, the knowledge imparted typically is available in a nonrivalrous fashion. That is, many students can simultaneously consume the course without adversely affecting the level of education available to any individual student. Similarly, school events such as basketball games or plays are typically price excludable but nonrivalrous in consumption.

Although the classification of a given good or service is often more a matter of art than science, and more a matter of interpretation than litmus tests, the four categories of goods and services are clear from a theoretical standpoint, and each has goods and services that can be placed in its classification through general consensus. Unfortunately, the notion of excludability is slightly richer than our examples might lead one to believe, thereby further complicating the classification of goods and services. A more in-depth look at externalities will help illuminate this complication.

EXTERNALITIES

Externalities are benefits or costs related to the production or consumption of a good or service that flow to parties outside of the production or consumption transaction and are not priced as a part of the transaction. For example, pollution created as part of a production process is an externality. So are the public health benefits of immunizations and the nutritional benefits of school lunches. The presence of externalities is sufficient to characterize the good as nonexcludable. Externalities represent benefits or costs that flow to individuals without regard to whether the individuals pay for those benefits or are compensated for those costs, and they cannot be withheld feasibly from individuals who choose not to pay for the benefits. The fact that externalities are not priced as part of a market transaction and that they flow to parties outside a given transaction means that market prices no longer accurately reflect the true costs and/or benefits from a societal standpoint. Thus, an unfettered market system will not necessarily achieve an efficient outcome when externalities are present.

In the case of positive externalities, there are societal benefits to the production or consumption of a particular good or service in addition to the private benefits that are part of the individual firm's or consumer's decision of what and how much to produce or consume. For example, let us assume that production of a given agricultural crop has the additional societal benefit of cleaning up the groundwater in areas near the production fields. In general, the farmer will make his or her decision as to how much of the crop to produce after comparing the market price for the crop (based upon its use) and the marginal cost of producing a given unit of the crop. In an unfettered market, the price offered to the farmer will only be a reflection of the private use value of the crop (i.e., a value not including the external effect on the groundwater). However, from a societal standpoint the true social benefit of the crop's production must include some valuation of the positive effects on groundwater. Thus, from society's standpoint, an unfettered market system will generally underproduce those goods and services with which positive externalities are associated, and it will overproduce those goods or services with which negative externalities are associated.

As we will discuss later, primary and secondary education is generally felt to be an example of a good or service with which positive externalities are associated. This and other characteristics of education will help us to more accurately assess the nature and appropriateness of government's role in school reform. But first, a better understanding of market roles and market role assessment must be developed.

MARKET ROLES

The key to market role assessment is an understanding of the nature of market roles and their importance in evaluating the appropriate roles for government and the private sector in producing, allocating, and distributing a particular good or service. Market role assessment begins from the premise that a number of different activities need to take place in order for a good or service to be produced, allocated to consumers, distributed to consumers, and monitored for necessary changes in product composition and quality. The key insights for evaluating government's role in the market for a good or service are that a number of roles exist in the market for any good or service, and that there is no necessity that these roles be played by a single economic actor or type of economic actor. It easy to give examples of different private sector actors serving a market through division of market roles[9] and of public sector actors doing so in particular markets, but the sharing of market roles between the public sector and the private sector is less common and perhaps less obvious.

The market roles required for effective production and provision of any good or service are a function of the characteristics of that product and its market. For example, the role of importer or exporter may be a very important one for commodities that are geographically constrained in their production, but it may be irrelevant in the market for other goods or services that are capable of being produced more ubiquitously. Furthermore, when the conditions of perfectly competitive markets are met, the unfettered system of markets can be expected to play many roles implicitly as part of its operation that would need to be explicitly played by government under the alternative allocation mechanism provided by political institutions operating within a collective choice system. An example is the role of regulator, a role that is explicitly played by government[10] in the case of markets like that of utility monopolies, but unobtrusively and automatically played through price adjustments[11] in a system of unfettered markets. Despite these idiosyncracies, the definition of roles in the market for any good or service is driven by providing answers to the following questions:

- Who or what entity identifies goods or services as candidates for production?
- Who or what entity makes and/or executes decisions about what, how, and how much to produce?
- Who or what entity makes and/or executes decisions about the allocation of goods or services to those individuals or groups who desire to have them?
- Who or what entity makes and/or executes decisions about delivering the goods or services to those economic actors to whom they have been allocated?
- Who or what entity makes decisions about how the production, allocation, and distribution is working; and how is this feedback incorporated into the system?

Consideration of these questions allows us to identify and define candidate roles for analysis. However, the previously mentioned idiosyncracies in market roles that are at least partially related to the rivalry and excludability attributes of the good or service in question suggest that a consideration of the good or service in terms of its attributes as an economic good should be a prerequisite to identification of candidate roles for analysis using market role assessment. It is to this task that we now turn, focusing on primary and secondary education.

CLASSIFYING EDUCATION AS AN ECONOMIC GOOD

As an aid to the identification and subsequent assessment of roles in the market for primary and secondary education, it is appropriate to classify primary and secondary education as an economic good along the dimensions of rivalry and excludability. We then utilize this classification discussion as a foundation upon which to conduct market role assessment with respect to primary and secondary education and education reform.

Some individuals in the education community find characterization of education as an economic good to be unpalatable. However, the simple fact is that any good or service can be classified along the dimensions of excludability and rivalry and placed into one of the categories defined in this chapter. This classification, in itself, although certainly requiring subjective judgments about the presence or absence of traits in the good or service, is not a normative process. On the other hand, the interpretation and implications of the classification may be intensely normative. Market role assessment provides a framework within which these normative judgments can be identified and evaluated. We now turn our attention to the classification of primary and secondary education along the dimensions of rivalry and excludability.

Is education rivalrous in consumption? Yes . . . and no! Whereas the lectures of an instructor are nonrivalrous, and the amount of education consumed by a given student in theory does not reduce the amount available to be consumed by other students in the same classroom, other aspects of education are clearly rivalrous. Any written materials, including textbooks, used as a part of education are rivalrous in consumption, at least at any given point in time.[12] The physical facilities through which education is provided, including desks and classrooms as well as schools themselves, are rivalrous even in a home school environment.[13] Therefore, even with shallow analysis, one can readily see that education has both public good and private good aspects when evaluated on the dimension of rivalry.

Unfortunately, classification of education with respect to excludability characteristics is no less ambiguous than that with respect to rivalry. Clearly, we can exclude nonpayers from direct consumption of the services of formal primary and secondary education. That is, in the absence of public education laws, it is feasible to exclude from our schools those individuals who do not pay their tuition. Evidence of this fact is provided by the presence of private schools. There would be no incentive for the existence of a private school if nonpayers could not be excluded. However, the externality aspects of primary and secondary education, in terms of spillover benefits in particular, threaten the universal application of the exclusion principle.

A substantial portion of the benefits of education flow to the individual who consumes the education. For example, research has shown that lifetime earnings increase substantially with educational attainment. In addition, evidence indicates that better-educated people make better health-related decisions and tend to live longer and more productively as a result. However, additional benefits of education flow to society as a whole. An educated populace contributes to productivity and societal stability, including lower crime rates (Hanushek et al., 1994 p. 17). An educated workforce is at the heart of economic competitiveness.[14] An informed populace will make better personal decisions and therefore assist in more efficient operation of markets and other economic and political institutions.[15] "Recent economic studies argue that education may provide benefits to society that are greater than the sum of its benefits to individuals; by providing a rich environment for innovation and scientific discovery, education can accelerate the growth rate of the economy" (Hanushek et al. 1994, p. 17). Furthermore, education is a major contributor to the achievement of greater social equality and reduced disparity in the distribution of economic resources. The external or spillover social benefits of education do not satisfy the exclusion principle because individuals cannot feasibly be excluded from receiving them.

Thus, based on the ambiguous results of our classification of rivalry and excludability characteristics, one should conclude that primary and secondary education is neither a pure private good nor a pure public good. Rather, education appears to be a mixed good, one that has attributes of all four of the general classes of goods and services discussed earlier in the chapter. Such goods and services provide the greatest challenge for analysis of the appropriate role of government and the private sector in their market.

In general, the case for the use of an unfettered market system is most easily and unambiguously made for pure private goods, and the case for government intervention is most easily and unambiguously made in the case of pure public goods. Moving to the realm of nonexcludable private goods and excludable public goods greatly complicates and adds ambiguity to the analysis. However, the analysis remains fairly straightforward in the sense that it is generally being conducted on a good or service whose characteristics are relatively well defined and pure with respect to rivalry and excludability.[16] When one moves to analysis of a good or service such as primary and secondary education, even the classification along the dimensions of rivalry and excludability becomes ambiguous, further complicating efforts to identify the appropriate functions of the private sector and government in the market for such goods and services. Market role assessment provides an alternative and complementary analytical tool to assist with the defining of appropriate functions for the public sector and private sector that can be particularly useful in such cases. This analytical tool provides a means of organizing this ill-structured problem.

The initial step in market role assessment is the identification of a set of market roles within which the efficacy of public and private sector activity can be compared and evaluated. Therefore, we now turn our attention to the identification of potential roles that might be played in the market for primary and secondary education, in an effort to better analyze the nature of what government's role and the private sector's role might be in the reform of primary and secondary education.

As noted earlier, regardless of economic system or commodity, the consumption of a good or service normally requires the interaction of several economic actors, each performing a role essential to converting a raw material into a consumable final product. Many of these roles are so familiar and natural that little or no attention is given to their performance or to the economic actors responsible for their performance. Yet, these economic roles help to clarify differences between goods and services, as well as government's role in a mixed economy.

Contemplating education as an economic good classified on the dimensions of rivalry and excludability led to the identification of at least seven roles that might be fulfilled by economic actors: regulator, administrator, distributor/allocator, producer, auditor, financier (including venture capitalist), and entrepreneur. Although this list may not be exhaustive and universal, it provides a starting point for broad analysis of government's role in primary and secondary education, as well as in education reform.[17]

The process of market role assessment begins with the identification of market roles we have just completed. Other parts of the market role assessment process include: definition of a "presumption rule" for analytical application, definition and delineation of applicable underlying values used for normative analysis, analysis of each market role, categorization of the result for each role, and development of conclusions regarding the overall role of the private sector and public sector in the market.[18] Each of these phases will receive greater attention as we learn more about market role assessment by applying it to the analysis of primary and secondary education beginning in Chapter 3.

A LOOK AHEAD

In subsequent chapters, each of the identified market roles will be discussed in some detail, along with an evaluation using market role assessment of the *prima facie* case for government's performance of the role versus private sector involvement or exclusive performance in the market for primary and secondary education. This evaluation should assist in framing and organizing the ill-structured public policy debate about school reform, and in focusing discussion on areas with greater probability for successful reform.

NOTES

[1]Indeed, the market and the government are the two primary choices available when considering allocation mechanisms in a mixed economy. Of course, some intermediate combinations of these two choices might be identified and implemented.

[2]In the interests of brevity, only the strongest and most straightforward linkages between the characteristics and market failure will be developed. Thus, the subsequent discussion should not be viewed as exhaustive.

[3]This normative statement is grounded on the foundations of government's functions in a mixed economy that were developed in Chapter 1. Namely, government interventions are designed to aid in the efficacy and efficiency of voluntary economic transactions, to adjust undesirable but economically efficient market outcomes, and to assist in addressing market failures. In circumstances where a good has strong rivalry

and excludability characteristics, these types of interventions are less likely to be necessary, given that rivalry and excludability improve the workings of the market for any good or service. This point should become more evident as these concepts are explained in more detail.

[4]The more nonrivalrous and nonexcludable is a particular good, the more likely it is that market failure will be encountered in the market for that particular good or service. Therefore, in terms of the discussion presented in Chapter 1, government intervention will commonly be sought out as an alternative mechanism designed to help mitigate the failure of the private market to provide the good or service and/or provide it in a socially desirable quantity.

[5]A zero-sum game is one in which all gains to winners are exactly offset by the losses suffered by the losers. Hence, the sum of the gains and losses is zero.

[6]A narrow exception to this would be the case in which an individual builds a solar collector that interferes with the ability of neighbors to access sunlight.

[7]It should be noted, however, that one of the arguments supporting a school lunch program cites the spillover effects of improved nutrition and health. For example, a better nourished child will generally be a healthier child and less likely to infect other students with communicable diseases. Thus, even with a seemingly clear-cut example of a private good, definitional ambiguity still can occur at some level.

[8]Of course, nonexclusion may also mean that in some cases individuals are forced to consume goods or services in greater quantities than they would have chosen to consume on their own.

[9]For example, it is not uncommon for a private sector company to distribute its products through an unaffiliated network of distributors. In the health care industry, it is not uncommon to have third party administrators for employer-provided and -funded health insurance. In the public sector, Medicaid is an example of multiple levels and units of government (and the private sector, for that matter) playing different market roles that result in the delivery of health care services to eligible recipients.

[10]Indeed, regulation is one of the major forms of intervention undertaken by government in response to perceived market failures.

[11]These include profit adjustments, because the "price" paid for entrepreneurial services is profit.

[12]Textbooks, for example, can be used again in a subsequent semester without any direct loss in their contribution to learning

[13]One might argue that the aspects of rivalry that are identified do not correspond to education itself, but rather to goods and services related to education. However, few would argue that one of the crucial basic skills taught in primary and secondary education is reading. It is impossible to teach reading or to utilize any written or published materials in the classroom without facing rivalry in consumption at some level. Similar arguments can be made with respect to physical plant and other goods and services that are an essential part of primary and secondary education.

[14]For example, see Reich (1991).

[15]Nobel laureate George Stigler makes a cogent argument for the benefits of literacy. See Stigler (1983).

[16]That is, the classification of the good or service is generally unambiguous with respect to *each* of the characteristics; the ambiguity is in the combination of the classifications *across* the characteristics.

[17]The list of market roles is not unique to education and can be used effectively as a starting point for any market role assessment. However, given the idiosyncracies related to particular goods and services, analysts using market role assessment should be encouraged to adapt and supplement this list to best meet the needs of their analytical undertaking.

[18]This step should include some evaluation of the relative level of ambiguity associated with the choice of the economic actor or actors recommended to perform the given role. That is, one should try to identify the potential nature and intensity of disagreement with any given market role assessment conclusion. The reason for this is to attempt to focus public policy debate so that points of agreement can be quickly discerned and greater attention given to aspects of the policy issue that involve more conflict in value systems and more conflict in the interpretation and application of analysis. This approach is consistent with the need to provide assistance in the resolution of ill-structured problems.

CHAPTER 3

The Regulator
Who Makes and Enforces the Rules?

This chapter begins our explicit consideration of individual market roles as part of the market role assessment of primary and secondary education. Before considering the first market role, that of regulator, it is important to have an understanding of the context in which our assessment will take place.

Conducting market role assessment requires: identification of a set of market roles that will be investigated for a given good or service, definition of a "presumption rule" for analytical application, acknowledgment of applicable underlying values used for normative analysis, analysis of each market role, categorization of the result for each role, and development of conclusions regarding the overall role of the private sector and public sector in the market. Identification of a set of market roles for consideration with respect to primary and secondary education was accomplished in Chapter 2. With the exception of defining a "presumption rule" in this chapter only, the other components of market role assessment will be introduced and performed as encountered during the analysis of each role already identified with respect to the market for primary and secondary education. A "presumption rule" must be explained and chosen prior to beginning analysis of the first market role—that of regulator, the maker and enforcer of rules.

A "PRESUMPTION RULE"

The terms of analysis are influenced by the starting point from which the analysis begins and the decision rule used to evaluate results of the analysis. For example, a lawyer preparing a case for litigation might be influenced by the side favored by the "presumption rule." That is, does the presumption lie with the prosecution or plaintiff, or does it lie with the defendant? Furthermore, does the case need to be proven "beyond a reasonable doubt" or by a "preponderance of the evidence"?

Even though market role assessment is not blessed by the centuries of tradition that have led to established rules such as those in civil and criminal law, the importance of well-defined and well-articulated presumption and decision rules should not be diminished. The functions of government in a mixed economy are all related to the facilitation of better market operations or to interventions designed to aid market outcomes in better meeting agreed-upon standards of fairness or equity. Thus, the benchmark that is generally used for analytical comparison is one that corresponds to the outcome that is, or would be, produced by a system of perfectly competitive markets. Therefore, market role assessment begins from the presumption that the private market performance of a market role is preferred to government performance in the absence of strong evidence in favor of government performance that is consistent with government's functions in a mixed economy.[1] Alternatively, the private market will be presumed innocent until proven guilty (or inferior). We now proceed to analysis of the regulator role, an area in which certain other parts of market role assessment are first encountered.

The notion of a regulator in the market is a complex and multifaceted one. It involves activities that are designed to facilitate voluntary economic transactions, as well as activities that are designed to regulate private behavior through efforts to maintain competition or to preserve health and safety. This can be seen by looking at some of the linkages between the functions of government in a mixed economy and the performance of the regulator role in the market.

GOVERNMENT INTERVENTION AND THE REGULATOR ROLE

On the one hand, the role of regulator can be related to the first function of government in a mixed economy that was identified in Chapter 1: establishment and enforcement of a legal framework that makes voluntary economic transactions within a price system a viable means of economic interaction. This is a role that government plays in a mixed economy without regard for differentiation by good or service; generally, this notion of "regulator" is a well-established and accepted governmental role. Given the universality of this aspect of the role and its apparently widespread acceptance, the regulator role provides a good place to begin a market role assessment that seeks to define the appropriate role for government in primary and secondary school reform. However, analysis of the regulator role must concentrate not only on the ubiquitous notion of government as a regulator (defined within the context of government's widely accepted role of providing a framework for the operation of a price system) but also on less universal and less universally accepted aspects of government's regulatory role.[2] This will better allow the highlighting and justification of possible unique or unusual regulatory roles or activities for government in the market for education. For candidate activities, we look initially at some of the regulatory roles government currently plays in certain markets.

Government performs a regulatory role in markets inhabited by natural monopolies. Natural monopolies are, in general, markets in which the economically efficient quantity of production is such that the production or output of only one firm is sufficient to serve the entire market. That is, ". . . when the production of a good or service is subject to continually decreasing average costs (the greater the level of output, the lower the cost per unit), . . . a single firm can take advantage of economies of scale and supply the entire industry output, at least for a sizeable region" (Rosen 1992, p. 338). Under such circumstances, public production of the good or service is often undertaken. In other circumstances, the natural monopoly conditions are addressed through government regulation of a private producer. Typically, utilities such as natural gas, electric, and local telephone service are used as examples of regulated natural monopolies.[3] With respect to government-regulated natural monopolies, regulation typically involves the granting of a franchise or license for exclusive service of the market. In exchange for this license, the firm is usually required to meet some combination of standards related to universal service within the market, quality of service, and customer rates. Furthermore, firms are often asked to make payments, provide services, or make in-kind contributions as compensation for their exclusive franchise.

In general, the market for primary and secondary education in most areas of the United States is not characterized by natural monopoly conditions.[4] Exclusive franchises for primary and secondary education do not exist, and in most urban markets, educational alternatives do exist.[5] Thus, at least at first glance, there would not appear to be a *prima facie* case for government intervention as a regulator in the market for primary and secondary education on the basis of natural monopoly conditions. However, other reasons for government intervention in a regulator role must be considered.

Government regulation in markets is also sometimes based upon the existence of market power or monopoly power that is not derived from natural monopoly conditions, as suggested by the note in the previous paragraph. Regulatory intervention in such cases includes antitrust laws designed to eliminate or limit actions such as collusive behavior, predatory pricing, tying contracts, and other forms of anticompetitive behavior. As implemented in the United States, these laws typically are not selective in terms of the products or markets to which they are intended to apply,[6] although numerous industries have been exempted from compliance[7] with aspects of these laws on a selective basis over time, and some others have had particular industry-related statutes applied.

The effectiveness of reform of primary and secondary education in the United States would not be expected to be dependent upon a change in the application or provision of these antitrust laws. One can expect that competition in the market for primary and secondary education will continue to be protected like any other market through this existing governmental regulatory role.[8] That is, the federal government already has a well-established regulatory role in administering laws against anticompetitive behavior. This role can be expected to continue in the future and will be important as a means of protecting competition in the market for education. However, it is unlikely that progress in primary and secondary school reform, including that of facilitating increased competition for public schools, is significantly related to provisions of antitrust laws and their enforcement. Thus, in-depth analysis of this aspect of the regulatory role is not likely to bear much fruit in our search for insight.

Another major means of regulation in markets involves measures to protect public health and safety. Such regulation is typically justified in one of at least three ways: (1) threats to health and safety are posed owing to market imperfections that lead to incomplete information being provided to consumers or workers regarding potentially dangerous products or product attributes; (2) labor market power on the part of employers may lead to uncompensated or undercompensated hazardous conditions in the workplace; or (3) societal norms do not allow lives to be explicitly traded off in the name of economic efficiency.[9] Although government interventions in these matters have a long history and a certain degree of success (e.g., the Food and Drug Administration, Attorneys' General consumer offices, and Occupational Health and Safety Administration (OSHA)), it should be noted that the need for regulation in these cases must not always be, nor is it always, met by *government* regulatory measures. Private sector alternatives are sometimes used to fill certain regulatory functions.

For example, gaps in the market for information have been met by private efforts such as Underwriters Laboratories and the Consumers Union. The labor market power of employers has been offset in markets by means of unionization and collective bargaining of working conditions, hazard pay, and other forms of compensation and protection. In theory, our insurance and tort systems are designed to assist with the need for monitoring and regulating of health and safety conditions without direct government regulation.[10] The use of private substitutes for government regulation and intervention is also evidenced by the growing use of alternative dispute resolution mechanisms.

With respect to primary and secondary education, the issue of appropriate regulations for health and safety (and their enforcement) is somewhat complicated by the fact that the primary consumers of the services in question are children. On average, a child can be expected to have more years of productive life ahead of him or her than the average adult does. In addition, children are generally less experienced and less capable of identifying and evaluating risky situations for themselves than are adults. Finally, the generally acknowledged paternalistic[11] responsibilities of parents and society as a whole suggest that decisions about health and safety conditions not be left to children. The question therefore remains as to the extent to which government needs to be involved in the regulation of health and safety as it applies to primary and secondary education. The answer to the question is further complicated by the precise nature of the market for primary and secondary education as institutionalized in the United States.

The market for primary and secondary education in the United States is one in which education is mandatory for children up to a certain age, and one in which "free" public education is considered a right by many people.[12] This drastically changes the context within which regulation and the regulatory role (as well as other market roles) in primary and secondary education are considered. This is because consumers cannot generally opt out of market participation, although they can elect to change providers and can use home schooling as an option in certain cases.[13] As an analytical prerequisite one must ask:

- Are mandatory education and "free" public education appropriate or at least sustainable public policies?
- Should our discussion of government's role in primary and secondary education and education reform assume continuation of these policies?

The analysis in this book assumes a "yes" answer to both questions, at least initially. Although one might argue with these assumptions, analysis within the context of mandatory and free public education allows the market role assessment to be conducted within the same rules of the game under which the status quo is operating. Thus, comparing and contrasting systems and approaches is more straightforward and appropriate. Furthermore, mandatory and "free" public education can be defended on its merits.

Basic skills education, a major component of primary and secondary education, has significant positive externalities. The lack of basic skills often makes a person unemployable or otherwise unproductive.[14] Thus, a strong argument can be made regarding society's stake in primary and secondary education. In light of the growing realization that global competitiveness in the twenty-first century is intimately tied to an educated and productive workforce, society's stake in education is even more clear and profound. Indeed, even many antigovernment libertarians have expressed continuing support for mandatory public education, albeit with the qualification that such mandatory public education need not be government produced or operated.

In an era during which unfunded mandates receive great attention and vehement opposition, mandatory education would be a tough sell without the corresponding provisions for "free" public education. The justification for free public education comes from two perspectives: (1) because society is a main beneficiary of primary and secondary education, society, rather than the individual, should take primary responsibility for financing that education; and (2) if a certain level of education is to be legally required, some provision must be made for those individuals who do not have the financial ability to meet this mandated responsibility. However, the meaning of "free" public education is subject to interpretation. This is a theme that will recur throughout the analysis in this book.

Returning to the issue of the regulatory role in the market for education, mandatory primary and secondary education makes compulsory the participation of children in the market for education. This heightens the regulatory requirements of the market, because compulsory attendance laws reduce the ability of students to opt out of unsafe or hazardous situations faced during the school day or school year. Therefore, it follows that in support of a mandatory education system, government also takes the responsibility for making and enforcing rules to ensure the health and safety of students.[15] As explained earlier, given that the clients in the market for primary and secondary education are children, the market-based alternative to external government regulation of health and safety is probably not feasible or desirable. The death of even one child in such an unregulated environment[16] would likely be viewed as one too many by a significant portion of society.

Furthermore, mandatory and free public education requires provisions to guarantee educational access to all students, including those who are disabled in some way or those whose special needs otherwise require greater resources to successfully educate. These forms of regulation are based on adjusting market outcomes to make them more just or equitable. That is, these interventions are not necessarily based on a market failure.[17] Although the necessary laws are already on the books to address issues of access, issues of finance are raised again with respect to servicing special needs students. From a regulatory point of view, government's involvement in ensuring equal access to education is well settled,[18] whereas financing issues are not. These will be discussed in Chapter 8.

Government's regulatory role in the market for primary and secondary education has typically extended well beyond health and safety and equal access issues. At some level, government regulates transportation, teacher certification, collective bargaining and the right to strike, curriculum, length of school day, length of school year, administration of achievement tests, and numerous other factors related to primary and secondary education. For the most part, these government interventions are not based on any market failures or compelling public interest. Evidence of this is provided by the willingness and ability of government to relax these types of regulations as part of the charter school movement.[19] Increasingly, reform proposals are based upon reduced government regulation in favor of outcome-based performance measures. In the realm of charter schools, "there is an up-front waiver from rules about curriculum, management, and teaching. States may specify student outcomes. But determining how the school operates should be up to the people who establish it and operate it" (Nathan 1995, p. 99). Currently, government regulations may act as a barrier to some school reform efforts.

"Schools are bound by state regulations that dictate the length of each class period; school day; class size; the subjects to be taught; and the qualifications of those who teach them. Schools also are bound by state and federal regulations that prescribe which children with special needs must be served and how funds should be spent" (United States General Accounting Office (GAO), April 1994, pp. 1–2). As the GAO study preface goes on to point out, principals who want to lengthen the school day to provide children with more time to learn, teachers who want to reallocate subject time to basic skills, and school administrators who wish to try innovative means of combining classes to help the mainstreaming of special needs students, may all be stymied by current government regulations.

As mentioned previously, many current efforts in school reform begin with regulatory flexibility by (1) reducing and eliminating regulations for schools through legislative action, and (2) allowing for schools to apply for waivers of specific regulations that are granted on a case-by-case basis. Unfortunately, little if any systematic evidence is available on the results of these flexibility efforts (U.S. GAO, April 1994), and there is little hope for generalizable results until regulatory flexibility is undertaken on a more widespread and universal basis, and until the regulatory flexibility is explicitly tied to accountability measures that allow student performance to be accurately gauged and compared across regulatory situations. Some of the initial results from charter schools indicate success in limited, small-scale cases.

CONCLUSION

Government's performance of the regulator role in a market can be justified on the basis of any of the three overarching functions of government in a mixed economy. Government's interventions as a regulator in the market for primary and secondary education can be distributed among these functions. However, government interventions in primary and secondary education based on each of these functions are not equally meritorious or justifiable.

Government's function as provider of a framework that allows for the smooth operation of the price system is an important one, but it requires no special regulatory intervention in the market for primary and secondary education. Also, primary and secondary education is not characterized by natural monopoly conditions or by barriers to entry of the type that merit government regulatory intervention on the basis of seeking to maintain competition. This leaves consideration of government intervention in primary and secondary education as a regulator under the justification of either seeking to promote health and safety or adjusting market outcomes to make them more just or equitable.

Government's role as a regulator to promote health and safety in the market for mandatory primary and secondary education seems well grounded. Indeed, government's role as a regulator of health and safety in this market appears to be one that needs to be maintained even in the face of the most drastic moves to a greater reliance on the market and the private sector in the provision and production of primary and secondary education. The reasons for this conclusion reflect several factors. First, the principal consumers or participants in the market for primary and secondary education are children, who would not typically be capable of making the required evaluation of health and safety tradeoffs that an unfettered market approach requires. Second, based on societal reaction in many similar situations, one would not expect that society is willing to accept the efficient outcome produced by unfettered markets, one that typically does not eliminate unsafe or unpleasant conditions. Finally, with mandatory education, the ability to opt out of dangerous or unhealthy conditions may be greatly reduced. Thus, government performance of the regulator role in the market for primary and secondary education seems necessary, at least in terms of basic health and safety issues and concerns.

Government's role as a regulator to alter market outcomes to make them more just or equitable also presents some elements that appear to be relatively noncontroversial, well established, and well accepted. In particular, regulation to guarantee access to education is well grounded in government's function of improving market outcomes on the grounds of justice or equity, but it also can be justified on the basis of facilitating a system of mandatory and free public education. This may be especially important in protecting the rights of special needs students. The protection of civil rights in settings such as educational institutions can be expected to remain in the hands of the federal government, though not through any explicit need to impart special regulations for primary and secondary education beyond those generally promulgated as enforcement of the Constitution.[20] Of course, in terms of ensuring access, government's role in financing education may be as important as or more important than equal opportunity laws and similar regulatory interventions.

Government has also performed as a regulator under the status quo in the market for primary and secondary education on dimensions that are not easily justified, based on reference to government's functions in a mixed economy. There does not appear to be any compelling rationale[21] for government regulation of curriculum, length of school day, or other elements related to the methods of preparation and education of students. These dimensions of regulation appear to be aspects of the production and provision of primary and secondary education that can be effectively regulated through normal market operations.[22]

As we discuss other market roles, one may find that government's more active performance of the market role of auditor may offset any diminution of its previous regulatory role. This possibility is discussed further in Chapter 7. In Chapter 4, we turn our attention to the administrator role.

NOTES

[1] It should be noted that this presumption rule does not necessarily reflect the author's personal feelings about the merits or demerits of governmental activity in the economy.

[2] The analytical approach employed here will be replicated in subsequent chapters and should be explicitly noted. Where possible, the parameters of the market role that is to be analyzed will be established by making reference to some of the ways in which government has been known to perform the chosen role, and by relating government performance of the role back to the functions of government in a mixed economy. This approach allows the realm of governmental activity to be circumscribed and enables the role to be more concretely identified and understood through reference to examples of cases in which the collective choice system has produced government performance of the given role.

[3] It should be noted that these three markets, which are typical examples of natural monopolies, have been greatly deregulated in recent years. One of the major factors that has made deregulation feasible has been a recognition that the unbundling of market roles is possible. With the realization that new technologies are making smaller scales of production economically viable, the existence of integrated delivery systems that make local generation of services less essential, and the recognition that control of the delivery system need not imply control of all market roles, greater opportunities for competition and sharing of market roles have been recognized and implemented.

[4] Although many rural and sparsely populated areas of the country may offer only a single provider of primary and secondary education, in most cases this lack of competition is not driven by natural monopoly per se. Even though the form of competition may be greatly limited by the resources and geography, education can be and is efficiently produced in small quantities through means such as home-based education, education cooperatives, and a variety of distance learning techniques. It should be noted, however, that a number of other barriers to entry besides efficient output considerations may produce anticompetitive results (e.g., simply the economies of being established).

[5] One could argue that from a market perspective the home schooling alternative *always* exists.

[6] That is, the market role is being played generally with respect to the market system rather than to particular markets.

[7] Major League Baseball is an example.

[8] It should be noted that this analysis does not presume the existence of free entry and exit of firms in the market for primary and secondary education. Public education systems as formulated in the United States generally provide significant barriers to entry for private competitors, including those who desire to home-school. Perhaps chief among these is public schools' access to subsidy through tax dollars. However,

in the context of the regulatory role discussed in this chapter, these barriers to entry
are neither the result of natural monopoly status nor forms of anticompetitive behavior prohibited by the antitrust system. Rather, the benefits of being established
and having access to tax dollars provide a competitive advantage for public schools,
an advantage that will be discussed further in Chapter 8 on financing primary and secondary education.

[9]It should be noted that the U.S. experience has been one of a double standard
with respect to this third justification. Although tremendous outcry is heard in response
to revelations such as the safety tradeoffs in the Ford Pinto gas tank case, little or no
outcry is heard when safety standards for products such as automobiles do not require
the *elimination* of fatal injuries owing to collisions. On the one hand, market forces
seem to be acknowledged; while on the other hand, they are abhorred—with no obvious demarcation between the two other than the luck of litigation and sensationalism.

[10]Of course, government's role in enforcing contracts and property rights, as well
as its regulation of the insurance industry, are all important contributors in enabling
this private sector alternative to be viable and effective.

[11]*Paternalistic* is a term of art used to justify certain forms of government intervention in areas in which individuals are incapable of or unwilling to make appropriate decisions. The term is not used with any noninclusive intent or meaning.

[12]The meaning of "free" public education has been the centerpiece of several
court cases and public debates, including *Serrano v. Priest* (1971) in California, *Edgewood v. Kirby* (1989, 1990, 1991, 1992, 1995) in Texas, and *Committee for Educational Rights v. Edgar* (1996) in Illinois.

[13]A parallel analysis is that according to administrators and school board members from Illinois, a special education student (at least in Illinois) cannot be expelled
(even for serious weapons violations!) from public school as long as the behavior can
in any way be traced or attributed to the special need condition. The student may be
removed from class, but the school district must continue to provide the student with a
publicly funded education at no extra charge.

[14]It should be noted that even though basic skills education has a very large
spillover benefit, in the assessment of increasingly advanced levels of education it
becomes apparent that the public good aspects of education diminish as one moves to
progressively more advanced levels of education.

[15]Regulation for the protection of the health and safety of faculty and staff in the
schools is no different from any other regulation for workplace health or safety.
Schools should be subjected to the same workplace rules as other job sites are, with no
special exemptions or provisions.

[16]It should be noted that the discussion of death and serious injury is not idle
speculation. Recall that one of the virtues of the competitive market system is the production of efficient market outcomes. In general, the efficient outcome in a market
with respect to any unsafe or unpleasant condition does not *eliminate* the condition or
adverse consequences, but rather it reduces them to the level at which further reductions are not merited on the basis of comparing the added benefits of reduction with
the costs of achieving that reduction. To put it bluntly, the efficient outcome will generally accept some deaths or injuries, on the grounds that simply paying compensation
to those who are still harmed under the safer condition will be less expensive than
eliminating the condition. Though this approach may be efficient, many would find it

to be exceedingly undesirable, as evidenced by the reaction to this behavior in the aforementioned case involving the safety of gasoline tanks on the Ford Pinto.

[17]Although some individuals might argue that special needs education involves overcoming market failure, particularly that of incomplete markets or of public goods, the existence of successful private providers of special education is a counterexample to the assertion of these types of market failure. The crux of the access and provision problem appears to be financing. This suggests an intervention based on considerations of equity or justice rather than efficiency.

[18]It is reasonably well settled that government should enforce laws designed to prohibit unfair discrimination and to promote equal opportunity (not to be confused with affirmative action). Opinion is less well settled as to appropriate interventions by government in enforcing these laws or operationalizing them through administrative regulations.

[19]Charter schools represent a reform effort undertaken in several states, including Massachusetts, Minnesota, and Michigan. Charter schools are run by organizations (normally required to be nonreligious) that receive a charter from the state government to administer the school. The school is relieved of most regulations outside of civil rights and health/safety, but it is held to outcome-based performance standards. Charter schools generally must take students on a first-come, first-served or lottery basis to prevent "creaming." Charter school experiments are designed in part to evaluate the effects of relieving the schools from what are perceived by some people to be undue levels of government regulation.

[20]Realistically, education is such an important area for opportunity in our society that it is likely (and probably appropriate) that more attention be paid to the market for primary and secondary education than to the market for certain other goods and services.

[21]That is, there appears to be no compelling rationale for these interventions that is based upon the established functions of government in a mixed economy.

[22]It should be noted that educational outcomes can still be audited and evaluated without regulating dimensions such as class size, length of school day, length of school year, and similar elements of educational process and input.

CHAPTER 4

The Administrator
Who Is Responsible for Day-to-Day Operations?

According to *The American Heritage Dictionary,* the verb *to administer* means "to have charge of; direct; manage." In terms of market roles, the administrator is responsible for the day-to-day management of the economic enterprise, for the execution of policy, and for directing the enterprise toward the achievement of its goals and objectives. This market role is one that is simultaneously broad and narrowly constrained. In some of his recent writings and addresses, James M. Banovetz, a noted city management scholar, has drawn an analogy between public managers, specifically city administrators and managers, and baseball managers. His analogy is useful here in helping to explain and differentiate the role of the administrator.

A baseball team is typically run by an owner, a director of player personnel (commonly known as the general manager), and a field manager (commonly known as the manager).[1] In the context of this chapter, the field manager is the one who most directly and regularly plays the role of administrator. The field manager is responsible for setting the lineup, determining day-to-day game strategy, making strategy decisions during the course of the ball game, making personnel changes during the ball game, setting daily schedules for team workouts, and establishing day-to-day team rules.

Analogously, a primary or secondary school system is run by a school board (the "owner's" representatives), a superintendent (the "general manager"), and principals (the "field managers").[2] A problem with this analogy is that in many school systems principals do not have control over many of the day-to-day decisions that might be associated with other field managers. As we discuss later in the chapter, school-based or site-based management systems are more precise examples of cases in which principals truly act in the role of day-to-day administrators with requisite powers. In the case of site-based management, the principal typically also inherits the general manager's powers for administration of his or her school. Although it is easy to get

41

wrapped up in definitional minutiae, the intended general notion of the administrator's market role should be reasonably clear even if certain lines of demarcation remain ambiguous or somewhat undefined.[3] Thus, it is time to turn to assessment of the administrator market role.

In the context of market role assessment the fundamental question is whether there is any reason, grounded in the functions of government in a mixed economy, that primary and secondary education needs to be governmentally administered. The fact that private and parochial schools already exist and flourish on a fairly ubiquitous basis provides incontrovertible evidence that nongovernmental administration of schools is feasible in at least some circumstances. But what about traditional public schools: Can they or should they be privately administered?

Clearly, public schools *can* be privately administered. Indeed, privately administered public schools are already a reality. Nationally, several school systems have contracted out to private firms for services that were traditionally the purview of government in the public schools. For example, the lead private sector partner in the management of the Baltimore schools, Education Alternatives Incorporated (EAI) of Minnesota, also had contracts to run a school in Miami and the entire school system (comprising thirty-two schools) in Hartford, Connecticut. However, none of these contracts were renewed or are currently in place.[4] Christopher Whittle's Edison Project vowed to open 200 new for-profit schools by 1996 and at least 1,000 by the beginning of the next century, but "as of January 1996, the Edison Project was running four schools—one each in Boston; Mount Clemens, Michigan; Wichita, Kansas; and Sherman, Texas—and preparing to run four more, two in Miami, one in Colorado Springs, and one in Springfield, Massachusetts, beginning in the fall of 1996" (Schrag 1996, p. 68).[5] Boston University was hired under a ten-year agreement signed in 1989 to run the entire Chelsea, Massachusetts, school system. Alternative Schools, Inc., has been running a public elementary school in Wilkinsburg, Pennsylvania.

However, privatization efforts remain relatively rare and novel, and the success of previous efforts is at best debatable. In fact, efforts at privatization of administration have yet to produce any unqualified long-term successes that can be cited as indicative of the long-term feasibility of private administration of public schools (Bushweller 1997).[6] Indeed, as of March 1997, "the Public Strategies Group—a St. Paul, Minn., Education Maintenance Organization (EMO) that runs the Minneapolis public schools—is currently the only private company managing an entire public school district" (Bushweller 1997, p. 20). As of July 1997 this three-year experiment in private administration also had ended. With this in mind, the administrator role should be assessed from the perspective of the functions of government in a mixed economy in an effort to identify characteristics that might explain the notable lack of success of previous privatization efforts.

GOVERNMENT INTERVENTION
AND THE ADMINISTRATOR ROLE

Recall that one overarching function of government in a mixed economy is to establish and enforce a legal framework and social environment that makes voluntary economic transactions within a price system a viable means of economic interaction. The primary ways by which government performs this function in a mixed economy are through establishment and enforcement of property rights, judicial enforcement of contracts, and police powers. Although all these activities are crucial to the smooth operation of the price system, there is nothing obvious about the market for primary and secondary education that would suggest any need to make a special intervention into the market as justified by providing a framework for the smooth operation of the price system. Indeed, this reasoning for government intervention in the market for primary and secondary education is not among the plethora of reasons cited for the involvement of government in primary and secondary education as documented in the wide-ranging, often heavily normative literature on education and education reform. Proponents of government-run schools instead tend to focus on reasons for government intervention that fall under other functions of government. These functions are now considered in the context of the market role of administrator, the economic actor who is responsible for day-to-day management and for execution of policy.

A second function of government in a mixed economy is to adjust private market outcomes to make them better conform to collective notions of fairness and equity. Issues of fairness and equity are seemingly at the heart of many arguments in support of traditional means of funding, running, and evaluating public schools (McKinney 1996; Fennimore 1996). One author makes the argument with respect to educational access for special needs students. "The marketplace concept that drives charter school legislation is stood on its head and proves to be a disincentive when it comes to serving students with disabilities" (McKinney 1996, p. 25). Beatrice Fennimore is more global in her equity argument. "In the absence of equal and excellent public schools for all children, citizens become competitors for the best (or even adequate) resources. Those in the position of justifying their advantage may denigrate the intelligence and worthiness of others. . . . Educators must be concerned about the lack of regard for 'other people's children' and the subsequent denial of responsibility for universally adequate educational opportunities" (Fennimore 1996, p. 54).

Yet, no matter how compelling one finds arguments like those suggested by McKinney and Fennimore, one must be careful in conducting market role assessment to consider arguments and evidence as they relate to the specific market role under consideration. When one considers equity justifications in the *context of the administrator role*, the need for intervention becomes less clear. This is true even in situations in which the notion of equity being applied is objectively supportable and the inability of the market to produce an equitable solution is stipulated. As defined, the administrator role does little in and of itself to promote or improve equity outcomes. Although it is true that the administrator could engage in discriminatory behavior[7] that impedes equitable outcomes, there is nothing to suggest that the tendency toward such behavior is a function of the administrator coming from the private or public sector. Furthermore, there is no reason to expect that government will improve the equity outcomes in the market for primary and secondary education through its performance of the *administrator* role.[8] For example, recall that the administrator is nominally charged with the *execution* of policy and not the *making* of policy, a distinction that is the purview of the classic politics and administration dichotomy familiar to students of public administration. As a result, one would expect less influence on equity outcomes by the administrator. One should also recall that the analysis of government's role as *regulator* in the market for primary and secondary education indicated the need for interventions such as those designed to ensure equal access and opportunity to education. Such interventions through the regulator role will also affect equity outcomes in the market, and they are not dependent on whether the administrator role in the market is played by the public sector or the private sector. However, efficiency considerations may lead to a different set of conclusions about the administrator's role in the market for primary and secondary education.

Interventions justified on the basis of improvements in economic efficiency are driven generally by the identification of one or more forms of market failure. Government interventions related to economic inefficiencies introduced by market failures usually are justified on the grounds of seeking to maintain competition, seeking to protect health and safety, or providing goods and services that the market cannot or will not provide. Each of these justifications should be examined in terms of its application to the administrator role in the market for primary and secondary education. Once again, we maintain a presumption rule in favor of the unfettered market, and we seek a justification for government intervention that applies to the role in question.

Government intervention designed to help maintain competition in a market is driven by the existence of market power in the unfettered market. As mentioned in Chapter 3, market power that promotes government intervention is usually attributable to natural monopoly conditions or explicit anticompetitive behavior such as collusion, tying contracts, or predatory pricing. The nature of primary and secondary education is such that natural monopoly conditions are rarely present. However, even if the market were characterized by natural monopoly conditions, these conditions would not be improved or addressed by government's intervention in the *administrator* role. A similar conclusion can be reached by considering the possibility of a government intervention to address market power that is derived from anti-competitive behavior. That is, even if one finds anticompetitive behavior in the market for primary and secondary education, the means of intervention chosen to address the behavior would not require government to act in the administrator role as a primary determinant of success of the intervention. There is nothing inherent in the administrator role that gives substantial and meaningful control over those decisions and policies that might be the foundation of anticompetitive behavior.[9] At minimum, there appears to be no compelling *prima facie* case based on market power considerations that would require government to play the role of administrator in the market for primary and secondary education. However, the existence of such a case based on health and safety concerns, or on the inability or unwillingness of the private market to provide primary and secondary education, must be considered and analyzed.

As mentioned in Chapter 3, government intervention to help ensure health and safety can be well justified in the market for primary and secondary education. Indeed, our conclusion was that government performance of the regulator role could be justified in areas related to health and safety. The need for government intervention through performance of the administrator role would not appear to be as well supported. Although the administrator can play an integral role in maintaining health and safety in the workplace or the place of service delivery, there does not appear to be any meaningful distinction between the government's ability to adequately perform in this regard and that of a private sector administrator. That is, once the rules, regulations, and policies are set, there is no inherent reason why private sector performance of the administrator role should be inferior or inadequate—in either absolute or relative terms—to that of government. In the absence of such an expectation, the presumption rule of our analysis directs a finding against government intervention. This reasoning and finding also apply to the inefficiencies that result from discriminatory behavior in the market.

Even though private sector education administration firms remain rare, the existence and experiences of private administrators such as Education Alternatives, the Edison Project, Alternative Public Schools, the Public Strategies Group, and Ombudsman Education Services suggest that private performance of the administrator role is not only feasible but also receiving increasing attention—not only in school board deliberations but also in the Wall Street investment community (Bushweller 1997; Jones, March 1997). This provides *prima facie* evidence that the private market is willing to perform the administrator role in the market for *public* primary and secondary education. The success of numerous private schools indicates the more general willingness and ability of the private sector to perform as an administrator of primary and secondary education. Thus, at the most basic level, government intervention on the basis of incomplete markets[10] can be rejected, and the public good aspects of primary and secondary education also do not require public administration in the market, as evidenced by the widespread success of private education.

Thus, assessment of the administrator role in primary and secondary education fails to discern any compelling reason that government needs to intervene in this market through performance of this role. Not only does private performance of the administrator role seem feasible, but our presumption rule would argue that in the absence of evidence to the contrary, private performance would be desirable. Unfortunately, the track record for private administration of public schools is not good. A look at some of the recent experiences with privatizing the administration of public schools should offer insight into the divergence between theory and the realities observed thus far.

PRIVATE ADMINISTRATION EXPERIENCES

Sammis White studied the early experience in Baltimore (see White 1995) and indicated that preliminary reviews were positive but that definitive results needed to wait for the passage of a bit more time. Unfortunately, the privatization experienced ended in failure[11] not long after White's paper was published. "EAI's management . . . ended on March 4, 1996, a year and three months short of the original five year contract" (Williams and Leak 1996, p. 57). Nevertheless, it is still appropriate to look at a few of the basic features of the Baltimore approach so as to better understand one model for turning over administrative control of public schools to private firms.

"Frustrated by continuing difficulties making educational progress, the Baltimore City Public Schools (BCPS) began searching for alternative ways to operate that might lead them to higher levels of student achievement" (White 1995, p. 224). White notes that Baltimore's efforts included both internal and external solutions. A site-based management system was established, and individual schools were charged with exploration of solutions under the system's administrative freedom. At the same time, bids were entertained from outside corporations to operate the schools (White 1995, p. 224). In the summer of 1992, after signing an agreement with the teachers union, the BCPS signed a five-year agreement[12] with a consortium of private sector, for-profit firms called the Alliance for Schools That Work[13] ("the Alliance") to operate nine of the city's schools, schools that were considered to be among the most difficult and risky in the system. These nine schools included one primary school, seven elementary schools, and one junior high. "In January 1994, three additional schools, exercising their power as site-based management schools, also signed contracts with the Alliance" (White 1995, pp. 224–225).

The Baltimore contracts were very broad-based, turning over virtually 100% of the operational control to the private firms. Basically, the Alliance received a payment for each student in its schools that amounted to the average cost per pupil of educating students in the BCPS. According to White's figures, about 12.7% of the original contract was to be paid back to the district for its administrative overhead and approximately 6.4% was taken for administrative overhead by the headquarters of the lead Alliance partner. As noted, the Alliance was responsible for the day-to-day operations of the schools. However, at least one notable constraint was placed upon the Alliance in terms of its operational decisions. "Under the agreement with the BCPS the Alliance used BCPS principals and teachers. The Alliance had no control over which of these was assigned to their schools. In the agreement with the union, however, teachers have the right to transfer to other Baltimore public schools if they do not want to participate in the experiment" (White 1995, p. 227). In the first year of operations, fourteen teachers made transfer requests, "fewer than had done so before the agreement with the Alliance had been announced."

In a preliminary look at the Alliance's approach, White (1995) notes that the approach:[14]

- put $1 million more annually in direct expenditures into nine schools than BCPS would have;
- put over 1,100 new computers with new software into these nine schools;
- rehabilitated the buildings inside and out and maintained them at that improved level;
- created a respect for the buildings among students that had not previously existed;
- instituted weekly teacher training as well as summer teacher offerings;
- put a second college-degreed adult into most classrooms;
- put a much higher level of materials and supplies into the classrooms;
- established a standard, proven approach to education that all schools use; and
- significantly raised the level of parent participation in their children's education.

Results from the early stages of the Baltimore experience indicated that student attendance rates at the nine schools were above the district average and that parental satisfaction was rising. On the other hand, the American Federation of Teachers instituted both a national and a local campaign to discredit the effort (White 1995, p. 225). In any case, the Baltimore effort was not successful, at least in terms of long-term sustainability of private management.

The University of Maryland—Baltimore County (UMBC) conducted an extensive evaluation of the first three years of the Tesseract Program in

Baltimore. Among the findings delineated by Williams and Leak (1996), the co-principal investigators for the study, were the following:

- Comprehensive Test of Basic Skills (CTBS) scores for all groups were at levels similar to the year before EAI came in. For comparison schools and all Baltimore schools, the scores were relatively flat. For the Tesseract schools, scores had dipped sharply in the first year, then risen over the next two years to about their pre-EAI level.
- Baltimore City was paying about 11% more per student in the Tesseract schools than in the comparison elementary schools.
- EAI was very successful in providing staff development as part of the Tesseract Program. Teachers and principals both evaluated the staff development program highly. Principals noted a new level of professionalism among their staffs, as most teachers responded to staff development by making real changes in their teaching strategies.
- After some start-up pains, classroom interns proved increasingly satisfactory. As second college-degreed adults in the classroom, interns were able to share responsibility for teaching student groups and monitoring classroom activities.
- The Tesseract Program places emphasis on the use of integrated learning system software. Unfortunately, adequate numbers of computers to implement the Tesseract Program were not provided in all schools.[15] The experiment provided no demonstrated success for use of the software.

"Although our finding of no CTBS test score gain . . . has been publicly viewed as a determining factor in the decision . . . to terminate the contract, it was the report's financial information that cut short EAI's effort" (Williams and Leak 1996, p. 57). Williams and Leak noted that although, at first glance, average per-pupil cost seems an appropriate funding basis for alternatives to public education in which "the funds follow the student," school systems generally spend less than their average per-pupil cost for elementary school students and more than their average for secondary and special needs students. Thus, the relevant cost comparison for EAI's seven Tesseract elementary schools that were studied by UMBC would be a figure that is less than the average per-pupil cost for the entire BCPS. "The unmasking of this artifice made a mockery of EAI's promise to improve schools at no extra cost to Baltimore City. We have since learned that EAI's inference that it directs a larger percentage of resources to the classroom is also a distortion" (Williams and Leak 1996, p. 57). Contract termination came after protracted negotiations in which Baltimore City offered continuation at a rate that was much lower than EAI was projected to receive under the original average per-pupil cost formula (and 5% less than the comparison elementary schools were to have received). According to Williams and Leak, EAI chose not to accept the lower offer.

An alternative explanation for the financial disagreement in Baltimore is offered by many observers. In the Baltimore case, EAI was paid a fee of $44 million to manage twelve schools. According to EAI and others close to the situation, "Baltimore Mayor Kurt Schmoke asked EAI to cut $7 million from . . . its contract. Schmoke wanted the money to help the city make up its budget shortfall" (Borger 1995, p. 1D). Michael Moe, a Wall Street analyst who followed EAI for Lehman Brothers, said that Baltimore was facing a $30 million shortfall owing to the election-year raise given to teachers by Schmoke. "And he wants EAI to make it up. EAI hasn't even made $7 million in the three years they've been there" (Borger 1995, p. 1D). Whether the lack of agreement between EAI and Baltimore City was related to cost-related performance issues that reflected adversely on EAI, or dissatisfaction on EAI's part from being asked to bear a disproportionate share of budget cuts in a financially strapped school system, is not objectively determinable. What is clear is that EAI's financial performance was inferior relative to its expectations and those of Baltimore City.

Nevertheless, "principals and teachers say that they plan to continue several elements of the program" (Williams and Leak 1996, p. 59). These include the use of Personal Education Plans, which provide a no-cost device for parental involvement; the keeping of student progress records in a visible notebook in the classroom; the use of student progress reports in place of traditional report cards; and twice-a-week multigrade community meetings/assemblies of students.

The Alliance in Baltimore was only able to provide comprehensive administrative services through the combined efforts of four firms with comparative advantages in different areas relevant to operating the schools: management of operations and resources for educational achievement, facilities operations, accounting and auditing, and educational computing software. Even with such expertise, it is evident that EAI failed to make its expected profits in any of its school system or subsystem endeavors. This issue may ultimately be at the heart of any future efforts to engage in privatization of the administration function, and it may provide some anecdotal evidence as to why the public sector was administering these school systems in the first place.

Other observers insist that the nonrenewal of EAI's contract in Baltimore can be traced to dissatisfaction with EAI's management performance rather than political vengeance taking. Further support for the plausibility of this view is provided through consideration of the case of Hartford, where the financial stakes were considerably different in structure but where officials also said that EAI did not fulfill its contract.[16] Officials in Dade County, Florida, also allegedly made the same claim of poor performance against

EAI. Another look at some of the facts in the falling out between EAI and the Hartford public school system may help to further our understanding of why private administration of public schools has yet to be sustainable on a wide-spread basis.

Cancellation of the Baltimore contract followed nonrenewal of EAI's contract in Dade County, Florida, in May 1995 (Borger 1995, p. 1D). After only one and one-half years had passed on its five-year contract, EAI pulled out of its largest contract, an agreement to run the entire Hartford, Connecticut school system, "leaving the fiscally and academically troubled Hartford system in a lurch" (Kirby 1996, p. 8). At issue in Hartford, like Baltimore, was money: whether and how much EAI would be paid for the expenses it incurred while managing the district's finances and operating six of its schools.

The Hartford experience was especially noteworthy because of its scope and the relatively unique fee structure under which EAI was to work.[17] "The firm would assume full management of the state's largest school district. Instead of being paid a set fee for their management, EAI would take its pay from the savings the school system would realize" (Kirby 1996, p. 8). In return, EAI would manage the district in a cost-effective manner, which was advertised to provide the school board with extra moneys to improve the programs and curriculum. In addition, EAI was allegedly committed to investing up to $20 million of its own money in improvements to local district infrastructure.

After less than two years, EAI conceded that it had been overly ambitious in evaluating the project and its ability to deliver what had been promised. Indeed, by 1995 its efforts in Hartford had been scaled back to concentrate on five schools. "The Hartford contract unraveled, as city and company officials could not agree on if or how much EAI should be paid. EAI officials, threatening litigation, claimed they invested $11 million in the district but have been paid only $343,000" (Kirby 1996, p. 8). "Instead of taking a specific fee for services in its contract with the district, EAI had agreed to be paid from savings. But officials in Hartford said there had been no savings from which to pay the firm" (Harrington-Lueker, April 1996, p. 28). Clearly, privatization did not offer the windfall cost savings anticipated by either side in the original agreement. In August 1996, a settlement was approved under which EAI would be paid about $6.2 million over five years in exchange for leaving the city. It seems rather ironic that in today's climate calling for privatization and more businesslike behavior on the part of government, a governmental unit was able to negotiate a favorable contract that for all intents and purposes left the private sector firm holding the proverbial empty bag. Although there is of course no reason to believe that this was intended or is in any way desirable, the reversal of fortune is a bit too obvious to ignore. Some observers suspect that EAI saw an opportunity to make a big splash with a success in a large school district where it had the benefits of full managerial control. Unfortunately, these EAI undertakings and experiences with other managerial experiments have not provided much indication of widespread or generalizable success in privatizing all aspects of public school administration.

Even in today's favorable privatization environment of reinvention; distrust of government; and emphasis on productivity, quality, and customer service; the privatization of public schools, and public school administration in particular, has moved slowly and in an isolated fashion. In the high-profile Baltimore case, only a small portion of the school system was contracted out originally. In Hartford, EAI's efforts were quickly scaled back to concentrate on a small number of schools; and no additional schools were added or have been added to any new privatization effort. The notable underachievement of the Edison Project is a further example of the snail's pace at which privatization has proceeded. "At the forefront of the privatization movement was the Edison Project, a venture begun with much fanfare by entrepreneur Christopher Whittle. More than four years and $40 million later, the Edison Project operates only four schools nationally" (Kirby 1996, p. 8). The Edison Project received a new infusion of money in 1999, but the results of its self-described "watershed year" are yet to be determined (Billings 1999).

This slow movement cannot entirely be attributed to an unwillingness to change or to an opposition to privatization. Rather, it should be noted that the viability of private administration of schools varies from system to system and may even vary from building to building in heterogeneous school systems. In addition, there are simply very few private, for-profit firms that are currently in a position to credibly and confidently bid for private management of schools.[18] Furthermore, there is a paucity of research on privatization through contracting out (Uline 1998, p. 176). The fallout from the lack of success in many high-profile cases serves to heighten anxiety and frustration among those firms struggling to enter or remain in the market for private administration of schools and school systems, as well as among policymakers seeking to explore or undertake privatization of their public schools.

In attempting to evaluate the empirical results thus far, it is important to try to discern the link between the private manager's degrees of freedom in administration and the results of the privatization experience. Unfortunately, this is difficult to assess with any degree of confidence in the absence of good baseline data and a comprehensive review of each management contract. Even with such data, the degree of management control and degrees of freedom may be extremely difficult to discern. Nevertheless, despite relatively limited success in the privatization of administrative services, interest in privatization as a tool of education reform remains high.

DeSpain and Livingston (1996) present the results of a national survey of school board presidents and chamber of commerce executives. Over two-thirds of the chamber executives favored privatization as an option for school reform, and nearly one-third of school board presidents favored this option. A recent survey of 3,000 school board members from 354 districts by the National School Boards Association found that "62% have considered privatizing their overall district operations or specific areas of administration or instruction" (Henry 1996, p. D1). Despite this indication of interest, the association also notes that a majority of school districts still use private contractors only for support services such as maintenance, food, and transportation.[19] Clearly, support services do not present the same accountability problems, problems with success evaluation, or unpredictable profit situations for either the district or its private contractors. The same survey indicated that big city districts use private firms more frequently for *instructional* programs, with 19% contracting for special education services and 12% for at-risk services.

There remains significant disagreement about the perceived effectiveness of privatization on the management of public schools. According to DeSpain and Livingston (1996), board presidents were skeptical of the effectiveness of privatization.[20] This creates a significant obstacle to privatization efforts and may explain in part the short-lived nature of many privatization contracts.

Furthermore, the criteria by which to evaluate school privatization efforts are not well established. However, Joseph Murphy, a noted expert on school privatization, suggests judging "school privatization efforts on the basis of five criteria: cost savings, efficiency, improved quality, effects on employees, and values in terms of choice, equity, and community" (Uline 1998, p. 176). The existence and interpretation of evidence based on these criteria has not been well documented in most previous privatization efforts.

In evaluating the heretofore relatively limited evidence with respect to privatization, one should recognize that there are currently significant differences in the administrative structures and administrative environments present in primary and secondary schools and school systems across the United States. In many cases this means that significant administrative reforms can be undertaken without going to the extreme of external intervention through contracting for administrative or consulting services. School-based management initiatives are a good example of such intermediate reform efforts.[21] As of 1994, some of the states and localities using school-based management included: Cambridge, Massachusetts; Chicago; Colorado; Kentucky; Martin County, Florida; and New York City (Zinser 1994, p. 5). With reference to our original analogy, school-based management means shifting authority and power away from the ownership and general management (i.e., the school board and central administration in the case of public primary and secondary education) to the principal and his or her local administrative team. In school-based or site-based management, decisions about educational goals, curriculum, discipline policies, budget, and personnel can be made at the individual school level. For reasons of morale and local control, it may be appropriate to exhaust such major internal reform alternatives before moving to external contracting. "School-based management gives flexibility to those closest to the students, allowing them to design the most appropriate education for students. It is also suggested that making decisions locally fosters within the community a greater sense of ownership and responsibility for the quality of education and increases the accountability of schools" (Zinser 1994, p. 5). Furthermore, there is some evidence that decentralized district decision making may result in stronger education programs and higher test scores (Ferguson and Nochelski 1996). However, school-based management presumes the availability of people, including professional staff, with the interest, time, and expertise to make wise decisions. Furthermore, one must be careful to differentiate among the issues of site-based management of primary and secondary schools, private contracting for certain administrative services for public schools, contracting for support services such as maintenance and food service, the issue of whether public schools are necessary, and the issue of the relative administrative roles of the public sector and the private sector in the market for primary and secondary education.

One major area of reform that has received increased attention in today's environment of fiscal stress, pressure for lower taxes in local government, and a demand for accountability from government at all levels is some verification as to where school dollars are being spent and some assurance that they are being spent wisely. "Many voters believe that their school dollars are going into a black hole" (Mandel, Melcher, Yang, and McNamee 1995, p. 67). Indeed, evidence exists that those voters might be right in this assessment. Bruce Cooper of Fordham University, perhaps the school accounting guru of the twentieth and twenty-first century, notes that only 52% of every school dollar actually gets into the classroom in the typical large school district (Mandel et al. 1995, p. 64). As a result of these concerns, an increasing number of school districts are moving to "site-based reporting," a system developed by Cooper and now nationally distributed by Coopers & Lybrand and the U.S. Chamber of Commerce. Site-based reporting provides disaggregated data that allows school district spending to be accounted for by category of spending (e.g., instruction v. support services), as well as by building or other accounting center (e.g., central administration). Site-based reporting is a logical teammate of site-based management in that it provides the accounting data necessary to evaluate the effectiveness and deficiencies within a site-based management system. Reform targets and priorities can then be set on the basis of this improved information.

One of the major concerns raised by past experiences with private administration of public schools is the seeming lack of valid and reliable cost data for public primary and secondary education. This lack of cost data makes it difficult for private firms to accurately assess the potential for cost savings and profits.[22] Correspondingly, school boards are less able to evaluate the relative merits of privatization and the performance of administrative contractors in the absence of benchmarked cost information. This is a notable deficiency that continues to act as a barrier to greater use of private administration of public schools.

There is much to be done in terms of administrative reforms with respect to primary and secondary education. Nevertheless, it appears that progress is being made toward overturning traditional management and accounting structures that some people maintain have allowed our schools to stagnate. Even the limited experience with reform alternatives should indicate that there is nothing magical about centralized governmental administration of primary and secondary education. At the same time, the highly publicized Education Alternatives Incorporated and Edison Project experiences do not offer overwhelming evidence for the success or sustainability of the private alternative, or of contracting out. Nevertheless, numerous examples exist of successful publicly administered school systems and of privately administered schools. Thus, a clear path for reform remains undefined or poorly defined. However, some progress may come with patience.

"Part of the problem, analysts say, is that the education industry is an immature market. Many of these companies are still learning from their mistakes as they go along, because there is no real track record for privatization of public education" (Bushweller 1997, p. 20). Bushweller goes on to compare today's education industry with the health care industry of the 1970s. "Hospitals . . . were experiencing serious financial problems as expenses outpaced revenues. The shortfall opened the door for health maintenance organizations (HMOs), whose primary motive was to turn a profit" (Bushweller 1997, p. 20). Bushweller notes that some of the same kinds of criticisms that were launched against HMOs[23] are now appearing as arguments put forth by critics of privatization in education. Although success was relatively slow and painful, HMOs, though still controversial and detested in many circles, are a well-established part of the health care industry. "The HMO parallel has already become a rallying cry for education privatization advocates. The comparison is made often, and industry advocates and analysts have begun using the acronym EMO (education management organization) to categorize companies like Education Alternatives Inc. (EAI), Alternative Public Schools (APS), and the Edison Project" (Bushweller 1997, p. 20). Reformers remain vocal, but there is some question as to whether the deck might be stacked against them.

"Reformers of educational services are arguing for a return of control and choice to customers and away from centralized bureaucracies. However, while centralized authority can often be clumsy and inefficient, central administrations are often best-suited to provide certain services at the lowest cost" (Downes and Testa 1995, p. ix). At least tangentially, this raises the question of school district consolidation, on top of the already complex administrative issues addressed in this chapter.

CONCLUSION

Our market role analysis of the administrator role did not succeed in identifying any binding or compelling rationale for the universal administration of public schools by government. Based on the presumption rule adopted for the analysis, private administration of public schools should be feasible and desirable. From the standpoint of theory, vast opportunities for reform of the administration of public schools (and schools in general) appear to exist and seem economically and politically viable. From the standpoint of practice, a track record of private management success has not developed commensurate with the broad opportunities that market role assessment suggests should be available and feasible.

Given the nature of current empirical evidence, it is plausible that what is being observed is a comparative advantage for the public sector in the efficient management of public schools. As we move through discussion of other market roles, the parameters for privatization of administration should become even more well defined and narrowed. Some of our most useful information may ultimately come from the analysis of ongoing charter school programs that have been instituted in a variety of states. Given the seemingly private administration of "public schools" that is inherent in the charter school model, even small-scale, potentially idiosyncratic results may be both interesting and useful in investigating the role of the administrator in primary and secondary education.

A further related question that needs to be explored, in terms of our previous discussion of government's regulatory role in the market for primary and secondary education, is the extent to which the extensive current regulatory role of government in the public schools may make administrative reform through privatization impossible. It is possible that when one is faced with adhering to laws about length of school day, length of class period, class size, requirements for the service of special needs children, and so on, there is no significant freedom left to allow improvement in administration through competition, or contracting out, or other forms of privatization. Again, charter school results may help to clarify the answer to this concern. Thus, we leave our discussion of the administrator role for the time being, but not before identifying the administrator role as a priority area for further investigation, policy debate, and investment in reform experiments. This discussion is resumed in the comprehensive evaluative summary that appears as Chapter 10.

Chapter 5 considers the dual market roles of distributor and allocator, crucial roles in determining access to and availability of educational services.

NOTES

[1]Other similar analogies come to mind. For example, the making of a movie involves a producer, executive producer, and director.

[2]This analogy is also appropriate for private and parochial schools in that most have a similar administrative structure (albeit with different names for some of the actors), even when one considers an example like a single parish-run school.

[3]In the interest of narrowing the debate and analysis, the principal focus of this chapter is on the administrator role as it relates to the general administration and educational administration of schools and school systems. Thus, issues like that of privatizing support services are neither emphasized nor directly analyzed in any detail.

[4]EAI did land a contract in early 1997 to lease and operate twelve charter schools in the Phoenix area. This reflected a new focus by EAI on running its own new schools and on managing schools in suburban areas.

[5]There is, however, some recent evidence that the Edison Project has found new life and had a new infusion of resources (Billings 1999).

[6]Given that privatization efforts are not costless in terms of time, effort, and expenditures by both the private sector and the public sector, one might logically inquire about the true cost of failed privatization efforts.

[7]It should be noted that discriminatory behavior typically is considered to be a market failure and therefore has both efficiency and equity dimensions. Therefore, discrimination will be revisited as we assess the administrator role and its relationship to market failures.

[8]However, government may, as pointed out in Chapter 3, improve the outcomes through its role as regulator or through its function in providing a legal foundation to assist in the operation of the price system. Furthermore, government's role as financier may have a great impact on improving equity outcomes, as will be discussed later chapters.

[9]That is, within the context of our definition of the administrator role, the administrator will not be the primary source or participant in most forms of anticompetitive behavior.

[10]Incomplete markets exist when a good or service is not produced by the private market even though the marginal social benefits of the good or service exceed the marginal social costs of its production. Traditional examples of incomplete markets are deposit insurance and flood insurance.

[11]For example, see Williams and Leak (1996).

[12]The contract with the Alliance gave the school district the right to back out of the contract at the end of each school year if it so desired.

[13]Education Alternatives, Inc. (EAI), is the instructional management arm of the Alliance for Schools That Work, which also includes Johnson Controls World Services (custodial, maintenance, food, and clerical personnel); Computer Curriculum Corporation (computer-assisted instruction software); and KPMG, Peat Marwick (financial services). "EAI and its 'Tesseract' program, however, have become synonymous with the whole package of services. *Tesseract* is a word from a children's book implying a rapid journey to previously imagined heights, and Baltimore's nine EAI schools have been known as Tesseract schools" (Williams and Leak 1996, p. 56).

[14]It should be noted that many of White's descriptions of the Baltimore program have been challenged in subsequent research findings (e.g., Williams and Leak 1996).

For example, several researchers and commentators on the Baltimore experience have disputed the assertion that EAI invested many more dollars in the Tesseract schools than BCPS would have. In fact, there is some disagreement in the literature about the amount EAI actually was spending in Baltimore (Harrington-Lueker, April 1996).

[15]"Although never described as such, the use of this software was seen as a demonstration project embedded in the Tesseract program to show that full use of an integrated learning system would boost student achievement" (Williams and Leak 1996, p. 59).

[16]EAI president Philip Geijer was widely quoted in asserting that the problem in Hartford involved finances and contractual disagreements rather than his company's performance.

[17]For a more detailed description and evaluation of the Hartford experiment, see Uline (1998).

[18]However, there seems to be growing interest in the education industry by for-profit firms and private investors (Bushweller 1997).

[19]Among school board presidents who favored privatization, 64% said it was alright to privatize support services, but only 25% said it was alright to privatize instructional services (DeSpain and Livingston 1996, p. 19). Contracting for support services is much more widely accepted as a form of privatization in primary and secondary education. It also has a much longer and more successful track record of sustained contractual relationships (Bushweller 1997).

[20]Whereas 48% of chamber of commerce executives believed privatization would hold administrators more accountable, only 14% of board presidents believed this to be the case. More than 60% of chamber executives thought privatization would save money for taxpayers, and a similar proportion expected privatization to motivate teachers to work harder and more efficiently. In contrast, only 18% of school board presidents thought privatization would save money, and 23% thought it would motivate teachers to work harder. It is interesting that nearly two-thirds of school board presidents felt that privatization would encourage corruption, and 38% of chamber executives concurred in this judgment. In one point of agreement, 56% of both groups thought privatization would control the influence of unions (DeSpain and Livingston 1996).

[21]For example, see United States General Accounting Office (August 1994).

[22]There is widespread speculation in the literature that this factor contributed to the failed EAI contracts.

[23]For example, that cost controls will result in diminished service quality.

CHAPTER 5

The Distributor/Allocator
Who Is Responsible for Allocating Access to Education and Ensuring Its Delivery to Students?

The role of distributor/allocator is a market role that may be hard to define owing to the implicit nature of the role in a competitive market. Actually, calling this a distributor/allocator role blurs the distinction between two different and often separate economic roles, but in the context of a market such as primary and secondary education there is little to be gained by attempting to formally analyze these roles individually. Although distributor and allocator are different economic roles, the relationship between them is such that there are economies in the same institution or organization playing both roles in many markets. Defining each of these roles will aid in understanding their importance as well as their nature in the context of primary and secondary education.

The first role, which we will refer to as the allocator, deals with performing a resource allocation function. The allocator, subject to the existence of an initial distribution of resources that is assumed to be outside his or her formal control,[1] determines which resources will be made available for the production of which goods and services. In addition, the allocator determines to whom goods and services will be made available once they are produced. Thus, the allocator takes the resources that are available for production in the market of interest[2] and allocates them to the production of particular goods and services in that market. Once the goods and services are produced with the allocated resources, it is the allocator's job to determine how the finished goods and services will be allotted among the consumers desiring some quantity of the product. Generally, the allocator sets up a priority structure that is applied until the supply of the good or service is exhausted.

The second role, which we will refer to as the distributor, deals with performing what can be considered the marketing and delivery functions for the good or service. In this nomenclature, the distributor acts as a middleperson between producers and consumers, marketing the producer's products and ensuring that the products are transported in some fashion from producer to consumer.[3] The distributor in this conception of economic roles is the economic actor who is responsible for the information flow between the producer and the consumer. From a strategic standpoint, and assuming an imperfectly competitive market[4] (otherwise product differentiation or supplier differentiation has no economic function), control of this information flow involves not only developing a product description that will be of interest to consumers, but also designing a marketing system, including a marketing network through which information is disseminated to consumers and feedback is received in return.

Beyond his or her marketing function, the distributor is responsible for implementing the economic allocations of the final good or service according to the decisions made by the allocator (or his or her allocation mechanism). That is, the allocator determines who will receive the production of the firm during a given period and the payment the consumers must make in return for the product. The distributor takes the allocation decisions as given and has the responsibility for making sure that every buyer designated by the allocator receives his or her designated quantity of the good or service. One would also expect the distributor to be the logical "customer service" agent in terms of handling complaints about the quality of the good or service, or the timeliness and reliability of its delivery. In today's era of increasing attention to customer orientation, quality services, and responsiveness to constituents, the role of the distributor is especially important for the contemporary public administrator to understand. As the public sector continues to come under fire and scrutiny related to efficiency and quality of service, the ability to deftly and effectively play the marketing role of distributor becomes increasingly important.

Despite the crucial nature of the allocator role, the average person rarely would have reason to give any independent thought to it. In a market system, prices generally serve the allocator role in a relatively invisible and automatic fashion. Resources flow to those uses where they receive the greatest return, that is, where the price paid for them is highest. Goods and services are purchased and consumed by those individuals willing and able to pay the market-determined price.

In a system of perfectly competitive markets, prices serve the allocation function. In such a system, economic efficiency is achieved through (1) all resources being put to their highest and best use, and (2) all goods and services being purchased and consumed by those consumers who placed the highest value on those goods and services.

Even in imperfectly competitive markets, the price system generally plays the role of allocator. Prices, both resource and product, still allocate resources between production alternatives, and prices still determine who will receive the typically limited units of the good or service, with those consumers who are willing to pay the highest prices being the ones to receive highest priority. The primary difference in an imperfectly competitive market is that the prices at which the goods or services are traded are not necessarily a reflection of social benefits and costs, and therefore an economically efficient outcome cannot be guaranteed. This loss of efficiency is one factor that motivates interest in alternative allocation mechanisms and alternatives to private market performance of the allocator role. Indeed, despite our familiarity and comfort with market allocation schemes based on prices, alternative allocational mechanisms exist and are widely utilized in conjunction with or in the place of market prices. Some of these alternatives involve government intervention in the market through performance or facilitation of the allocator role. Market role assessment of the allocator/distributor role enables us to evaluate these interventions in the context of government's functions in a mixed economy.

GOVERNMENT INTERVENTION AND THE ALLOCATOR/DISTRIBUTOR ROLE

For example, with respect to natural monopolies, the role of allocator is not (exclusively) played by the price system. Typically, in exchange for a monopoly franchise, a natural monopoly is required to make concessions that do not allow it to merely provide its product to the highest bidder. Indeed, most regulated natural monopolies are required to provide their services on a non-discriminatory basis to their market area, are regulated in the price they can charge and/or the profit they can make, and are required to have special accommodations to ensure access for low income households.[5] Although at the margin there may be some flexibility in rate structures and private contracting for services, in general the allocator role in the case of natural monopolies is at least partially performed through external government intervention that holds prices below the market outcome expected in the face of monopoly power.[6] This type of intervention can be justified through government's function of intervening to correct market failure owing to monopoly power.

In addition to the case of natural monopoly, government plays the role of allocator for goods and services that are not generally produced in private markets, or for which government is a dominant producer outside of the main market system. Once again, this intervention directly corresponds to one of the previously discussed functions of government in a mixed economy. Generally, interventions of this type are justified on the basis of market failure owing to the public good aspects of the good or service in question, or owing to incomplete markets.

As an example, intergovernmental grants and welfare payments are generally distributed through a government-based allocation system that substitutes for the price system.[7] The government, through a set of eligibility guidelines, typically determines who receives the benefits of these programs and in what amount. Such eligibility guidelines often include a "means test," whereby the applicants must prove that their economic capacity is below a some predetermined floor. In other cases, allocation decisions require a "status test," whereby the applicants must prove membership in some targeted group to whom assistance is aimed (e.g., head of household with dependent children, senior citizen, have less than a high school education). Furthermore, the level of government making the allocation decision often differs from program to program, or from level of program to level of program.

In the former CETA jobs program, the federal government made the allocation decisions that resulted in funds flowing from Washington to each of the states. Urban counties received their own allocation of these funds directly from the federal government and had the responsibility for allocating the funds among recipients.[8] Similarly, the governor's office in each state received the allocation of funds for each state except for the urban counties just mentioned and discussed. The governor's office made the allocation decisions for the "balance of state" area. These allocation decisions followed the same general pattern as those discussed for urban counties; but one should note that in "balance of state" areas, members of targeted groups were typically much more difficult to find and enroll.[9] Before assessing the allocator/distributor role in the market for primary and secondary education, some idiosyncracies related to the distribution of services should be explored.

With respect to most *services,* the distributor role is less well established and less broad than with respect to the distribution of manufactured products. Many services are produced and consumed on a face-to-face or direct basis.[10] Thus, physically moving the product from producer to consumer rarely takes place. To the extent that the services are produced and consumed at the producer's place of business (e.g., a barber shop), there is no need to physically distribute the service from producer to consumer. However, to the extent that services are provided to the customer at the customer's residence, place of employment, or other customer-chosen place, there is a necessity to move the service producer from his or her place of business to the customer. Dispatching services, such as those used by taxi drivers, who are often independent contractors, or by tow truck operators who service national automobile clubs, are service-based distributors. When there is excess demand for services, as is often the case for jump starts during a winter cold snap, the dispatch service may also play an allocator role.

However, whereas the "delivery" aspect of the distributor's role may be less important in service markets, the marketing aspect of the distributor role may be even more important to service producers than it is to traditional goods producers. Service producers often need to make their services better known to consumers, and many service producers actively seek to secure business in an often very competitive market. This helps to explain the affiliation of service producers with national chains or firms (e.g., H&R Block, Coldwell Banker, Ernst & Young, Rainbow Carpet Cleaning). Such affiliations produce name recognition, marketing clout, and some degree of perceived product familiarity to the mobile consumer. Indeed, most national real estate firms now employ relocation experts who seek to gain business on both ends of a customer's move through references and availability of franchisees in both the origin and destination communities. To some extent, this marketing goal also appears to be at the heart of many managed health care firms. A recent radio ad campaign suggests an effort to instill the concept that one major national managed care provider wants to be your "health care system" (a portable concept) and "not your doctor" (a nonportable concept). This is a modern marketing approach to differentiating a service product while simultaneously allaying people's fear of change.

As one can see, the allocator/distributor role is broad and rich in its formulation. It is particularly complex and interesting role in the market for primary and secondary education. The market for primary and secondary education features an interesting amalgam of the allocator and distributor roles. One reason for this is the variety of conditions under which primary and secondary education services are offered. For example, some primary and secondary education in the United States is supplied by private not-for-profit and private for-profit providers. Access to education services supplied by these private providers typically is allocated on the basis of some combination of academic achievement/promise, and willingness and ability to pay the requisite tuition. Although the allocation system for private education is not generally based purely on price or willingness to pay, universal or random access to private schools is not generally claimed or sought, and private school tuition is generally market responsive. That is, even though it may be unfair to characterize access to private education as exclusively, or even predominantly, market determined, it is fair to say that access to private schools is based on willingness and ability to pay. Private tuition is a general reflection of market conditions even if it is not directly market determined. Tuition must be commensurate with parents' ability to pay as measured within the school's market, and those students whose families are unwilling or unable to pay the required tuition, regardless of form,[11] need not be accepted or retained. With respect to the distributor role, private schools typically have distribution mechanisms that enable them to be marketed to their prospective clientele through in-house marketing programs, through the marketing resources of organizations related to their clientele (e.g., for parochial schools such resources might include church bulletin announcements, sermons and homilies, and advertisements or stories in religious magazines and newspapers), or even through marketing services provided by directly contracting with a private firm or a school association. The track record of private education in the United States provides incontrovertible evidence that private performance of the allocator/distributor role is both feasible and sustainable in the market for primary and secondary education.

The typical allocation and distribution mechanisms for traditional public schools differ significantly from the more market-based model of private schools. Some of these differences are attributable to the nature of the conditions under which public education is provided in the United States. For example, there are greater legal constraints placed upon public schools with respect to open access and equal opportunity. Whereas a religiously affiliated school might give preferential consideration to students of the same faith as the affiliated church, public schools have no comparable ability to choose the students they want to enroll or continue, with the exception of their expulsion powers (which are actually quite limited) to remove a student from the public schools.[12] The right to a "free" public education plays into this debate.

"Free" public education is a well-established tradition in the United States. In the 1820s a few states began to put public monies and public lands into education. "By the 1850's, many Northeastern and Midwestern states had established systems of free public schools, including high schools in some locations. In the latter half of the 19th century, free public schools became accessible to most children in the South and the West, and education became compulsory in most states" (Center on National Education Policy 1996, p. 6). Many people would argue, and have argued in recent educational finance cases, that "free" public education is a basic right and not merely a privilege, requiring that greater diligence and energy be devoted to its furtherance and protection.[13]

Though education may be considered a right (at some level) by most Americans, the collective choices made by these same Americans through our collective choice institutions (i.e., government) have also made education a responsibility. Basic education is mandatory in the United States. Typically, school attendance is required of all children under the age of 16. Truancy laws are enforced against students and parents who fail to comply with mandatory education requirements.[14]

Americans' commitment to education as a basic right and as a basic responsibility has led to numerous government interventions designed to ensure equal educational opportunities regardless of race; creed; ethnic origin; and social class; as well as without regard to physical, mental, or emotional challenges. The government interventions to ensure access to the market can be justified in several ways related to the functions of government in a mixed economy. Owing to the significant positive spillover benefits associated with primary and secondary education, government is responsible for the drafting and enforcement of laws compelling education until a minimum age. Government's intervention as an enforcer of compulsory education can also be justified under government's paternalistic function. This function supports government interventions to compel individual behavior that is in an individual's best interest but that may not be undertaken if not mandated (e.g., immunization and school physical requirements can be justified on similar grounds). Furthermore, government performance as allocator in the market for primary and secondary education can also be justified on equity grounds. Government intervenes to adjust private market outcomes to make them more just or equitable. Through performance of the allocator role, government can ensure a level of access for special needs students, underprivileged students, and members of other groups who may not have access through an unfettered private market owing to relative cost considerations or discrimination. For many years, it has been government policy to try to mainstream students with special needs, that is, integrate them into the regular school population and curriculum as much as possible while being sensitive and adaptive to their special needs. Although numerous federal and state grant programs have been developed to help local communities offset the relatively high cost of educating special needs students, the responsibility for educating these students has fallen overwhelmingly on public school systems,[15] as has the task of educating problem students and students rejected by alternative education providers. It is interesting that many charter schools have been approved under the guise of alternative schools that provide a last resort attempt to educate problem students. However, many reform efforts and proposals neglect to significantly address the issue of special needs students. Few charter schools are teaching students with disabilities at rates comparable to the surrounding public schools (McKinney 1996).[16] The Illinois law authorizing charter schools does not make the special education funds for special needs students portable to the charter school.[17] This potentially creates some serious problems regarding incentives and resource allocation.

Thus, in practice the allocation mechanism utilized for the largest segment of the market for primary and secondary education is a government-developed and -enforced (nonmarket) system of universal and compulsory access to education for all students below the age of 16, as well as for those above age 16 who desire to continue their primary and secondary education. "Free" public education has generally been interpreted to mean that this universal access is provided on a tuition-free basis. As we will learn in Chapter 8 devoted to the financing of primary and secondary education, increasingly parents are being asked to bear increased fees and charges, outside of the realm of traditional tuition, in exchange for this "free" public education. Government remains the allocator of last resort in the market for primary and secondary education, the allocator from whom any student can gain access to the market and can choose to exercise the rights and responsibilities associated with primary and secondary education. As last resort allocator, government provides access to the market for those who are unable to pay the required price for access from a (more) market-based allocator such as a private educational institution.

It is unlikely that the need for a last resort, nonmarket source of access to the market for primary and secondary education will ever disappear. Therefore, with respect to the role of allocator, government may always have a role in the market for primary and secondary education in terms of allocating educational opportunities as a means of ensuring universal access to free and mandatory education. However, until relatively recently government's role as allocator was primarily implemented in a passive fashion through geographically based rules that ultimately determined attendance and attendance patterns.

In most traditional public school systems, government allocated educational opportunities on the basis of geographic attendance zones that were generally nonnegotiable for students in any systematic way. The original challenges to these attendance zones came primarily as a result of civil rights–based complaints and lawsuits charging that unequal public education opportunities were being provided based on *de facto* racial lines. This was because of racial and ethnic segregation of neighborhoods that was not overcome through the use of geographically based attendance zones. Furthermore, accusations of unequal resources provided to minority and white schools exacerbated conflict that allegedly had its primary roots in attendance zones that segregated students on racial or ethnic lines. In fact, breaking down the geographically based attendance zones may have *increased* government's role as allocator of educational opportunities by way of court-imposed busing plans, mandatory integration measures, and other equal access prescriptions that were externally imposed through laws, regulations, and court orders; not to mention the increased discretion given to local school districts to actively manage enrollment for social purposes.

Magnet schools, special interest public high schools with competitive admissions, and expanded school choice programs were initiatives designed to allow quasi-market mechanisms to help allocate public classroom seats on other than a purely geographic basis. Such quasi-market mechanisms can be justified in part as improving the efficiency with which students are matched to preferred schools and academic programs. With the diversity of one's student body as a contributing criterion, allocative solutions superior to those of geographically based attendance zones seem to be both possible and achievable. However, the success of such quasi market reform efforts generally requires a reevaluation of both government regulations and parental expectations. Some students will be denied access to their preferred program or school. In a public school system, this may be the source of significant tension, especially if a large number of students are denied admission. "On the surface, these [school choice] options were innovative and often designed to support important social goals such as school integration. Beneath the surface, however, the new programs developed identities that seemed more elitist than egalitarian. I was troubled by my perception of a diminished commitment to equal opportunity and successful education of all children" (Fennimore 1996, p. 53). Thus, community "buy in" to a well-articulated and well-designed program is an essential precursor to the success of such reform efforts designed at altering traditional allocative methods.

For example, transportation of students to a distant school is an essential part of distributing education in the market and is generally considered under the traditional model to be the responsibility of the school system. This clearly makes sense in a system where government is allocating classroom space and students/parents do not choose their school.[18] Quasi market reforms, including school choice programs, put several wrinkles into the traditional school transportation model. Elimination or relaxation of geographically based attendance zones would be expected to increase by some measure (large or small, depending on a number of intervening factors) the average length of the school commute for students. Furthermore or alternatively, the area from which schools draw their student body would generally be expected to increase. Thus, the density of students within a given school's attendance area would be expected to decrease. All of these factors would be expected to increase a school system's transportation costs. These increased transportation costs may be acceptable to the district and its residents, but they do in any case represent increased operational costs for the school system that are driven by changes in the allocation rules. Other options may exist.

For example, given that not all school districts are required by law to provide transportation to their pupils,[19] especially in situations where student or parental choice of school is allowed, it is possible to consider options whereby parents are generally responsible for their students' school commute, with provisions made for students from low income households for free or low cost transportation. Additionally, it would be possible to make transportation to the nearest school free of charge, with incremental costs charged back to parents for longer commutes by students (with an option for parentally provided transportation). The point is that even with such transportation barriers, adjustments can be made so as to approximate market allocation and distribution mechanisms. Once again, a key to the success of such programs is parental understanding and support that has been developed prior to the program being announced and implemented. The implications of approximating market mechanisms through government initiatives are significant in terms of the discussion of the allocator/distributor role in this chapter.

In the presence of interference or imperfections that prevent or hinder attainment of unfettered market efficiency (i.e., market failures), economists suggest that efforts to restore efficiency focus on designing interventions such that the external intervention[20] leads economic actors (i.e., producers and consumers) to adjust their market behavior so as to mimic an efficient market solution. In the literature, this is known as internalization (of an externality). For example, by charging a transportation fee proportional to the additional transportation costs imposed by a student's school choice, internalization is approximated and a more efficient and comprehensive school choice system can be operated. Each individual consumer then compares the costs of the additional transportation with the perceived benefits to be received by attending the more distant school, and he or she makes a decision as to the merit of paying an additional sum for transportation to the distant school.[21] This process mimics that which the consumer goes through in making market decisions. The better the information that the parent is provided with in terms of transportation alternatives and the potential differences in the educational experiences at competing schools, the greater the likelihood that the end result will approach an economically efficient outcome. Although the relative value of different educational experiences may vary from individual to individual and be difficult to quantify, good information about the content and differences in the schools' programs should be sufficient to make an informed quasi market decision that represents an improvement over unilateral government allocation made wholly by nonmarket methods.

The key point to be made as a result of this analysis is that even a publicly controlled school system does not necessarily require that government play the role of allocator, even as a last resort. Government can make rules to guarantee universal access to primary and secondary education and enforce those rules through its role as regulator. In charter school experiments, government has typically set up rules requiring equal access through either a first come, first served system or a lottery system, to prevent "creaming" of students. In strict terms, government is not acting as allocator but once again is acting in its role as regulator. A similar framework can be used for reform alternatives such as school choice programs. To the extent that issues of access are related to affordability, vouchers could be used to ensure financial access in a quasi market system.

In summary, government need not play the role of allocator in the market for primary and secondary education, although it seems likely that government will need to be involved in setting rules to regulate the allocation of public educational opportunities as long as free and mandatory public education remains as a collective choice. To the extent that government can set and enforce rules for universal access to primary and secondary education, allocation at a more micro level can be handled through market and quasi market mechanisms with expected efficiency gains. The distributor aspect of the role appears to be more complex.

With respect to defining the nature of and the degree to which government should perform the distributor role in primary and secondary education, the analysis is much more subtle. This is especially true given the wide variety of instructional technologies that are now available, including distance learning technologies that allow simultaneous and interactive multiple site delivery of educational programs.[22] However, to the extent that true competition is ever introduced into primary and secondary education, the role of distributor, especially in terms of marketing, becomes even more important as schools compete for students.

The role of distributor is a viable one in the market for primary and secondary education, whether education is privately or publicly provided. Educational services and educational programs should be marketed to their clientele, and information with respect to the availability, content, and quality of educational programs should flow freely.[23] Furthermore, part of ensuring universal access to primary and secondary education would seem to include utilizing innovative delivery mechanisms as appropriate to broaden access to educational programs. Such delivery mechanisms might include interactive television, teleconferencing, use of the Internet, and computer networks. However, despite the importance of this distributor role, there is nothing in the description or content of this role that suggests that any sector need have a monopoly on its performance. Specifically, there is nothing to suggest that the distributor role as we have defined it needs be performed by government, even in the case of public schools. Government could make the allocation rules and make the allocation decisions, but the marketing and delivery functions that define the distributor role could be contracted out to a private firm. *Prima facie* evidence that this is feasible is provided by the success that private schools have had in performing these functions. Further evidence is provided by the development of successful distance learning networks that centralize delivery and marketing functions for coursework of multiple academic institutions. But it is possible the distributor role has been underdefined and underutilized with respect to public primary and secondary education. Government has a responsibility to assess and evaluate the truth of this perception and to pay as much attention to issues of distribution as a private manufacturing firm might. The market role assessment in this book can provide a starting point for administrative analysis of possible improvements in efficiency related to the performance of the distributor role for public primary and secondary schools.

CONCLUSION

The allocator/distributor role is at the heart of our system of mandatory, free education. Such a system requires open and unbiased access to educational opportunities. Any reform effort carried out in the context of preserving such an educational system will need to provide an allocator of last resort, an undeniable means of access to the market for primary and secondary education. In view of our societal concerns about equal educational opportunity, the chosen allocation mechanism must be one that does not promote allocation decisions that are discriminatory in intent or effect with respect to dimensions such as race, ethnicity, or special needs. This allocation mechanism need not be government based but would likely need to be government regulated and audited to ensure that the responsibility of last resort, nondiscriminatory access to the market, was being upheld. That is, a market or quasi market allocation mechanism that complies with appropriate regulations about nondiscrimination and fair access would be a plausible alternative. Indeed, given the absence of a compelling rationale grounded in the functions of government in a mixed economy, the presumption rule requires a finding in favor of such a market or quasi market outcome. Government's performance of the regulator role can set appropriate rules within which the allocator role can then be performed by the private sector.

The distributor role is also an important consideration in the design of reform proposals. There appears to be significant interest in undertaking measures to expand the range of choices that parents have in selecting the school that their child attends. No matter how such expanded choice is facilitated through reform efforts, the role of distributor is central to the success of any choice effort. Good choice is based on quality information, and a good distributor can be the source of quality information. Especially in the situation of a market that delivers its services to children outside of the presence of their parents, reliable and extensive information is a crucial input into making good choices among educational alternatives. The private sector already effectively performs the distributor function for private education. There is no reason, grounded in the functions of government in a mixed economy, why government is required to act as distributor in the market for public primary and secondary education. In order to facilitate the operation of a market or quasi market allocation and distribution system, it may be necessary for government to regulate the information format in the distribution channels by requiring that a certain template be followed to more readily enable parents to make informed choices among education alternatives.[24] However, such an intervention would likely be a relatively minor intrusion in the market and would be justified under the regulator role as opposed to that of allocator/distributor.

In Chapter 6 we address the central market role of producer. The producer is the economic actor who is responsible for taking the allocated inputs and converting those inputs into the desired set of goods and services.

NOTES

[1]For example, income will have much to do with the allocation of goods and services, but we assume that the allocator of primary and secondary education services does not directly control the initial income distribution in the market.

[2]That is, the market in which the allocator function is being performed.

[3]Transportation may involve placing orders with the firm so that it knows where to ship its products, or it may involve the distributor taking physical custody of the goods and moving them from place to place (e.g., a soft drink or beer distributor), or some intermediate arrangement.

[4]In a perfectly competitive market, the product is homogeneous among all firms in all respects. Thus, firms cannot even compete on the basis of customer service. This means that all buyers are indifferent as to the seller from whom they purchase the generic product.

[5]These are familiar types of rules under which electric and natural gas services have been often provided through regulated monopolies. Increasingly, though, these industries are being deregulated, and many of these rules no longer apply as multiple firms are allowed to compete to deliver services in a given market.

[6]It should be noted that the monopoly outcome here is basically the same as the adverse outcome expected in the case of a monopoly driven by a barrier to entry other than market size. That is, the outcome results in a production level lower than that achieved in perfect competition (i.e., the efficient level of output) and at an unfettered market price greater than that which would prevail under perfect competition. Thus, one gets the worst of both worlds: fewer goods, and at a higher price.

[7]Consistent with the theme of market role assessment, it should be noted again that the primary focus in the current analysis is on the allocator/distributor role. This means that issues such as the appropriateness of public welfare, administrative efficiency of the welfare system, and welfare fraud are tangential to the current discussion.

[8]These counties had to prove that their allocation system resulted in the funds flowing to eligible and targeted groups, but the counties had great flexibility as to how to do this within the confines of the broad administrative rules.

[9]During 1980 the author worked for the Executive Office of the Governor in the State of Iowa in the area of balance of state CETA administration. His primary responsibility was to develop an allocation mechanism for field staff such that the CETA funds for the state would be spent each year (i.e., a method that would not turn down an inappropriately high number of applicants, but would likely not exhaust funds so early as to have them run out for even highly targeted groups). As one might imagine, such a task was extremely difficult and was indicative of the administrative and delivery problems that contributed to CETA's demise in the early 1980s.

[10]For example, personal grooming, health care services, and home repair services.

[11]Some schools now accept a combination of sweat equity and cash payments in satisfaction of tuition requirements.

[12]Recall that with special needs students, expulsions become very difficult, if not impossible in many cases. Furthermore, with special needs students, an expulsion may carry with it a continuing responsibility on the part of the district to educate the child.

[13]As of April 1997, thirteen states' Supreme Courts had declared that education is a fundamental constitutional right, and eleven state Supreme Courts had declared that education is not a fundamental constitutional right (Hickrod et al. 1997).

[14]It should be noted that the mandatory education requirement does not generally require that the student be enrolled in an educational institution. Numerous home schooling arrangements have been approved over the years in fulfillment of mandatory education requirements.

[15]However, it should be noted that in many areas special education consortia are often formed to provide a more critical mass and specialized resources for serving special needs children across school districts. For example, one consortium in the southwestern portion of the Chicago area serves the students from fifty districts, according to information provided by a former director of the consortium. Bushweller

(1997) notes increased interest and success in privatizing specialized services including special education, although greater success has been seen in alternative schools for other types of at-risk students.

[16]One of the major factors determining whether a charter school educates significant numbers of children with disabilities is the school's legal status. If the school is considered a legally autonomous school district, it has a legal duty to provide a free appropriate public education for children with disabilities under the Individuals with Disabilities Education Act (IDEA). If the school is part of a traditional district, as an individual school site its level of responsibility is significantly lower. Few states with charter schools have addressed the issue of the precise legal status of these schools (McKinney 1996, p. 23).

[17]One other problem reported to me by a parent spearheading a "core skills" charter school effort in the Chicago area is the fact that the Illinois law requires the approval of the school district before a new charter school can receive its license/charter. Given that the school district would be signing on to a loss of state aid for every pupil that went to the charter school, it is not surprising that few charter schools have been approved in Illinois. The approval requirement also makes it more likely that the first charter schools to be approved will be something like the alternative schools for problem students that were just described (indeed, according to recent reports from legislators and the news media, some districts are erroneously interpreting the Illinois charter law to only allow such alternative schools). Although this may be a good use of charter schools, it is not the full intent of charter school legislation, and it would be tragic if such schools ultimately were the only (or even a great proportion) of the new schools chartered under the state law.

[18]Transportation represents a part of the distributor role defined at the beginning of the chapter. The current discussion represents a good example of the difficulty in separating the allocator and distributor roles.

[19]For example, high school districts in Illinois are not actually required to provide transportation for students and can charge back such costs to parents according to the Illinois School Code.

[20]For example, a tax on every unit of production from a manufacturing plant that is set in the amount of the estimated pollution cost imposed by production of each unit of the same product.

[21]Of course, a portion of the transportation cost for low income families may be borne by the school district or another government in order to ensure access and to make market outcomes more just or equitable. In such cases, the parents would compare their out-of-pocket cost of transportation with the perceived educational benefits.

[22]For an overview of some of these technologies, see Bennett and Peddle (1998).

[23]Recall that such an information flow is essential to the effective operation of a free market system.

[24]Such a template and regulatory intervention should become less necessary with the passage of time. Once the system is up and operating, market flows of information in the forms desired by parents should increase and be self-regulated as part of the normal market mechanisms.

CHAPTER 6

The Producer
Who Is Responsible for "Producing" the Education?

In the simple circular flow model of an economy taught to students of economics, the product market is inhabited by producers on one side of the market and consumers on the other side of the market. One of the simplifying assumptions inherent in the circular flow model is that in the market for goods and services, households are assumed to be the only consumers and private businesses are assumed to be the only producers.[1]

Although more sophisticated economic models provide an enhanced view of the economy and market operations, rarely are market roles disaggregated and dissected to the extent required for a market role assessment such as the one conducted here. For example, the role of producer in simpler (i.e., more aggregated) economic models often requires that a single economic actor fulfill two or more of the individual roles we have identified (e.g., administrator, distributor, and producer). Such is the case with the circular flow model. In conducting our market role assessment, it is once again imperative to differentiate clearly among the individual market roles we discuss. This is especially true in the case of a role like that of producer, where alternative meanings and usage of the term are somewhat common.[2]

The word *produce* has rich and varied meaning.[3] Even in the context of economic usage, several different meanings must be combined to accurately capture the essence of economic production. Doing so, we define the producer for the purpose of market role assessment as *that economic entity that brings a product into existence through mental and physical effort involving the combination of economic resources*. Owing to the wide variety of goods and services that are produced, production, and thus the notion of a producer, remains rather broadly defined. Precise application of this definition to the production of primary and secondary education is an important part of our market role assessment. In addition, the link between the producer role and other market roles must be explored and evaluated. But first, a more general look into the producer role is required.

GOVERNMENT INTERVENTION AND THE PRODUCER ROLE

Government's role as producer in a market can conceivably be justified in a number of ways related to the functions government plays in a mixed economy. For example, government intervention as a producer may occur as part of government's function to provide goods and services that the private sector cannot or will not provide in sufficient quantities (i.e., public goods). Intervention as producer may also be justified to offset the negative effects of incomplete markets. Furthermore, government may intervene as a producer so as to make more units of a good or service available to those unable to access the good or service through the private market. Such an intervention might be classified as one designed to adjust market outcomes to make them more just or equitable.

Even though each of these justifications for government intervention is reasonable and well founded on its face, whether the intervention requires government performance of the producer role is less clear. Evaluating the evidence related to the need for government performance of the producer role requires an understanding of the distinction between *provision* of a good and *production* of a good. In simple terms, production involves actually manufacturing a good or directly performing a service; provision involves making arrangements to ensure the availability of a good or service. An example of the distinction between provision and production can be seen with reference to garbage removal services for residential properties in a municipality. The municipality could produce solid waste removal by buying trucks and using public works employees to drive the trucks and to pick up garbage at homes in the community. In this case, the municipality would both produce and provide garbage service. However, the municipality could also contract with a private firm in order to provide garbage service[4] to homes. In this case, the municipality would provide garbage service but would not perform the producer role in the market.

Analysis of the functions of government mentioned previously as possible justification for interventions in the producer role suggests that although government provision of goods and services may be important in all of these cases, government performance of the producer role may not be essential. Government intervention in each case is driven by ensuring availability of certain goods or services, either to the market in general or to targeted groups. In the case of public goods or access/opportunity issues, the government could generally ensure availability of the goods through contracting with private firms for production of the goods or services. That is, government could maintain its provision responsibilities without playing the producer role. In effect, this is what government has done with Medicare and Medicaid as a means of providing medical services. Other examples include small municipalities contracting with a county sheriff for police services or with an ambulance company for emergency medical services.

The issue of government intervention in the case of incomplete markets is somewhat different. Recall that incomplete markets are characterized by a failure of private markets to produce a good or service, even though the marginal social benefit of the good or service exceeds the marginal social cost of producing it. In such cases, normal economic incentives such as profits are insufficient to induce creation of a private market for the good or service. Flood insurance and deposit insurance are typical examples of government intervention in incomplete markets.

Incomplete markets provide a case wherein government performance of the producer role seems unavoidable. Because private firms have not provided the good or service, one cannot reasonably expect them to be willing to contract with government to provide the good or service except at a price that exceeds their marginal private cost of production. Thus, the existence of incomplete markets provides a *prima facie* case for government performance as producer.

We now turn our attention to the market for primary and secondary education. Market role assessment begins with a general look at education production.

THE PRODUCTION OF EDUCATION

The production of education—or, more precisely, educational services—is multifaceted and somewhat amorphous. One's notion of education can include classroom learning, out-of-class course-related learning, intramural noncourse activities, life skills training and experience, and physical and emotional learning, just to mention some of the variety of components often associated with the primary and secondary education experience. Viewing education in this broad manner makes it clear that the classroom teacher is not the sole or even the ultimate producer of education, although he or she is an essential part of primary and secondary education and its production. Similarly, although the school principal retains responsibility for educational services at a level above that of the classroom teacher, the principal remains equivalent to low or middle level management in a manufacturing firm. That is, the principal has some level of control over the way that resources are used within his or her school (depending upon the management system employed within a particular school system), but overarching resource decisions are made at a level above that of the individual school,[5] as are many educational policy decisions including curriculum and general educational philosophy. Ultimately, in most schools, it seems that the producer of education is thus some combination of teachers, parents (alone and collectively), the school level administrative team, high level central district administration, the local school board (and thus the local community at some level), and the state school board.[6]

Education is currently produced at all levels by nongovernmental producers. Indeed, education services prior to kindergarten are still dominated by private providers, some of which are national chains (e.g, KinderCare). This is *prima facie* evidence that governmental production of primary and secondary education need not be universal. However, the characteristics of primary and secondary education and the market for such education suggest that it may be unreasonable to expect all school systems to function in the long term with private producers of education, at least for-profit producers. The experiences of Education Alternatives Incorporated offer some evidence of this fact, especially in terms of the Hartford experience outlined in Chapter 4. However, given the multifaceted nature of primary and secondary education, including the need for active parent and student involvement in education that occurs outside of the classroom, it is equally clear that the production role cannot be borne exclusively by government at any level. However, to what extent does government need to play the producer role in the market for primary and secondary education?

As one may recall, primary and secondary education is characterized by positive externalities. That is, the benefits of primary and secondary education do not exclusively accrue to the student receiving the education. In Chapter 2 we outlined some of the societal benefits of primary and secondary education. These benefits include: preparing people to become responsible citizens, improving social conditions, and helping people to become more economically self-sufficient (Center on National Education Policy 1996, p. 5). Recalling our discussion from Chapter 2, the presence of significant positive externalities with respect to the consumption of a good or service leads to an undervaluation of the commodity by the consumer[7] and, therefore, underproduction of the good in the market. Thus, in an unfettered market, producers would be unwilling to supply the socially optimal amount of education because consumers of education would be willing to pay a price that would only reflect the marginal private benefits of education rather than the full social benefits of education. This situation is illustrated in Figure 1. A request from government for proposals from firms that wish to run a market-based franchise to produce the socially optimal level of education in an unfettered market would likely remain unanswered, because the firm(s) under such circumstances would not be expected to be profitable in a competitive market system wherein production of education would be wholly sustained by tuition and fee payments.

Alas, this particular problem is probably one of only theoretical concern. Few, if any, schools in the United States provide education such that the full

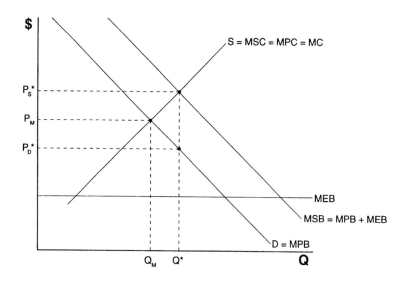

KEY

P_D^* = demand price at Q^*
P_S^* = supply price at Q^*
P_M = market price at Q_M
MPC = marginal private cost
MSC = marginal social cost
MPB = marginal private benefit
MEB = marginal external (spillover) benefit,
        which is assumed constant in this example
MSB = marginal social benefit
Q_M = quantity in unfettered market
Q^* = socially optimal, efficient quantity where
        MSB = MSC, but MPC > MPB

Figure 1.

cost of that education is supported by tuition and fee payments by students. Public schools are heavily supported by tax revenues and grants; private schools often receive in-kind government subsidies and grants, as well as private donations and endowments.[8] Thus, profitability concerns that might normally arise in the case of a service with positive externalities are reduced somewhat by the fact that a market-based price is not the sole revenue received by the producer. Indeed, returning to the Baltimore example, recall that the Alliance received a payment equivalent to the average per-pupil expenditure in the Baltimore City Public Schools, a payment that does not represent the equivalent of a market price determined through the interaction of supply and demand. Furthermore, under mandatory education laws students cannot opt out of the market if they do not place the appropriate value on education. Thus, the demand for education in any given market is tempered by the fact that a segment of the market is forced to participate even if the marginal cost of education exceeds the benefits in their private evaluation. On the other hand, our conception of free public education in the United States generally means that primary and secondary education is available on a tuition-free basis. The individual student or his or her family is not even asked to pay tuition that represents a portion of the *private* benefits that accrue to all students as a result of receiving education.[9]

Thus, the issue of government's role in the production of education must be discussed in terms of the parameters set out for the role at the beginning of this chapter, as well as in the context of the likely role that government would play in a fully reformed system of primary and secondary education. To the extent that we maintain a system of mandatory and free education that is universally available in the United States, fully free and unfettered market production of primary and secondary education is unfeasible. Given the positive externalities of primary and secondary education, along with the requirement of mandatory and free universal education, one must expect that a substantial portion of the bill for our primary and secondary education system will be borne collectively through compulsory contributions/exactions made through taxes and fees administered by government, as opposed to voluntary private tuition payments. Nevertheless, the resources collected by government to support a system of primary and secondary education need not be retained by government for production of these services. In other words, the need for a compulsory system of finance[10] does not imply the need for government performance of the producer role. It would be possible to make transfer payments to alternative producers to either (1) account for the collective benefits of primary and secondary education, or (2) pay producers for the full "costs" of producing education.[11] The role of producer should be played by the entity that can achieve the greatest educational results with the least exhaustion of resources. Given the relative newness of contracting out administration and production, most public school systems have well-entrenched resource patterns and levels of operational spending. Experiments with private production would seem desirable, especially in cases such as Baltimore and Hartford where problem schools might be radically improved. Reasons for the failures of the EAI and other private contracts must be explored and to the greatest extent possible not allowed to be repeated. On the other hand, public sector success stories like the one that appears to have unfolded in Chicago must also be given significant attention, so as to clearly understand the nature of and reasons for the relatively rapid financial and performance turnaround of the schools. Thus, some benchmarking against current government production results will be essential; but there is no theoretical reason, based on government's functions in a mixed economy, that educational production should necessarily be government's province, even in a traditional public school system. However, there is also little or no empirical evidence to indicate that the private sector will necessarily do a better job, especially on a widespread and ubiquitous basis. Once again, evidence from charter schools may begin to provide a picture of the feasibility of private production of public education, as well as barriers to effective and sustainable privatization of the producer role.

It should once again be noted that government likely will need to remain involved in oversight of the schools through the performance of the regulator and auditor roles,[12] even if government is removed from active production of educational services. Furthermore, the effective performance of the producer role in the market for primary and secondary education may be dependent on substantial regulatory relief for local schools in exchange for some type of outcome-based measure of achievement and success on the part of local districts and their students. Charter school experiences may offer evidence regarding the need for and effectiveness of regulatory relief.

Thus, to a great extent we return to the realm of uncertainty about the appropriate actor or set of actors to be involved in the performance of an economic role, in this case the role of the producer. This ambiguity is far from bad news, especially to an economist. In the absence of an inability to make performance of the role profitable for a private sector producer, a position for which there is no theoretical or reliable empirical support, the possibility of a market-based determination of the role division between government and the private sector remains viable.

CONCLUSION

Effective private sector performance of the producer role in private schools provides evidence that primary and secondary education can be produced privately. The existence of private schools also indicates that a private market exists for primary and secondary education. Thus, there is no evidence of the need for government intervention as a producer to alleviate a condition of incomplete markets. In the absence of incomplete markets, assessment of the producer role found no justification, grounded in the functions of government in a mixed economy, that indicated a necessity for government to perform the producer role in the market for primary and secondary education. As mentioned previously, the presumption rule used in our market role assessment requires a finding in favor of private performance of the producer role. However, there is no evidence of successful and sustainable private production of public education. Thus, careful monitoring of charter school reforms and successful private production of education in private schools should be undertaken and careful evaluations performed. In addition, the role that government regulations and rules have played in creating barriers to private production of public education should be considered and assessed.

One role that may be useful to consider in terms of its ability to facilitate privatization of roles such as allocator/distributor and producer is the market role of auditor. We turn to the auditor role in Chapter 7.

NOTES

[1]Alternatively, in the resource market, households are assumed to be the sole owners/suppliers of economic resources and firms are assumed to be the sole source of demand for economic resources. Neither assumption is particularly violent in terms of analytical outcomes, and both go a long way in simplifying the theoretical structure required to depict a macroeconomy. The model is called a circular flow because the core of the model is depicted by a physical flow of resources and goods, and a financial flow that runs in the opposite direction. These flows appear circular when represented in a figure.

[2]However, it should also be noted that individual, disaggregated roles may be combined and performed by a single entity, even though differentiation of the roles remains conceptually useful and meaningful for market role assessment.

[3]For example, *The American Heritage Dictionary* gives at least nine definitions for the word.

[4]The cost of the service could be covered through general taxation or through user fees and charges.

[5]For example, aggregate staffing levels, capital budgets, and large equipment purchases or preferred vendors for such are often determined at the district level.

[6]Generally, a state school board's role in production is limited to regulatory interventions that limit production function decisions.

[7]Undervaluation occurs when a consumer values the good or service on the basis of the benefits he or she receives from its consumption and does not include additional societal benefits in the calculation.

[8]For example, the tuition at the local Catholic and local Christian elementary schools in the author's area are $1,850 and $3,000 per year respectively, whereas the state-determined foundation level of operating funding for public schools is over $4,250 per pupil. Although there may be efficiencies in private education, nontuition and nonparent revenues are an important source of funds for all schools, including private schools.

[9]It should again be noted that the proportion of the total benefits of education that accrues to the individual student (rather than society as a whole) increases with each level or year of education. That is, the benefits of college accrue generally more to private individuals and less to society than do the benefits of elementary school. Therefore, these uncharged private benefits increase with each year of an individual's education.

[10]The financing system for primary and secondary education will be discussed in more detail when the financier role is analyzed in Chapter 8.

[11]Obviously, a major factor influencing the appropriate amount of payment is whether the payment takes place under a system of compulsory, free public education.

For example, if one could accurately measure the collective benefits of education, one could provide assistance to private schools in the amount of the collective benefits. Tuition charges at private schools could then be a reflection of the private benefits of the education (and education at that school in particular). Public schools would continue to be tuition free but would be forced to compete on a more even playing field with private schools. Alternatively, a benchmark cost of educating a pupil in each grade could (theoretically) be calculated, and government could make a payment in this amount to public or private producers in the market.

[12]The auditor role is analyzed in Chapter 7.

The Auditor
Who Provides Quality Control for the System?

Accountability is an increasingly important issue with respect to government and its relations with constituents.[1] The contemporary public administrator must be well versed in means by which to provide accountability to his or her constituents, while at the same time maintaining good relations with staff and efficient operations of the governmental unit. In light of the well-documented push for the privatization of many governmental services (Murphy 1996), it is even more important to understand the appropriate means of providing accountability, even in situations in which government contracts out or privatizes previously publicly produced goods or services. One of the major means of providing such accountability is through the auditor role. A clear knowledge of the audit function, its possible forms, and appropriate uses can go a long way to aiding the modern public administrator in doing his or her job and in being responsive to both market conditions and constituent concerns.

Audits and auditors are generally associated with independence and credibility. Auditors are responsible for examining and verifying results, perhaps most commonly with respect to financial statements but often with respect to other outcomes such as beauty contests, sweepstakes, examination results, and the accuracy of weights and measures.[2] An audited outcome or statement typically is viewed with greater confidence and exudes greater veracity from the perspective of the reader or consumer when compared with an unaudited alternative.

According to the General Accounting Office's *Government Auditing Standards*, which apply to governmental units and many not-for-profit organizations, two broad types of audit[3] are recognized: financial and performance (Holder 1996). "A financial audit determines whether the financial reports of an audited entity are presented fairly and whether the governmental unit has complied with applicable laws and regulations" (Holder 1996, p. 195). Financial audits in *Government Auditing Standards* are actually divided into two categories: financial statement audits, a term that is equivalent to the AICPA's (American Institute of Certified Public Accountants) financial audit; and financial related audits, a term introduced in the GAO standards "to describe special audits over, for example, segments of financial statements, information in budget requests, budget-actual information, internal controls over compliance with laws and regulations, internal controls over computer systems, and general compliance with laws and regulations and allegations of fraud" (Engstrom and Hay 1999, p. 351). On the other hand, performance audits come in two varieties: economy and efficiency audits, and program audits. Holder notes: "Economy and efficiency audits determine whether the governmental unit is acquiring, protecting, and using its resources economically and efficiently and whether it has complied with laws and regulations on matters of economy and efficiency. Program audits determine the extent to which desired results are being achieved and analyze related matters of compliance" (p. 195). Both independent external auditors and internal auditors play an important function in evaluating results and procedures through financial and performance audits. In addition, both play an important role in monitoring and ensuring compliance with applicable laws and regulation. The link between the auditor and regulator roles is evident, but their differences should be noted.

    The role of auditor should be differentiated from that of regulator, although auditors generally play an important role in any regulatory system. Perhaps the most significant difference between a regulator and an auditor is that regulators generally exercise control or direction through rule making and enforcement, whereas auditors apply a set of rules developed by another party in order to examine and verify some type of outcome. Thus, one can see the importance of the auditor as a complement to the regulator and the regulatory function. One can also see the potential need in many circumstances to have different economic actors play the regulator and auditor roles so as to avoid appearance of conflicts of interest. This can also increase the ability of the auditor to be viewed by outsiders as independent in investigation, conclusions, and reporting. This type of independence or appearance of independence gives the audit function a measure of essential credibility.[4] A competent and independent internal audit department is also an important component of planning, management, and control in an organization. A description of general auditing standards will help elucidate some of the basis of and reasons for the credibility associated with the auditor role.

    When discussing the auditor's market role, it is very important to keep in mind those characteristics that constitute good auditing practice and allow its credibility to be established and maintained. The American Institute of Certified Public Accountants (AICPA) identifies ten generally accepted auditing standards (GAAS),[5] the auditing equivalent of the more familiar generally accepted *accounting* principles, or GAAP. The AICPA's ten auditing standards include three general standards, three standards of field work, and four standards for reporting. "Auditing procedures relate to acts to be performed while auditing standards pertain to the quality of the performance of those acts and the audit objectives to be attained by the use of the procedures" (Newkirk 1988, p. A-3). Whereas most audits performed by accountants are financial in nature, the audit *standards* are much more generally applicable. This is especially true of the three general audit standards.[6]

The three general audit standards can be summarized as follows: (1) the audit should be performed by a person or persons with appropriate training and proficiency as an auditor; (2) with respect to all matters associated with the audit, the auditor shall maintain an independence in mental attitude; and (3) the audit examination and preparation of the audit report shall be performed exercising due professional care. The universality of these standards makes them easy to apply beyond the financial audit environment. We will examine in more detail their applicability to the audit role in primary and secondary education after summarizing the field and reporting audit standards.

Standards of field work under GAAS are related to the actual performance of audit procedures while in the field. The three standards of field work are: (1) the work should be adequately planned, and any assistants to the auditor should be properly supervised; (2) the audit shall include a proper study and evaluation of the existing internal controls as a basis for determining the appropriate level of reliance on such controls, as well as for determining the extent of the tests to which auditing procedures are to be restricted; and (3) "sufficient, competent evidential matter is to be obtained through inspection, observation, inquiries, and confirmations to offer a reasonable basis for an opinion regarding the financial statements under examination" (Newkirk 1988, p. A-3). For the most part, field audit standards are also very useful in providing guidance for audits other than those of financial statements and transactions. In contrast, the four standards of reporting generally relate to the audit of financial statements.[7] In the interest of brevity and precise discussion, reporting standards are not discussed in detail at this juncture.

Both financial audits and performance audits are important in evaluating organizational operating results. The inappropriateness and unavailability of profit-based measures of government performance give greater significance and importance to the notion of performance audits in the public sector.[8] Yet, less guidance is provided in terms of standards for such audits. "The use of performance auditing techniques is increasing, but generally accepted standards for conducting audits with a broad scope have not yet been established at the level that exists for financial and compliance audits" (Holder 1996, p. 195). This lends a special complexity to defining and assessing the auditor role with respect to government and government activities.

"An audit is an examination of records, facilities, systems, and other evidence to discover or verify desired information" (Mikesell 1995, p. 45). Yet, the auditor role is much more complex in its function than the mere formal performance of audits, especially when nonfinancial auditing is considered. This is in part because of the lack of well-established standards for performance audits. In the absence of well-established standards, the auditor has the responsibility for (1) establishing, explaining, and justifying an audit methodology that examines evidence appropriate to the content area, and (2) developing benchmarks to allow the audit findings to be contextualized by users of the information. In the case of compliance audits, the regulator has primary responsibility for identifying and articulating the rules and regulations against which compliance will be measured. But what does this say about the need for government to play the auditor role in markets?

At the most simple and perhaps trivial level, an economic actor participating in a market in any role has a responsibility to engage in internal auditing in order to assess the nature of and quality of his or her performance in the market, using appropriate measures. "At the federal level, the General Accounting Office supervises audits of agencies, although the actual auditing is done by agency personnel. States frequently have elected auditors or independent agencies that audit state agencies and local governments. Local governments sometimes have audits done by independent accounting firms as well as by governmental bodies" (Mikesell 1995 p. 45).

External auditing demands a level of independence that is incompatible with a government, business, or other organization performing its own audit. Nevertheless, even the independence requirements for external auditors fail to offer guidance about the need for or merits of government performance of the audit function in general or the auditor role in a particular market. We now look to the functions of government in a mixed economy for guidance.

GOVERNMENT INTERVENTION
AND THE AUDITOR ROLE

Government performance of the auditor role is not compelled by government's function of providing for the smooth operation of the price system, although government regulations that compel the open provision of information, licensing, and reporting involve important audit-related uses of the regulator role to improve the operation of private markets. For example, Securities and Exchange Commission (SEC) reporting and filing requirements can improve the smooth operation of the stock market.

Government interventions to improve market outcomes in terms of justice and equity may be motivated by information produced in performance of the auditor role,[9] but such information need not be produced by a government auditor, and the intervention will not generally be one that comes in the form of the auditor role. In terms of interventions to mitigate private market failures, more interesting and disaggregated analysis is necessary.

A characteristic of a free and unfettered perfectly competitive market system is the presence of full and free information. Full and free information theoretically negates the need for external auditing, because all producers and consumers in the market would have all evaluative information necessary to make informed decisions.[10] Unfortunately, asymmetric information and costly information are the rule rather than the exception in the markets for most good and services. Thus, the need for external auditing cannot generally be dismissed on grounds of the existence of full and free information.

The need for an external auditor in response to asymmetric or costly information must be determined on a market-by-market basis, and the identity of the appropriate actor to perform as auditor in the market must be similarly determined.

Interventions to mitigate other market failures can be analyzed in a similar fashion. Natural monopolies often require government regulation and, whether regulated or not, also require evaluation by an external auditor to assess a variety of issues (e.g., costs, prices, profits, price discrimination, supply reliability, and product quality). Given the availability of independent private auditors who could perform such evaluations, there is no requirement that government perform the auditor function, even though government may set the parameters for a given audit.

The presence of externalities does not necessarily compel an external audit function in and of itself. However, an external audit may be required in the case of externalities, such as pollution, that are caused by an economic activity. Even in the presence of laws and regulations, compliance, economy/efficiency, and performance audits may be required to assess pollution levels and the success of mitigation efforts. However, such audits could be conceivably contracted for, and there is no rationale that would *compel* the audit function to be government performed given the presence of competent private independent auditors.

The nature and availability of independent private auditors generally mean that government need not be required to perform the auditor role in the case of any of the other market failures such as discrimination, incomplete markets, or unemployment. It is conceivable that there will be markets in which the audit function will need to be performed by government owing to safety or security considerations,[11] but in general these cases can be expected to be isolated.

As noted, the idiosyncracies of markets and the performance of market roles in particular markets may affect the need for and appropriateness of government performance of the auditor role. It is from this perspective that our analysis now turns to market role assessment of the auditor role in primary and secondary education.

EDUCATION AND THE AUDITOR ROLE

In education, the role of auditor is becoming one of greater and greater importance, as well as one of broader responsibility. For example, the auditor role is central to any education reform effort that includes most typical forms of accountability measures, especially those that trade regulatory flexibility for a system of accountability that is grounded in outcome-based measures of learning or student achievement. Any form of national standards, whether the Clinton administration's Goals 2000 or another program, will have its success grounded ultimately in the type of accountability mechanism it contains and the nature of the audit function used to document that accountability. Indeed, this type of measurement and accountability issue is at the heart of some of the criticism of our current approach to national standards, including Goals 2000. "A new federal agency was created, the National Education Standards and Improvement Council. By statute, its membership has to represent the education establishment and historically low-achieving populations. . . . This is a formula . . . for reinforcing the very interest-group politics that have tolerated low academic performance in the first place" (Kramer 1995). The auditor role is also at the heart of the debate over the appropriate rules and regulations (if any) that should guide home schooling, an increasingly popular educational option for many families. "Since the late 70's the number of home-schooled kids has swelled from fewer than 13,000 to an estimated 1.2 million" (Sharp 1997, p. 4). Critics of home schooling argue that it is hard to believe that home schooled students would have the same level of expertise by high school in the absence of the science courses or technology available at most public and private schools. The auditor role is at the heart of providing the empirical evidence necessary to judge the efficacy of home schooling in general and the educational experiences of individual students in particular.

So, who needs to perform the auditor role with respect to primary and secondary education? A variety of people and organizations probably need to. First, to the extent that the auditor is to serve an attestation function (i.e., provide affirmation of truth or correctness), an *independent* auditor is needed and should be employed. The multifaceted and complex nature of primary and secondary education makes it likely that multiple auditors and audit organizations will be required to adequately perform the audit function. Splitting the audit function between a number of external entities will promote better compliance with the audit standard that requires an experienced and competent auditor to perform the audit.[12] This is especially important for program audits that require special skills or background. In addition to the provisions for independent auditors, internal audit mechanisms should be in place and utilized. Each economic actor should be interested in its performance and engage in self-evaluation procedures designed to assess the efficiency and effectiveness with which they are performing their role. For example, a producer might wish to audit its purchasing department not merely for compliance with procedural regulations but for effectiveness of operations that enable economies in purchasing to be realized. Furthermore, in addition to the independent and internal audits, external constituencies such as those representing persons with disabilities may engage in an audit function designed to enhance accountability on the part of education providers.

One can readily see the possibility that the auditor role has to be multifaceted and performed by a variety of economic actors. Nevertheless, some useful overarching conclusions can be presented through a brief analysis. Once again, it is assumed that the primary and secondary education system being analyzed is one like the status quo in which mandatory education and "free" public education are maintained as basic principles. This assumption is central to the assessment of the auditor role. Economic relationships between people and institutions are very different when consumers are compelled to consume a good or service and when every consumer is guaranteed "free" access to the market. At minimum, society becomes a very interested audit consumer in such circumstances.

As will be pointed out in Chapter 8 on the assessment of the financier role, government is likely to need to perform a significant portion of the role of financing primary and secondary education. Under such conditions, accountability for public funds must be maintained through the audit function, but the precise nature and focus of the performance of this audit function depends to a great extent on the roles that government plays in the market besides that of financier. For example, if a government is the producer of primary and secondary education, it is inappropriate for that government to be the only entity conducting outcome auditing of that school system. On the other hand, if a government has contracted out administration and production roles for schools in its area, it may be entirely appropriate for that government to be in charge of outcome auditing, at least from a loose reading of the independence criterion.[13] Despite the numerous idiosyncratic complications evident from this brief discussion, it is possible to develop some general rules for performance of the audit role in the market for primary and secondary education. Here is a set of rules that can provide a general starting point for discussion:[14]

Rule 1: The same economic actor should not be simultaneously responsible for educational production and for the auditing of the educational outcomes resulting from that production.[15] Following this rule helps to ensure the credibility and independence of the audit process.

Rule 2: Regardless of the audit method and auditor chosen, a governmentally constituted body[16] should play the role of the *audit committee* whenever the expenditure of public funds is involved. In a corporation, the audit committee is a standing committee of the board of directors. The audit committee has a number of duties and responsibilities, including:

1. reviewing the plan for the independent audit and related professional services;
2. reviewing audit results to help ensure that both management and the independent auditor are properly discharging their duties;
3. oversight of internal accounting controls and the internal audit function;
4. annual nomination of the independent auditors;
5. "investigation of special situations, such as conflicts of interest, questionable payments, and possible illegal acts by company officials" (Newkirk 1988, p. A-5).

Rule 3: The audit committee should implement a set of audit guidelines that allows for separate and independent audits of different aspects of the educational system, with full and free communication between management, the audit committee, and the independent auditors. A lead auditor should be hired and should coordinate the preparation of a comprehensive audit report.

Rule 4: Audit provisions should be built into any contract for services entered into by a government on behalf of its constituents.

Where does this leave us in terms of evaluation of the audit role in primary and secondary education? The audit function is a crucial and necessary one regardless of the division of other economic roles in the market. Evaluation of the financier role will indicate that the public finance of education probably should not disappear and is unlikely to disappear as a result of any currently plausible reform efforts. Thus, accountability for public dollars, if nothing else, requires that a financial audit of primary and secondary education schools and systems be performed regularly. Many implementation options with differing consequences are available for performing such audits and for determining the scope of and actor to perform other relevant audits.

The answer to the complex issue of precisely what to audit and the appropriate party to handle the different audit responsibilities depends in part on the allocation of the various economic functions that are the focus of this book. In the fairly common case in which primary and secondary education is financed, administered, and produced by government, audit standards and our general rules for the audit function require that an independent auditor be hired. However, what are the appropriate parameters for the audit assignment in terms of content and unit of analysis? Furthermore, how should internal audit functions be merged with the desired parameters of the independent audit?

Several areas of primary and secondary education can be suggested as candidates for audit:[17] (1) financial operations (including financial statements, internal controls, cash management, and cost accounting systems); (2) health and safety; (3) equal opportunity and civil rights; (4) educational outcomes (including school to work transition, college preparation, basic skills, and citizenship training); and (5) educator training and development. Each of these audit candidates requires different types of expertise and information for analysis and serves the needs of varying constituencies. Obviously, the nature and structure of the appropriate report will also differ by the type of audit being conducted.

It should be noted that auditing a program or service such as primary and secondary education bears close resemblance to the notion of program evaluation taught in schools of public policy and public administration. Indeed, the evaluation criteria and evaluation questions outlined in one of the widely used program evaluation texts seem especially useful in helping to formulate and implement the parameters of the audit role[18] we are currently discussing:

- Does the program or plan match the values of the stakeholders?
- Does the program or plan match the needs of the people to be served?
- Does the program as implemented fulfill the plans for its implementation?
- Do the outcomes achieved match the goals?
- Is there support for the program theory?
- Is the program accepted?
- Are the resources devoted to the program being expended appropriately? (Posavac and Carey 1992)

The answers to this set of questions can provide a good basis for the overall audit function and development of an audit program. One can see that the audit candidates for primary and secondary education that were identified previously fit well into this program evaluation framework. For example, the program evaluation framework suggests that an audit of educational outcomes should be able to answer questions about goal achievement, program implementation, and program acceptance, among other things. In addition, the use of the program evaluation perspective as a complement to the traditional (financial) audit perspective offers the possibility of using different frames of reference to assist in building a general audit description that can aid in the allocation of audit responsibilities between different economic actors. This also further strengthens the link suggested at the beginning of the book between the tools of contemporary public administration and the tools at the foundation of market role assessment. We now turn to analysis of each of the candidate audit categories.

FINANCIAL OPERATIONS

Traditional financial audits of operations should be conducted by an independent auditor who attests to the financial statements, financial results of operations, and accounting methods and systems of internal control. In addition, it would be prudent for an internal audit system to be in place as a more timely and direct component of an effective internal control structure. Finally, it may be appropriate for the economic actor responsible for the financier role to have involvement in the audit of financial operations. For example, it is common for a government agency that provides a grant to an organization to perform a field audit of the grant after the completion of the grant period.[19] The nature of the financial operations audit is such that a traditional accounting firm would be the appropriate contractor for performing such an audit. Internal auditors of organization finances should have accounting training similar to that required of CPA external auditors.

HEALTH AND SAFETY

The audit of health and safety conditions is likely to be multifaceted, including several different interested parties. To the extent that government acts as a regulator of health and safety conditions, it is reasonable that it take the responsibility for the audit function regarding these rules and regulations.[20] However, taking responsibility for the audit function should not be read to mean that government itself should perform the audits. Although the audit function could be and often is performed by a government agency, an independent auditor with appropriate expertise (e.g., an environmental engineering firm) could be hired by the regulator, or the regulator could compel the producer to hire an independent auditor as part of the regulatory framework. Government would retain the necessary police powers for enforcement even in the case of a contracted auditor.

In addition to a government regulatory body or agency, several other stakeholders may be appropriately interested in performing a health and safety audit of the schools. One would expect that a school board, and/or a parent/teacher council, and/or unions representing school employees would be interested in an ongoing audit of health and safety conditions in the schools. Similarly, one would expect interest groups representing special needs students and employees to have particular interest in the audit of health and safety conditions, especially as related to their constituencies. These parties would be significant stakeholders in information that may or may not be the same as the information of interest to government regulators. Therefore, an ongoing system of internal health and safety audits that includes representation from these groups[21] would seem appropriate and would likely be well received by representatives of stakeholders.

In today's litigious society, schools have a further incentive to audit health and safety conditions. Such audits can help to reduce lawsuit exposure, as well as make insurance premiums more manageable. Thus, one would also expect risk managers associated with both the schools and the insurance companies to be involved in an auditor role with respect to health and safety conditions.[22]

In addition to the audit of such conditions, one would expect the audit of health and safety in the schools to include the audit of programs designed to *improve* health and safety.[23] It is expected that such evaluations would be appropriately performed by the body that undertook the program initiative, at least to the extent that the initiative was voluntary and non–crisis related and offers no threat to participants in the audit.[24]

CIVIL RIGHTS AND EQUAL OPPORTUNITY

Although they are different in terms of technical aspects, from the perspective of auditing, civil rights/equal opportunity issues have much in common with health and safety issues. Civil rights and equal opportunity laws represent regulations by government designed to offset unfair or unjust market outcomes owing to unfair discrimination. This regulatory setting has analogues to that discussed in the section on health and safety, where regulations are made to provide assurances of health and safety beyond those available, or potentially available, in an unfettered market system.

The nature of civil rights and equal opportunity concerns (i.e., generally related to a problem or issue with its roots in some form of unfair discrimination[25]) suggests that external audit provisions may be essential to enforcement and the evaluation of success. Independent auditors with appropriate expertise are available and can be utilized to audit such entities as admissions procedures, hiring practices, and operations practices. Nevertheless, again one can argue that the regulator who makes the rules should retain ultimate responsibility for the audit process that is designed to attest to compliance with those rules. This would argue for government performance of the auditor role with respect to this area of interest. Once again, this responsibility can be discharged directly through actual audit performance by the agency or indirectly through a supervised audit process conducted by an outside auditor. The key factor is who retains control of the audit, and who staffs the audit committee.

As with health and safety audits, an internal audit process relating to civil rights and equal opportunity would seem advisable in addition to any external audit procedure. For example, diversity in the workplace is an important consideration even apart from the formal impact of civil rights and equal opportunity rules. A system of internal evaluation of the work environment, including issues related to civil rights and equal opportunity, is good management practice. Students, administrators, faculty, staff, parents, and the community at large are all important stakeholders in a school environment that fosters respect for diversity, as well as zero tolerance for prejudice and hatred.[26] An inclusive civil rights/equal opportunity audit is an important means of monitoring progress and remaining accountable with respect to these issues.

As with health and safety, civil rights and equal opportunity program evaluations are an important defense against potential litigation, as well as a means of remaining accountable to special interest groups concerned with ensuring protection of basic rights for members of groups who are traditionally discriminated against. Furthermore, ongoing program evaluations enable success to be documented as progress is made through continuing efforts to reduce prejudice and discrimination in institutions of primary and secondary education. Problems can often be identified prior to a time when they might surface and create undue tensions that explode into physical, verbal, or psychological confrontations.

EDUCATIONAL OUTCOMES

The audit of educational outcomes is probably the most rapidly growing—as well as the most controversial [27]—aspect of the audit function in primary and secondary education. It is important to understand the growing attention that educational outcomes seem to be receiving, as well as the controversy associated with any emphasis on outcome-based learning and education. "Current reform efforts . . . are primarily directed at the overall quality of educational services for all students . . . Replacing the equity language of the 1960s in a subtle way, current reform is framed in terms of better outcomes" (Wong and Sunderman 1995, p. 162). According to Wong and Sunderman, most reforms and reform proposals tend to reallocate power downward within the school district, like the site-level management initiatives discussed in Chapter 4. One real problem, at the heart of the lack of school reform progress in many areas such as Illinois, is the question of the temporal ordering of accountability and any improvements in school funding. As the only academic member[28] of the now defunct Illinois Business and Education Coalition (formed at the impetus of the Illinois Manufacturers Association), the author had an opportunity to be involved in this battle. Business leaders consistently argued that accountability measures had to precede any increased state funding for schools in Illinois. Education leaders consistently said that it was unfair to expect performance-based results until adequate resources were available to produce such results. Although education funding reform in Illinois remains in the nascent stage, 1998 brought the beginning of a large influx of new state dollars for primary and secondary education. The 1997 enabling legislation also brought accountability measures, including a new set of lifelong learning requirements for teachers and learning standards for students, with a new statewide test to assess academic progress. Governor George Ryan has also pledged that a majority of any new revenue dollars will go to education. However, other states have been far more successful in initiating accountability and outcome auditing, although descriptions of the auditing procedures are given little attention in the press or in other documents about even the most radical programs.[29]

The issues surrounding educational outcomes and their audit as a means of accountability and evaluation are at least partially grounded in fundamental measurement issues familiar to any student or practitioner of program evaluation. In the simplest terms, when one seeks to evaluate a primary or secondary educational program or innovation, one must be able to identify means by which to objectively judge when the program has been a success. Furthermore, even when one can agree on the standards by which educational achievement should be judged, it is a significant step to develop an audit procedure capable of measuring performance or compliance, as well as designating an appropriate and competent auditor. In general, this has been easier said than done; typically these types of audit procedures have been developed on a very subjective, or at least ad hoc, basis. A discussion of some of the fundamental measurement issues should help to clarify (1) some of the problems faced by program evaluators, and (2) the nature of possible solutions to these problems in terms of performing the auditor role.

Defining and measuring the success of primary and secondary education has proven to be difficult and controversial.[30] Various measures have been used, including: achievement test scores, college admissions test scores, number of students cited for excellence by the National Merit Scholarship Corporation, percentage of students who go on to college, dropout and/or diploma completion rates, winning athletic teams, winning scholastic bowl teams, pupil-to-teacher ratios, operating expenditures per student, operating expenditures per dollar of assessed valuation, and other measures. Renowned education author Diane Ravitch has advocated the use of the National Assessment of Educational Progress (NAEP) test, but she acknowledges its inherent weaknesses (Ravitch 1995). One problem with this diversity of measures involves manipulating results with the choice of achievement criterion.[31]

Increasingly, greater attention has also been focused on the education system's ability to produce productive citizens and workers. Indeed, this is a major justification for public education (Center on National Education Policy 1996). However, the success of an education system in producing productive members of the workforce or of society is unlikely to be measured by any of the variables mentioned in the preceding list, and there remains significant disagreement about the purpose of education itself.[32] Instead, increasing attention is being given to measuring educational success on the basis of standards and outcomes, some of which may or may not measure work-related skills sought by employers.[33] "The new basic skills that high-wage employers demand include: (1) hard skills (basic mathematics, problem solving, and reading abilities much higher than what almost half of today's high school graduates attain), (2) soft skills (the ability to work in groups . . . and to make effective oral and written presentations), and (3) the ability to use personal computers to carry out simple tasks" (Murnane and Levy 1997, p. 35). Students are expected to achieve competence in different areas at different points in their education, and an effective evaluation system would measure the success of education through outcomes related to relevant competencies.

As an example, early in their education students might be expected to demonstrate the ability to add a column of three digit numbers. A competency for more advanced students might be the ability to identify the location of countries in the world and their capital cities. Laboratory science classes might focus on knowledge exhibited in a lab practical. A student's ability to progress in his or her education would be related to mastery of skills, rather than passage of time. It would be a function of the auditor to assess the degree to which these competencies are achieved. Ignoring for the time being the logistical and political problems with identifying appropriate educational standards and outcomes, the need for an audit function in monitoring educational outcomes is clear regardless of the precise nature or definition of those outcomes. Given our focus on the auditor function, it is important to stay focused on the auditor role itself and to avoid digressing further into the standards debate.

Once again, it can be argued that the auditor who performs the attestation function should be independent of the economic actor who is responsible for the educational outcome. That is, the auditor should be independent of the producer of the education. However, it is highly advisable that the producer, administrator, financier, and other economic actors playing roles in the market all participate in the audit function through internal audit mechanisms and audit procedures designed to meet the special needs of their economic role in the market for primary and secondary education. Some of these audits will clearly be in the form of compliance audits; others will be the traditional financial type; still other audits will be the familiar program audit variety. Once again, one should expect multiple audits and auditors in a market as complex and important as that for primary and secondary education, but with a centralized process and means of oversight.

As mentioned before, the audit of and responsibility for educational outcomes is also the major *quid pro quo* for the freedom granted to charter schools through regulatory relief. In exchange for regulatory relief, the charter schools agree to meet or exceed agreed upon levels of educational outcomes. These educational outcomes are then subject to an audit procedure that is designed to attest to compliance and eligibility for charter renewal. One can readily see the centrality of the audit function, especially in terms of education outcomes, in evaluating charter schools and in offering a definable playing field for producing outcomes that can be evaluated as part of the terms for renewing a given school's charter. However, even in the currently limited realm of charter schools, the issue of appropriate definition of educational outcomes and standards remains.

EDUCATOR TRAINING AND DEVELOPMENT

The audit function envisioned for educator training and development is not, and should not be, merely a rehash of existing teacher certification regulations or collectively bargained rules regarding teacher training and development. In many ways the audit function that is envisioned is much more than the traditional teacher certification process, whereas in other ways it is much less, especially in terms of formality and rigidity.

At risk of stating the painfully obvious, good teachers and good teaching are an essential part of good education. Individuals who have the ability to enrich children's lives as educators should be encouraged to consider a teaching career. The education system must contain appropriate rewards and an appropriate environment to encourage teaching as a long-term career, as well as a second career for talented persons who have ended a first career. Furthermore, the system must encourage innovations in teaching and in educational methods that are designed to improve educational outcomes. However, in order to monitor teacher progress and the results of educational innovations, an audit system must be in place that enables educational results and teacher development to be linked and evaluated. This will not only allow problems to be identified and rectified, but also allow information about innovative teaching techniques to be developed. It will also offer an opportunity to identify outstanding teachers for well-deserved recognition. The audit system that is envisioned is likely to be very different from systems currently in place in traditional public schools (and probably most if not all private schools).

At present, a great deal of regulation of teacher certification takes place at levels of government higher than the local school system (e.g., teacher's certificates are issued through a state agency according to state regulations) and certainly higher than the local school itself. Furthermore, a great deal of the regulation of teacher certification has to do with education and experience requirements, typically including a requirement of coursework in education. In addition, most salary schedules in primary and secondary schools have education (along with experience) as a major component. Although few would argue that some amount of education is generally very helpful in developing the skills required in teaching, and that the characteristics of teaching are such that it could be considered a true profession, the education requirement for professional certification in teaching does not serve the same role as it does in the certification process in many other professions.

For example, certification as an accountant (i.e., as a CPA) requires one to have met basic education and/or experience requirements,[34] pass the National Uniform CPA Examination, and regularly show evidence that he or she is meeting the rather rigorous continuing education requirements of the profession. It should be noted that one can have a productive career as an accountant without being a CPA, because for all intents and purposes a non-CPA accountant can perform all accounting functions except the signing of an independent audit. Furthermore, the certification of public accountants in most states is two tiered: one can hold a CPA certificate, or one can hold a CPA license. In general, the CPA certificate is granted to those persons who pass the CPA examination and meet the education/experience requirement but do not require a license because they will not be actively pursuing audit functions and will not be actively meeting the continuing education requirements of the profession. On the other hand, the CPA license holder can perform all accounting functions and must meet the continuing education requirements of the profession.

Similarly, one can look to the legal profession. Although licensing requirements in nearly all states call for a law degree from an accredited law school,[35] all states require lawyers to pass a bar examination in addition to meeting the education requirement. Unlike accounting and the CPA examination, for most intents and purposes one cannot practice law without passing the bar examination.[36] The legal profession also has continuing education requirements for maintaining one's license to practice law.

It should be noted that strict professional licensure requirements are, not unintentionally, controls on entry to the profession as well as a quality control mechanism. Licensing artificially reduces the supply of persons practicing a given profession, thereby increasing the market price of services by those persons practicing the profession.[37] But how does this relate back to the audit function for teacher certification and continuing education in the realm of primary and secondary schools?

First, licensing of schoolteachers as part of the auditor[38] role in primary and secondary education should be revised, not abandoned. That is, the nature and function of the license should be changed. One can argue that the auditor and regulator functions of licensing of teachers should be mainly to help ensure the safety and well-being of the children within their charges. Issues related to the quality of teaching, teaching style, and so on should be left to the educational producer or administrator. That is, schools should be allowed broad latitude to hire those teachers they find appropriate to meet their educational mission and to successfully meet any standards or outcome-based measures of student achievement. As such, one might establish an audit function for teacher certification based upon a licensing scheme something like the following:

1. Prospective teachers would undergo comprehensive background checks like those performed by bar associations for prospective lawyers.
2. Ongoing, regular criminal background checks would be conducted on all school employees, including teachers.
3. Teacher certification programs would be instituted based upon knowledge of methods and procedures related to protection of the health and safety of students. For example, teacher certification might require demonstrated knowledge of first aid, recognition of signs of child abuse, recognition of signs of drug abuse, recognition of signs of emotional problems, and similar intervention referral and first response abilities.
4. Formal education requirements, beyond that of a high school diploma, would be eliminated, with the focus shifting to the educational outcomes produced by the teacher rather than the teacher's credentials.

The audit function with respect to teacher certification and continuing education in such a system should be bifaceted. An overarching statewide certification center could maintain records on all certified teachers in the state and would be responsible for the comprehensive background checks on persons entering the teaching profession. Such background checks should also be conducted on a regular basis for experienced teachers, perhaps on a random audit basis with a minimum and maximum length of time between comprehensive audits. It would probably be most effective for these background checks to be conducted by government law enforcement officials, owing to their existing police power and extensive databases and experience.[39] Beyond the background check, which will likely require government involvement, certification of formal education requirements and the record-keeping function for teacher certification could be privatized depending upon relative costs and the ability to find a willing private contractor. The hiring school would need to show due diligence in hiring by requiring teachers to have state certification and by conducting its own criminal background checks at a level at least comparable to that now done by many landlords. Obviously, such a system works best when states and localities cooperate to share information. Furthermore, such a system must have strong due process provisions to ensure that only persons who are likely to pose a threat are denied the basic credential.

Mandated continuing education could also be monitored by the state certification agency. However, continuing education mandates should be based upon the certification requirements of the system. That is, continuing education requirements should be aimed at the same health and safety issues (or expanded health and safety issues as they become important) required for teacher certification.

It should be noted that none of this discussion prevents, or should discourage, a school or school system from imposing its own hiring or continuing education requirements. These local requirements could be very similar to existing formal education requirements and could retain salary schedules that are based on such educational achievement. However, such items should not be negotiable as part of collective bargaining agreements. This helps prevent the use by unions of elaborate certification requirements as a means of creating (1) a barrier to entry in the district, and (2) job security for current teachers. The licensing structure suggested previously requires *all* teachers to be certified but greatly reduces the detail and educational nature of such certification. Furthermore, if more elaborate certification requirements are of value to consumers in the market, there is little reason to believe that districts or schools will not recognize this and compete in the market on the basis of stricter certification requirements for their teachers.

To some extent, the absurdity of some of the current certification requirements may be seen in those states that require full or partial teacher certification on the part of parents conducting home schooling. Although it is not hard to imagine the reasons schools might have for discouraging home schooling, it seems more appropriate to merely audit the home schooled students' progress rather than to bother with the credentials of parents who school their own children. Few states currently agree with this perspective on the issue. Evidence of this is provided by information from a recent article that defined five legal categories for governance (and, hence, audit) of home schooling and noted the number of states using each legal approach:

- *Home school–statute states:* Thirty-four states have legally defined home education and set criteria. Generally, student progress is assessed annually on the basis of examination or review by a certified teacher. "Parents may have to give the state details about curricula and textbooks and meet educational requirements themselves."
- *Private school states:* In ten states and the District of Columbia, home schooling is given the same legal status as private schooling. "These laws typically do not require parents to have certain degrees or children to take standardized tests."
- *Approved instruction states:* Two states "insist on previewing the curriculum and may also require an end-of-year evaluation."
- *Equivalent instruction states:* In three states, parents may be required to show that their curriculum is comparable or equivalent to that of the public schools, as defined by local school officials.
- *Constitutional right to home schooling:* In Oklahoma, home schooling is a guaranteed right, and no annual evaluations or parental qualifications are required. (Sharp 1997, pp. 4–6)

Thus, even in the extreme case of home schooling, states are generally divided on the appropriate nature and depth of the audit function. This offers further evidence of the complexity and disagreement over the appropriate role of government in the market for primary and secondary education, including the relatively passive role of auditor. Once again, in the case of teacher training and development, there does not appear to be a compelling need for government performance of the auditor role.

CONCLUSION

The audit function with respect to primary and secondary education is one of the most diverse and most important functions we will discuss. It involves all categories of audits defined under the GAO's *Government Auditing Standards*. The auditor must be able to competently and independently perform an attestation function. The complexity of primary and secondary education production requires that different economic actors perform the audit function for different aspects of the provision of primary and secondary education. For example, consulting engineers may need to be hired for a health and safety audit (at least as specialists), whereas a traditional accounting firm might be the independent auditor of the financial statements and financial outcomes. The identity of the economic actor performing the independent audit role is in part dependent upon the identity of the economic actor performing the role primarily responsible for the function that is being audited. Nevertheless, presumption still remains in favor of private sector performance of the role in the absence of a compelling rationale for government intervention.

Despite the importance of independent auditing, the role of internal auditing should not be ignored or underestimated. Internal auditing by the economic actors responsible for different functions in primary and secondary education provides a first-line and most timely response to potential issues of quality control, fraud, and safety. The audit role in primary and secondary education will therefore need to be performed by a wide variety of economic actors, both internal and external to the market, whose efforts together should produce a fair picture of the total operations of the education system.

Thus, there is no special dedicated role for government in playing the auditor role for primary and secondary education. Furthermore, it is likely that the auditor role in a given education system will be played simultaneously by public sector, private sector, and nonprofit entities with varying stakes in the educational system. As progress is made in the area of educational standards and outcomes, the audit function will gain even greater importance.

Nevertheless, the appropriate actor or actors to perform the auditor role with respect to the market for primary and secondary education remains dependent upon the division of the other roles in the market; the nature of the accountability that is being sought through the audit function; the ability to use, with reasonable faith in the information and results, the audits conducted by other stakeholders; and the nature of the definition of the items in need of audit. We will therefore return to the audit function, after our analysis of the remaining market roles, as part of our summary analysis of the appropriate role for government in school reform.

However, in Chapter 8 we turn to the issue of school finance and particularly to the role of the financier in the market for primary and secondary education. Given the great attention on financial aspects of schools and school reform, this is a particularly critical chapter in the development of our analysis through market role assessment of government and its role in school reform.

NOTES

[1]For example, the early years of the Clinton administration were home to Vice President Gore's National Performance Review and its recommendations with respect to national performance management. Ultimately, these initiatives were grounded in accountability-based improvement in the performance of government, much of which was directly related to audits performed by the Gore commission and a system of ongoing audits to ensure continuing compliance.

[2]Although some of these tasks are not performed by CPA auditors, they nevertheless represent legitimate audit *functions,* and the audit function is the focus of this chapter.

[3]It should be noted that alternative classifications of audit types are available. One such scheme is presented in Mikesell (1995). Mikesell classifies audits into: (1) financial audits, (2) management/operations audits, (3) program audits, and (4) performance audits. Although this classification scheme is interesting and useful, it and others like it do not significantly add to the parameters of the auditor role provided by the GAO classification.

[4]It should be noted, however, that not all situations require an external independent auditor. Auditor independence is most important in situations in which the audit results will be used by the public or by outside organizations. Internal auditors play an important audit function without having the same degree of independence required of outside auditors. Thus, evaluation of the need for an external independent auditor should be done on a situational and functional basis.

[5]The General Accounting Office (GAO) has been active in developing government audit standards. The GAO audit standards, published as *Government Auditing Standards,* "incorporate the AICPA standards and provide extensions that are necessary due to the unique nature of public entities. These extensions, for example, require auditor knowledge of government accounting and auditing (with continuing education requirements), public availability of audit reports, written evaluations of internal controls, and distribution of the reports and availability of working papers to federal and state funding authorities" (Engstrom and Hay 1999, p. 351). "Governmental units and many not-for-profit organizations are subject to the *Government Auditing Standards,* issued by the U.S. General Accounting Office in addition to the *Statements on Audit-*

ing Standards, issued by the American Institute of Certified Public Accountants" (Engstrom and Hay 1999, p. 351).

[6]This discussion of auditing standards is based in part on the material in Newkirk (1988).

[7]GAAS reporting standards require the following to be reported: whether the financial statements are presented in accordance with GAAP; circumstances in which GAAP have not been observed relative to the preceding period; any informative disclosures not deemed to be adequate; and an expression of an opinion of the financial statements as a whole. In contrast, the GAO audit standards include three standards related to reporting: compliance with laws and regulations as well as internal controls; restrictions on and omission of privileged and confidential information; and report distribution (Holder 1996, p. 196).

[8]Alternatively, the availability and acceptance of financial performance measures in the private sector have generally diminished the need for separate performance audits of most private activities. However, the desire for broader and non-financial audit of private business activities is suggested by developments such as (1) the growing interest in and availability of socially responsible investment vehicles, and (2) the concern over using after-market parts to repair automobiles that have been damaged.

[9]For example, audit of a program may indicate the need to intervene to provide access for low income families.

[10]The notion of full information means that producers and consumers in the market are all knowing about all relevant facts, and that this information is immediately and effectively acted upon.

[11]For example, auditing certain national defense programs or contractors, or assessing nuclear fuel programs.

[12]It should be noted that generally accepted audit procedures include the possibility of hiring specialists to provide expertise in assisting with an audit so as to centralize audit responsibility.

[13]However, it seems prudent for government to then contract out, in one fashion or another, the development of the standards to be audited. It is typically the case that the party making the rules is separate from the party performing the audit, although this need not always be the case, especially when the outcome measures are developed in a collaborative fashion that involves representation of important stakeholders.

[14]Although some of the rules are written from the frame of reference of government, they remain generally appropriate regardless of the division of market roles between the public and private sectors.

[15]This rule should not be interpreted as precluding or discouraging internal auditing of outcomes by an educational producer. However, such internal audits should not substitute for quality audits by an external independent auditor.

[16]Such a body might consist of representatives from a variety of stakeholders, including parents, school board members, administrators, and teachers, depending on the circumstances and nature of the audit.

[17]Even though this list of audit categories is broad, it should not be considered a definitive or exhaustive list of potential audit areas.

[18]These questions are most appropriate for program audits. For financial audits, the questions are complementary to those posed under general auditing standards.

[19]The Single Audit Act of 1984, as amended in 1996, provides statutory authority for uniform requirements for audits of state and local governments, public colleges and universities, and nongovernmental not-for-profit organizations (including hospitals and private colleges and universities) that receive federal assistance. Those entities receiving more than $300,000 in federal assistance are required to have a single audit. The Act provides for an audit process that enables auditors to assure the federal government that federal and state funds are expended in accordance with grant agreements, financial management standards, and other federal standards. The intention of the Act is to allow such assurances to be provided without decentralized program-by-program audits by each funding agency. The Act is discussed in some detail in Engstrom and Hay (1999).

[20]There is no compelling reason to separate the rulemaker from the auditor in this situation. Indeed, it may be preferable to have linkage between making the rules and enforcing the rules when it comes to health and safety. This is similar to the government both making and enforcing the laws related to physically harming or killing people.

[21]Representation may be provided through an audit committee or participation as part of an audit team. Audit procedures include conditions whereby internal auditors can be actively used, even in external audits (Newkirk 1988, p. 29).

[22]The increased involvement of governments and their agencies in risk management is noticeable and well documented. For example, *Management Policies in Local Government Finance,* 4th ed., one of the International City/County Management Association's "green books," has an excellent section on the use and components of risk management in local government. See Aronson and Schwartz (1996).

[23]For example, immunizations, protective equipment for sports, school lunch programs, sex education, and drivers education.

[24]For example, a nonconfidential interview of high school students about their sexual behavior may be quite enlightening and useful in evaluating the efficacy of some initiatives. However, the threat to high school students from being forced to discuss such topics openly and freely without the full protection of anonymity may affect one's results and cause psychological harm to the students. As such, a methodology of this type likely would not pass a human subjects committee review.

[25]The use of the term *unfair discrimination* is quite deliberate and quite precise. Unfortunately, the word *discrimination* has come to have negative connotations, even though the ability to discriminate appropriately is a greatly desirable skill, and the fact that our society has been built upon a system of (fair) discrimination. For example, few people are heard to complain that one must be a talented basketball player in order to be offered a contract to play for an NBA team. We typically view this as fair discrimination: generally, those who are able to play in the NBA are viewed to have earned that chance through their great ability to play the game of basketball. Similarly, smokers and nonsmokers pay different rates for life insurance on the basis of their different life expectancies. This is viewed as fair discrimination, as opposed to the unfair discrimination alleged in most civil rights or equal opportunity cases. Most of these cases contend discrimination based upon factors unrelated to performance or ability.

[26]In fairness, it should be noted that not all communities in the United States share this view.

[27]For example, see Harrington-Lueker (August 1996).

[28]The original intent was to have a colleague and me act as staff for the committee, but by the second meeting we were at the table as full participating members and by the third meeting my colleague had dropped out of the policy process. The coalition met for approximately two years, with little real progress made in terms of legislation. However, much progress was made in exploring the feasibility of different reform efforts, given the cross-section of interests (including those of the governor's office) represented in the room.

[29]For example, see Elmore, Abelmann, and Fuhrman (1996).

[30]For example, see Ravitch (1995).

[31]For example, a recent Ed.D. graduate of Northern Illinois University, Felicia Stewart, reported in her dissertation (Stewart 1996) that a significant issue during Ruth Love's tenure as school superintendent in Chicago was the move to the California Achievement Test rather than the Iowa Tests of Basic Skills in an effort to improve student outcomes (or, at least, reported student outcomes).

[32]For further insight into this debate, see the symposium "Rethinking the Purpose of Education" in the February 1997 issue of *Educational Leadership*.

[33]This is neither an argument for nor an argument against standards per se. Any effort to develop standards must be grounded in an understanding of the goals and stakeholders appropriate to our education system. The debate as to which standards should be idiosyncratic to specific schools and school systems is also ongoing. In Oregon, the new reform law imposes standards at the statewide level.

[34]The work experience must have been under the supervision of a CPA.

[35]It is possible to sit for the bar examination and be licensed with a law degree from an unaccredited law school. However, the ability to sit for the bar is typically limited to the state in which the law school is located, and the ability to transfer one's license to another state is significantly constrained.

[36]A notable exception to this is tax law, under which a CPA can represent clients in legal proceedings without being a member of the bar. This includes making appearances in tax court.

[37]Although this argument may be distasteful to some people, such stringent licensing would not be necessary in a system that is supported by quality judicial and insurance systems. The malpractice insurance system could compensate losers from incompetent or negligent professional behavior, as well as adjust the cost of doing business by professionals so as to make the cost of doing business higher for less competent or careful practitioners, eventually (one hopes) driving them out of business.

[38]It should be noted that the licensing of teachers is related to both the auditor and the regulator roles. The regulator role involves making many of the rules that will be monitored through the auditor role.

[39]The law enforcement officials could be hired as specialists under general audit procedures.

CHAPTER 8

The Financier
Who Pays the Bills, and How?

In a system of perfectly competitive markets, the role of financier is generally taken for granted and performed implicitly, at least in established markets. However, in other markets such as that for primary and secondary education, the role of financier is often not only important but also a market role that is rarely taken for granted. In such markets, the financier role can be the source of great debate and controversy. Before commencing market role assessment of the financier role in primary and secondary education, it is important to have a better idea of the general notion of the financier role.

The market role of financier is different from that of a venture capitalist or entrepreneur. The financier is the economic actor who provides the infusion of funds that compensates the producer for the costs of production. The financier also ensures that all consumers with effective demand for the product are satisfied at the market-determined price, or at the price determined through collective choice mechanisms. In a market meeting the conditions of perfect competition, market prices serve a rationing function such that producers are signaled to produce the appropriate quantity of a good that consumers are willing to buy at a given price. Consumers themselves act as the financiers in the market, with market prices serving to (1) allocate resources and final goods and services, and (2) determine the payment to be made by the financier. Recall the discussion of distortions like those created by externalities, wherein market prices are unable to efficiently allocate resources owing to conditions of market failure. In these cases, the given good or service will be underproduced or overproduced by the private market, depending upon the type and nature of market distortions that are present. Under such conditions, a Pareto efficient allocation of resources may be difficult or impossible to attain without outside intervention in the market. Furthermore, the spillover benefits and incentives to free ride (i.e., enjoy the benefits of a good or service without paying to do so) with respect to the provision and consumption of public goods have serious consequences for the appropriate means of financing the provision of these goods and services. An extreme example may help to clarify the relationship between the efficiency and the financing problem in the presence of market distortions.

Imagine that our national defense system did not exist, yet the threat of air attack was very real. A risk averse resident might feel significantly safer if he or she had an antiaircraft gun in the backyard to help protect his or her life and property and that of his or her family.[1] In fact, if one were sufficiently risk averse, he or she might prefer to mobilize a private air force to further reduce the chances of damage resulting from an air strike. In any case, the cost of such a response, whether an antiaircraft gun or an air force, would be prohibitive for nearly all individuals to undertake. Furthermore, the protection afforded by the gun or air force would extend well beyond the boundaries of one's own property, simultaneously protecting one's own life and property interests as well as those of neighbors for some distance. These spillover benefits to neighbors would reduce or eliminate the incentive for the neighbors to contribute to the cost of creating a defense system, because they would receive the benefits of the system without sharing in its costs.[2] This "free rider problem," the incentive to let other people pay for a good or service while you enjoy the benefits without paying, has serious repercussions relevant to our discussion of the financier role.[3]

In our example, no single individual is expected to have sufficient resources or willingness to pay to purchase the appropriate national defense type services on his or her own. Furthermore, the free rider effect is such that a voluntary contribution scheme would be unlikely to succeed in providing an equitable distribution of financing shares or sufficient revenues to finance a defense system. Hence, goods such as those required for national defense are typically provided by government through a means of compulsory contributions like taxes.[4] This introduces an explicit financier role for government in the market.

GOVERNMENT INTERVENTION AND THE FINANCIER ROLE

The need for government performance of the financier role occurs in markets in which conditions are such that sufficient resources/revenues to produce a socially optimal quantity of a particular good or service cannot be raised through voluntary channels. Several key factors[5] can be important in helping to recognize cases requiring government intervention as a financier: (1) the presence of significant positive externalities/spillovers associated with production or consumption of the good or service;[6] (2) a sufficiently high unit cost of production such that individuals generally would not be able to produce the good or service themselves;[7] and (3) a good or service whose production or consumption qualifies it as a "merit good," that is, a good that society through collective choice mechanisms deems should be provided even if the members of society do not always demand it or demand it in sufficient quantities. A good or service deemed to have all of these characteristics is likely to require government intervention as financier. The absence of all of these conditions suggests a good with few public good elements, implying a greater likelihood that the private market will be capable of performing the financier role through normal market system operations. In particular, a good with none of the aforementioned elements will have few positive externalities, reducing free rider issues; have lower unit costs, making private production and consumption more feasible; and be such that society has less paternal interest in its production or consumption. Unfortunately, the financier role is not so easily divided in practice between the public sector and the private sector. One reason for this is the normative nature of many of the key decisions that are often precursors to assigning responsibility for the financier role. In the midst of cries for reform of government, improved quality of public services, accountability to citizen consumers, and taxpayer revolt, the issue of financing public services[8] (including contracting out and privatizing) continues to draw great attention. The dimensions of this issue are broad.

At the most basic level, much discussion is devoted to the absolute and relative amount of public dollars that should flow to any proposed or established activity. This issue is at the heart of the evaluation of the financier role in a given market: What portion of the financing of a particular good or service should be provided by funds raised through the public sector? In answering this question, the contemporary public administrator must not only be keenly aware of the nature of the financier role in the market, but also be conversant in issues related to determining the appropriate private sector and public sector functions in performing the financier role.

Furthermore, the public administrator must have an understanding of public sector financial management, and revenue management in particular, so as to understand how to most effectively meet any financing responsibilities deemed appropriate to the public sector. This requires an understanding of the differences between those revenue tools that are based on the ability to pay principle,[9] and those that are grounded in the benefit principle.[10] In addition, public administrators and elected public policymakers should have an understanding of the differences in the nature and performance of different revenue tools that are within the same class in the ability to pay versus benefit principle dichotomy. Understanding these concepts is absolutely essential to performing effective market role assessment with respect to the appropriate role of government as a financier for primary and secondary education. Therefore, a brief introduction to some of these concepts is appropriate before conducting a market role assessment for primary and secondary education.

The ability to pay principle is the foundation for all of what economists call the Big Three taxes: property tax, sales tax, and income tax. However, each of these taxes is based upon a different operationalization of the ability to pay principle. That is, each uses a different measure of economic circumstances as a means of measuring ability to pay. The property tax is based on some measure of wealth, generally real property in most jurisdictions. The sales tax is based on some measure of consumption. The income tax is based on some notion of income as the appropriate measure of ability to pay. Despite the fact that all of these taxes are based on the ability to pay principle, the different measures of ability to pay that they employ have very different implications in terms of important issues such as evasion and avoidance, revenue elasticity, ease of administration, and measurement of the tax base.[11] Therefore, it is not at all surprising that debates over the appropriate level of reliance on each of these taxes as a means of financing primary and secondary education often have a central place in efforts at school reform and school finance reform. Furthermore, there is increasing controversy over the degree to which financing tools based on the benefit principle, such as user fees or commodity charges, are an appropriate part of the financing mix for public primary and secondary education. Whereas taxes based on the ability to pay principle have a strong justification in equity considerations, revenue tools that are based on the benefit principle are generally justified on efficiency grounds. The benefit principle advocates linking the cost of public services with the benefits received from those services. The greater the success in matching costs to benefits, the more closely the fees or charges will mimic market prices and perform a rationing function. This improves performance along efficiency dimensions. But how do these issues more directly relate to the market role assessment of the financier role for primary and secondary education?

The current financier role performed by government in the market for primary and secondary education is one grounded in, but not necessarily the source of, controversy. Contentious issues often get in the way of meaningful discussion of the nature of the financier role and the reform of primary and secondary school finance. First, probably more than any other role discussed, there is great intergovernmental controversy over the appropriate level of government that should have the primary financing responsibility for elementary and high school education. Tied into this question is the issue of whether financing from a higher level of government will (or needs to) carry with it a greater degree of oversight, and therefore a reduction in local control of schools. Thus, even if a rationale for government performance of the financier role is developed, intergovernmental issues may remain as an intellectual challenge.

Second, the intergovernmental controversy over the financier role in public education also involves disagreement over the appropriate public financing tools that should be used to raise the revenues to fund education. This issue was a factor in the reform efforts in Wisconsin and Michigan that shifted financing responsibility to the state level, as well as the earlier tax limitations in California and Massachusetts. All of these reform efforts significantly changed the distribution of funding between state and local sources while simultaneously altering some of the revenue tools that were used to finance primary and secondary education in each state.[12] "The goal of trying to achieve the right mix of revenues . . . can easily conflict with the goal of trying to relieve fiscal disparities through state grants-in-aid. The difficulty is that property taxes are local taxes, and income and sales taxes are largely, but not exclusively, state taxes" (McGuire 1995, p. 2).

Third, the financier role often gets wrapped up in constitutional challenges to the equity of educational opportunities afforded different groups in our society, including racial, ethnic, and religious minorities. Examples of major challenges include *Serrano v. Priest* (1971) in California, *San Antonio Independent School District v. Rodriguez* (1973) and *Edgewood v. Kirby* (1989, 1990, 1991, 1992, 1995) in Texas,[13] *Abbot v. Burke* (1994) in New Jersey, and *The Committee for Educational Rights v. Edgar* (1996) in Illinois. In some cases, these challenges have succeeded. "In states like California, New Jersey, Connecticut, and Texas, the respective state supreme court decisions in favor of the plaintiffs in school finance reform cases have marked the beginning of legislative battles that have easily extended to five, ten, and twenty years without successful resolution" (Ward, Colwell, and Kestner 1995, p. 3). In more general terms, "between 1971 and 1992, plaintiffs in 23 states alleged that funding and management was inequitable. Courts in eleven states overturned school funding systems" (Davare 1994, p. 8). By 1997, the litigation boxscore indicated that forty-one states had seen school finance lawsuits filed, with fifteen state supreme courts ruling in favor of the plaintiffs and no supreme court ruling yet rendered in seven of the states (Hickrod et al. 1997). However, Ward, Colwell, and Kestner go on to say that as a result of (or perhaps partially to explain) the delays they referred to, "legislatures have recognized that the courts may order, but they have few powers to compel compliance." It is interesting, that the school finance system in Michigan was upheld in two cases preceding the drastic and very rapid reform actions taken by the state legislature. The general consensus now is that a child's public education should not depend significantly on the wealth of the district in which he or she lives (McGuire 1995).

Fourth, financing primary and secondary education gets tied into arguments regarding the perceived advantage that public funding gives to public schools, as well as the appropriateness of this advantage.[14]

Fifth, government has been deeply involved in education finance, especially at the state level. Indeed, education takes a larger share of state budgets in the United States than any other program, and it has done so for a long time. Yet, over time schools' share of state budgets began to shrink,[15] an issue that continues to cause concern today in states including Illinois.

Sixth, efficiency questions regarding the relative performance of public and private schools, competitiveness issues raised in the debate over vouchers and school choice, and concerns about student outcomes often get related to arguments about the need to more closely tie educational funding (especially the increases in funding that accompany many equity-based reform efforts) to some kind of performance standards or expectations. In addition, the basic issue of accountability for public dollars remains. "Although few people balk at funding better education, taxpayers are subjecting these requests to greater scrutiny. . . . Before approving a proposal, voters want the assurance that their tax dollars will be efficiently raised, fairly distributed, and spent in a way that maximizes the return on investment" (Federal Reserve Bank of Atlanta 1994, p. 1).

EDUCATION AND THE FINANCIER ROLE

The characteristics of primary and secondary education as an economic good are again central to the analysis of the economic role of financier in its market. An intuitive analysis indicates that several aspects of primary and secondary education and its market in the United States make full reliance on an unfettered market an improbable dream. First, compulsory education requires consumption of primary and secondary education without regard to one's individual valuation of its worth. Second, "free" public education requires that primary and secondary education be provided to consumers at an out of pocket cost to the consumer that is less than marginal cost. Neither of these factors is compatible with finance directly through an unfettered market system. However, even in the absence of these artificial constraints, full private finance through the traditional operation of an unfettered system of markets would be impossible. As mentioned several times previously, a major reason for this conclusion is the spillover benefits associated with primary and secondary education.

The spillover benefits associated with primary and secondary education mean that the price an individual would be willing to pay for education[16] will be less than the total value of that education when social as well as private benefits are included in the calculation. In an unfettered market, education will be produced up to the point where marginal private benefit (MPB) is equated with marginal cost (MC).[17] If marginal social benefit (MSB) exceeds MPB because of positive externalities, it is likely that several units of education for which MSB exceeds MC (i.e., units which would result in a net gain to society) remain unproduced in the unfettered market. See Figure 2 for an illustration of this type of outcome. Thus, education would be underproduced in the unfettered market.

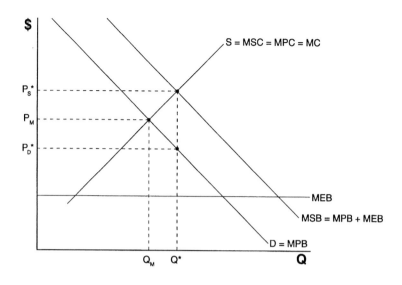

KEY

P_D^* = demand price at Q*
P_S^* = supply price at Q*
P_M = market price at Q_M
MPC = marginal private cost
MSC = marginal social cost
MPB = marginal private benefit
MEB = marginal external (spillover) benefit,
      which is assumed constant in this example
MSB = marginal social benefit
Q_M = quantity in unfettered market
Q* = socially optimal, efficient quantity where
      MSB = MSC, but MPC > MPB

Note that for all units between Q_M and Q*, MSB > MC,
making these units "profitable" from society's perspective.

Figure 2.

Making this point in another way, an inefficiently low amount of resources would be devoted to education by the unfettered private market. These are classic conditions defining a market failure for which some form of intervention by government should be considered, as supported by the functions of government in a mixed economy.

When this market failure attributable to positive externalities is combined with laws making education compulsory and "free," government intervention becomes even more compelling. Earlier in the chapter a set of three product characteristics was described that would offer *prima facie* evidence for the need to have government intervene in the financier role in a market. These characteristics included: significant positive externalities, a high unit cost of production, and "merit good" status. The intuitive analysis just completed, and the analysis in earlier chapters, suggests that at least two of these characteristics are present in the market for primary and secondary education. Primary and secondary education has significant positive externalities associated with its consumption, and it also has merit good status in a system of mandatory and free public education. These factors provide strong evidence of the need for government intervention as financier in this market. However, the appropriate *nature* of government's intervention is far less obvious than the need to intervene. The remainder of this chapter will consider the appropriate nature of government's role as financier in the market for primary and secondary education, the extent to which multiple sources of finance are appropriate, and the proper level of responsibility for the finance of primary and secondary education (i.e., local, state, regional, or national). Included in this discussion will be the nature of some challenges to school finance systems and their relationship to the equity issues related to access to primary and secondary education. This analysis will better allow policymakers to anticipate sources of disagreement and controversy over school finance and school finance reform.

The nature of government's role as financier is grounded in the factors compelling government's involvement in this aspect of the market. That is, the reasons for government's involvement in the market for primary and secondary education also give much information as to the features appropriate to government's means of participation as a financier in the market. As noted, some of these factors can be summarized as market failure issues related to positive externalities, laws making primary and secondary education compulsory, and laws requiring accessibility to "free" public education. As we will soon discover, the issues of equal educational opportunity and equity also enter in as key factors influencing the nature of government's role as financier. Once again, it should be noted that our discussion takes as a given the continuation of a mandatory and free public education.

Returning to basic principles of public finance, let us consider some of the alternative, general financial interventions appropriate for government in a market that is characterized by significant positive externalities generated by the consumption of a good or service such as primary and secondary education. A range of possible government interventions in the market might be considered, allowing parameters to be developed for government's involvement in the financier role for primary and secondary education. Once these parameters are established, it will be possible to more precisely discuss the particular form that the financier role, and government's involvement in that role, should take in the market. Three general forms of intervention will be considered: nonintervention,[18] subsidies, and exclusive compulsory collective finance.

NONINTERVENTION

One must always consider the option of nonintervention as a basic alternative. Choosing this option means allowing the market to work in an unfettered manner. This alternative produces a baseline solution against which other alternative intervention solutions can be compared and evaluated. As noted, the nonintervention alternative would be expected to result in underproduction and underconsumption of primary and secondary education from the perspective of society, owing to the positive externalities associated with primary and secondary education.[19] Furthermore, it is likely that (1) some prospective students who desire education would be priced out of the market, and (2) some students with a low valuation for education would choose not to enter the market. These two cases would be incompatible with mandatory and free public education policies. In addition, given societal values as expressed through the implementation of primary and secondary education systems in the United States,[20] the unfettered market solution would likely also fail equity tests, owing to the fact that those with an inability to pay would be turned away. Thus, greater promise is likely to be found in interventions that alter incentives in the unfettered market so as to allow the post-intervention market to produce more socially and economically desirable results than those of the unfettered market. One means of undertaking such an intervention in a market characterized by positive externalities would be through subsidies.

SUBSIDIES

An intermediate form of intervention would be that of an educational subsidy program, with subsidies payable either to producers or to consumers. In an otherwise unfettered market it does not matter for efficiency purposes whether producers or consumers are paid the subsidy.[21] However, for distributional purposes, or in the case of market regulation like that present in our current educational system, there may be a significant difference in economic outcomes (including efficiency aspects), depending upon the economic actor to whom the subsidy is paid.

At the most basic level, a subsidy can be used to internalize a positive externality. Internalization of an externality "occurs when the marginal private benefit or cost of goods and services is adjusted so that the users consider the actual marginal social benefit or cost of their decisions" (Hyman 1996, p. 604). For example, a subsidy that is paid to a consumer based upon his or her consumption of a good or service increases his or her marginal private benefit from consumption of the good or service. For each unit of the good or service that is consumed, the consumer receives not only the benefit that would normally accrue from the good or service, but also the subsidy payment. This increases the consumer's willingness to pay for a given unit and increases the number of units of the good or service that the consumer would be willing to buy at a given price. In economic terms, a subsidy will increase consumer demand in an otherwise unfettered market. That is, a larger quantity of the good or service will be sought by consumers at every market price, as compared with the pre-subsidy case.

Thus, the subsidy provides a theoretical and practical means by which the underconsumption and underproduction problem can be overcome. From the producer's standpoint, the buyer will be willing to pay a higher price for every given quantity of the good or service, increasing the profitability of all output levels for the producer. As a result, some higher levels of production that were not profitable in the unfettered market will become profitable in the presence of a subsidy. Furthermore, to the extent that the subsidy is an accurate reflection of marginal social benefit at the efficient level of production, the subsidy will also improve the economic efficiency outcome over that in the unfettered market. However, unit of analysis and measurement problems greatly complicate the practical application of a subsidy system and its ability to reach a Pareto efficient outcome.

Specifically, the ability to achieve a Pareto efficient outcome through the use of a subsidy scheme requires knowledge of both the marginal social benefit and the quantity of output associated with the economically efficient outcome.[22] In addition, those individuals producing the externality must be known, so as to be appropriately subsidized. Generally, this information is not known with much confidence. Thus, most subsidy schemes are undertaken blindly from the perspective of achieving economic efficiency. Nevertheless, to the extent that criteria other than economic efficiency are of importance, the problems of the amount of the appropriate subsidy are of much lesser importance. A subsidy will increase demand and is likely to also allow entry into the market by persons who would be unable to afford the good or service in an unfettered market.

A subsidy system represents only a marginal adjustment to an unfettered market solution. The subsidy is designed only to compensate the individual consumer for the excess of marginal social benefits over marginal private benefits; that is, government pays the consumer for the benefits society receives from his or her consumption above and beyond the benefits the consumer himself or herself receives directly from the consumption. For example, under a subsidy scheme, the consumer would still be responsible for paying a market price for education that represents his or her valuation of the education he or she consumes.[23] Thus, the efficient subsidy to each consumer will be dependent upon his or her individual valuation of the marginal unit of education. Under this scheme, the decision to participate in the market still remains driven by income and demand. This introduces some complications into the use of subsidies.

If a student has a very low private valuation of education, the student still may not choose to enter the market at any politically or economically feasible level of subsidy.[24] Furthermore, there may be a problem with truthful demand revelation if individuals are led to believe that their level of subsidy will be dependent upon their valuation of education.[25] Finally, some persons, even after a subsidy, may still not have sufficient income to pay their market share even with a high valuation for education, violating the mandatory free public education policy. One can readily see some of the complications that make instituting a true compensatory subsidy program difficult. Even if all of these complications could be overcome, the number of individual calculations and subsidies, along with the calculation of marginal social benefits, could make a subsidy program nearly impossible to implement and administer in any practical fashion. However, one must remember that this conclusion may be tempered depending on the intended purpose of the subsidy program. The greater the extent to which a subsidy is designed to stimulate greater demand and output without regard to considerations of economic efficiency, the greater the possibility one has of designing a practical and effective subsidy mechanism because the need for precisely calculated individual subsidies becomes unnecessary.

One additional complicating factor in the present system is the perceived lack of a level playing field in the market for primary and secondary education. Without making a judgment as to appropriateness at this time, the current market for primary and secondary education is such that public schools are subject to significantly more rules and regulations than most private schools, but public schools have monopoly access to nearly all locally generated education tax funds and to most of the education tax funds generated at the state and federal levels. If such monopoly power remained under a subsidy system, the potential gains from educational subsidies would be greatly reduced, especially in the case of subsidies to educational producers[26] because their accountability could be reduced by monopoly power. In the absence of such monopoly power, a scheme of subsidies to consumers or producers may have more positive competitive and efficiency effects. We will return to this possibility later in the chapter as we discuss reform efforts that include finance-related tools such as vouchers.

EXCLUSIVE COMPULSORY COLLECTIVE FINANCE

At the other pole from that of nonintervention is the exclusive finance of primary and secondary education through governmental funds raised by means of tools selected and administered through collective choice mechanisms.

The current educational system operates most closely to this finance method among those discussed thus far.

Compulsory collective finance is the finance method generally felt to be most appropriate for pure public goods. There are several reasons for this, some of which have been previously addressed. These reasons include the presence of significant positive externalities and, in some cases, the presence of merit good attributes. As previously noted, these are characteristics that apply to primary and secondary education. Indeed, primary and secondary education has significant benefits that flow to persons other than the individual who is the direct consumer of the education services. These positive spillover effects accrue to members of society without regard to any payment or contribution they might make in exchange for these benefits. Indeed, there would be no incentive for an individual to make payment in exchange for these benefits, because they will be received by the individual regardless of whether or not any payment is made.

Clearly, adequate payment for the full social benefits of primary and secondary education is unlikely to be produced through any voluntary financing scheme.[27] Thus, some form of compulsory finance scheme appears to be appropriate. However, a significant complicating factor to reliance on a compulsory finance mechanism is the substantial private good characteristics possessed by primary and secondary education. We shall return to this point shortly.

A second factor working in favor of reliance on a scheme of compulsory finance is the current treatment of primary and secondary education as a merit good and as some form of basic right. Mandatory education and free public education laws are reflections of this current treatment and basic policy position. Because all members of society, at least in theory, are required to consume primary and secondary education and have access to free public education,[28] some of the equity issues related to compulsory finance seem to be mitigated. Furthermore, there is even more concern today about unfunded government mandates. Although mandatory primary and secondary education training is probably not the most classic example of a government mandate, the analogy to the unfunded mandate discussion is fairly direct, and the notion of compulsory collective funding for mandatory consumption of merit goods is consistent with the traditional public policy in the United States.

As mentioned, the merit of a compulsory finance system for primary and secondary education is significantly complicated by the mixed nature of education as a good,[29] as well as by disagreement over the appropriate definitional parameters for the primary and secondary education experience.[30] The fact that education has both public and private good attributes complicates the financing issue because, in general, the use of compulsory collective finance is not appropriate for private goods. That is, the finance of the production and consumption of private goods should generally be undertaken through the natural operation of the price system in private markets. This is because public funding for private benefit is not generally palatable in the absence of other compelling rationales. However, in the case of a merit good such as education, public funding of private benefits may be accepted on the grounds that such a funding scheme is the only way to ensure adequate levels of production and consumption. In addition, collective funding may also be a means of making mandatory education more universally desirable and affordable. Disagreement over the identification of the basic components of primary and secondary education complicates the financing battle by making the definition of relevant costs and revenue needs more difficult and more subjective. A further complication involves contentious issues related to the revenue tools used for compulsory finance (e.g., the local real property tax) as opposed to the general appropriateness of using compulsory finance mechanisms. Unfortunately, some of these complications lie at the heart of much of the disagreement over school reform efforts and have stalled many attempts to improve our primary and secondary education systems before such efforts have been appropriately considered and discussed. Before going further, the relative merits of the three general types of financial intervention should be reviewed.

SUMMARY EVALUATION OF ALTERNATIVE GENERAL FINANCIAL INTERVENTIONS

As suggested by our analysis, reliance on the unfettered market for education finance generally will not result in production of an efficient quantity of primary and secondary education. That is, education will be underproduced and underconsumed. Furthermore, the unfettered market solution raises issues of equity, because a good that many people consider to be fundamental to future success and earning power would be distributed to a great extent on the basis of ability to pay.

The unfettered market solution would also be inconsistent with maintaining a system of mandatory education that offers the universal availability of "free" public education and that includes (in fact, requires) accommodations for students with special needs. An unfettered market solution would only provide revenues sufficient to cover the private benefits of education, which are represented by the demand price[31] for primary and secondary education. Furthermore, absent any intervention, some consumers would likely remain unfulfilled in the market at the equilibrium solution.[32] These unfulfilled consumers create a problem in a system of mandatory education, a problem that cannot be solved without outside intervention.[33] But outside intervention would bring the financing scheme out of the realm of a nonintervention, purely market-based solution. Thus, to the extent that primary and secondary education is a merit good for which we wish to maintain some form of mandatory consumption scheme, the nonintervention solution must be taken off of the table and attention must instead be focused on the other two alternative financing options: subsidy and compulsory financing.

Financing through subsidies may be feasible but would require significant administrative effort to determine appropriate levels of subsidy and an appropriate distribution mechanism for the subsidies. Furthermore, government would still be required to generate revenue to pay for the subsidies. Before considering the subsidy option further, we should review the relative merits of compulsory collective finance of primary and secondary education.

At the other end of the spectrum of financing alternatives from nonintervention is a system whereby all finance for primary and secondary education is provided through a compulsory finance system developed under a collective choice system[34] as opposed to a market system. Exclusive reliance on a system of compulsory finance would be feasible but would not be optimal, at least from the standpoint of economic theory. As suggested previously, the case of exclusive or nearly exclusive reliance on compulsory finance tools as a means of paying for the production and consumption of a given good or service is typically justified only in the case of pure public goods. Compulsory finance is justified in that case because of the significant positive externalities and the nonexcludability characteristics associated with public goods.

In general, education has both private good and public good characteristics. Specifically, the benefits of education are both personal and social. Even in the case of primary and secondary education, wherein the social benefits of education are substantial and dominant, private benefits are still significant and the exclusion of nonpayers is feasible and practical (although this may not be consistent with mandatory education requirements). This point must be examined further.

Much of the benefit of primary and secondary education is societal, owing to the basic and foundational nature of much of what is taught and learned.[35] However, even at the primary and secondary level, a portion of the benefits of education are captured by the individual as opposed to society. The presence of private, personal benefits suggests that exclusive reliance on collective compulsory finance may be neither required nor appropriate. That is, the presence of private personal benefits means that the individual consumer would be willing to pay a positive dollar amount for the right to consume the good. Furthermore, to the extent that some portion of the benefit of education is accrued personally and cannot be recaptured in whole by society, one can argue that public or collective dollars should only be used to pay for the benefits society receives from the primary and secondary education system above and beyond the benefits received by the individual. However, it should be noted the analysis in the previous section suggested that compulsory finance might still be justified on the grounds of merit good factors, which are present in primary and secondary education.

Thus, cursory analysis suggests that exclusive reliance on the market or on collective choice mechanisms for the finance of primary and secondary education is probably not feasible, not necessary, and not desirable.[36] One is left to consider finance mechanisms that combine compulsory finance and market prices, or their public sector analogues, as well as the opportunity for voluntary contributions.

Our discussion thus far has concluded that neither an unfettered market-based private system of finance nor a publicly based pure system of compulsory finance is appropriate for fulfilling the financier role in the market for primary and secondary education. Thus, the financier role need not be performed exclusively by the private sector nor exclusively by the public sector. Given that the current system represents such a mixed approach to the financier role, it is appropriate to explore some of the alternative means by which the financier role has been undertaken, as well as the resulting division of responsibilities between economic actors.

DIVISION OF RESPONSIBILITES

We begin with a discussion of the current general division of the financier role between the public sector and the private sector, and then we continue with a discussion of the division of responsibilities between different governments and government agencies. These divisions are at the heart of most of the recent controversy over school finance reform.

For the purpose of tractability, our discussion must focus on broad generalities, noting that there are exceptions to nearly all of the points made. By doing so, our analyses become more generalizable and, one hopes, more useful.

The financing of primary and secondary education is currently done through a variety of means. One of these is the purchase of educational services in the private market with private funds. The most common instance involves parents paying a market-based tuition to send their child to a selective, closed enrollment private school, either parochial or nonsectarian. Another means, at the other end of the continuum, involves parents who send their child, at little or no cost to the parents, to a closed enrollment residential public high school financed through public dollars that includes room and board.[37] Thus, the present system of primary and secondary education finance includes situations in which the financier role is almost exclusively played by the private sector in a manner very similar to that in an unfettered market. At the same time, the status quo also includes numerous other situations in which the predominant, if not exclusive, role of financier is played by government using tax dollars. Most situations today represent a mix between public and private finance of schools, regardless of whether we are talking about public or private schools. The fungibility of funds (i.e., the ability to commingle or substitute funds among accounts) and the conduit nature of many government programs sometimes make government's role as a financier more difficult to discern[38] than in cases in which government makes direct payments or grants to educational institutions or districts, or even private contractors. Therefore, careful analysis of fund sources may be necessary in order to evaluate the relative importance of public and private financing for a given school or school system. On the other hand, government imposition of user charges or fees (using this term very strictly and technically) amounts to a publicly imposed *private* finance methodology. A further twist on the division between public and private finance is provided by an example from Indianapolis. "The public is helping to finance private schools' very brick and mortar. Consider the $38.5 million in municipal bonds that the Archdiocese of Indianapolis issued in November 1996 through the Indianapolis Economic Development Commission. . . . This bond issue gives the archdiocesan schools access to money at below-market rates, since the interest paid to bondholders isn't taxable" (Mellish 1997, p. A22).

Government often provides in-kind services, shared by both public schools and private schools in the same geographic area, at a below market cost for the private institutions. In such circumstances, there is at least an implicit element of public finance of private schools, albeit one that will not generally be evident in a review of financial statements. Such services include community libraries, interlibrary loan services, transportation services, rental of lab facilities or sports facilities, allowing the private institution to contract with the public schools for specialized classes or teachers, and the rental of surplus facilities or equipment.

The division of responsibilities between levels of government is no less ambiguous nor any less contentious or interesting. Indeed, the division of responsibilities between levels of government is central to equity arguments about primary and secondary education and therefore to school finance reform. As of the 1996–1997 school year, National Education Association statistics indicated that expenditures per pupil in daily attendance ranged from a low of $4,387 in Arizona to a high of $10,393 in Alaska. The state's share of school revenues was lowest in New Hampshire at 6.6% and highest in Hawaii at 90.0% (where an additional 8.1% of funds come from the federal government, leaving less than 2% for local and other sources to provide). For the same period, fifteen states provided more than 60% of the revenues for primary and secondary education, whereas thirteen provided 40% or less of the revenues to local schools (National Education Association 1997). In Illinois, the state currently provides a little more than 30% of the revenues for most districts, a figure that has precipitously fallen over the past twenty years and is a source of great concern in the ongoing school finance fight in the state. Recent efforts have begun to reverse this trend.

Several different issues permeate the discussion of the division of education financing responsibilities between levels of government. These include:

the relative revenue-generating powers and abilities of different governmental units; the differing fiscal capacities of governmental units of the same type and level,[39] equity issues related to the provision of different quantities of merit goods depending upon the jurisdiction in which one lives; the relationship between fiscal capacity and poverty and/or protected class status; the link between financing responsibility and control over local schools; and the nature and level of social benefits from primary and secondary education. Some of these issues are relatively easy to deal with at a positive level, whereas the resolution of others is very dependent upon the underlying value system of the areas involved.[40] Nevertheless, in recent years the general policy trend has been toward greater state-level responsibility for the finance of primary and secondary education. This has happened for a variety of reasons linked to the issues we have just outlined.

In general, the higher the level of government the greater is its revenue-generating authority and ability. Indeed, in theoretical terms the only binding limit to the federal government's revenue-generating capability is gross domestic product.[41] Thus, in general, state governments, especially under Dillon's Rule,[42] will have greater fiscal power than local governments. Furthermore, redistribution is easier to carry out, though maybe not easier to administer, at higher levels of government. This is because redistribution can be spread over a larger number of persons, and the need for redistribution may be somewhat ameliorated with a greater number and variety of taxpayers. As a result, equity issues may also be easier to handle at a higher level. Furthermore, the nature of educational benefits and the mobility of human beings in the modern world means that the benefits of a given student's education are unlikely to flow primarily to the local community in which he or she is educated. In an effort to more accurately match benefits and costs, educational finance at the state level may be more efficient than that at the local level because more of the spillover benefits can be captured at the state level.[43] Despite these arguments, the move to state level (or even federal level) financing of primary and secondary education remains controversial for several reasons. Among these are: the degree to which local areas will be allowed to supplement state funding to provide an enhanced educational experience for the community's students; and the issue of whether state funding means giving up local control over fundamental educational decisions.

Based upon our discussion thus far, we can dispose of the second issue fairly easily: there is no reason for a change in the financier role to necessitate a reduction in local control. The financier role can be separated from that of producer, regulator, auditor, and the other roles we have already discussed. Therefore, it is realistic from an economic standpoint, although perhaps not from a political standpoint, to have state government finance education while local governments are given the freedom to produce the education (or contract for its production) as long as certain outcome measures or standards are met. We will discuss this issue further in Chapter 10 as we summarize our findings and make judgments as to some of the most appropriate ways to divide the economic functions between the various candidate actors, including state and local governments.

With respect to the issue of local communities being allowed to supplement some foundational level of education provided by a statewide financing mechanism, insight can be provided by digressing to examine some of the forms of government-based public school finance that are currently used in the United States.

School finance programs in the United States range from full state funding of schools to flat grant programs. In between are foundation programs, percent equalization programs, and guaranteed tax base/yield programs. Several states have shifted their type of financing program over the past fifteen to twenty years. "A direct result of a court mandate or the threat of such a mandate led over thirty-five state legislatures to enact fundamental changes in their school finance structures between 1971 and 1985" (Odden 1992, p. 4). A number of states, such as Wisconsin and Michigan, have made major changes in the school finance systems over the last five years or so.

Although there is some disagreement as to the appropriate classification of certain basic state support programs, there is general agreement that the most popular state financing program is a foundation program "under which the state sets both a minimum expenditure level and a required tax effort and pays the difference between the expenditure level and the amount that districts raise at the required tax rate" (Augenblick 1986, p. 12). The most common variant of the foundation program defines expenditures in terms of operating expenditures per pupil. It should be noted that the foundation level that is defined need not represent the full cost of an "adequate" education but generally is based upon provision of some percentage of that defined full cost figure.

Guaranteed tax base or tax yield programs are also used in some states. "Under this system, the state specifies a rate at which it will match local taxes; the rate varies inversely with the wealth of the school districts. . . . The basic difference between this approach and the foundation program is that the state does not specify the spending level beyond which state aid will not be available" (Augenblick 1986, p. 13). However, such guaranteed tax base or yield programs are rarely used in isolation. Far more popular are hybrid programs that combine foundation and guaranteed tax base programs into a multi-tiered system. "These multi-tiered systems specify a minimum spending level, with an associated minimum tax effort requirement, while helping to equalize the ability of districts to provide funds beyond the minimum level" (Augenblick 1986, p. 13). Augenblick argues that such programs retain a level of local control over spending while enabling the state to meet its responsibilities for adequacy and equity in school finance.

States typically have separate programs for administering and financing the education of special needs students. The most common method provides additional categorical grants (some originating at the federal level) for the provision of high cost educational programs like those required by many special needs students.

Some of the most drastic school finance reform measures are of very recent vintage. We look at two of these, Wisconsin and Michigan, in Chapter 11 when we assess the nature and outcomes of recent school finance reform efforts in an effort to help point primary and secondary school reform in the right direction. As a prelude, one should note that recent efforts in school finance reform have been dominated by approaches that return, or radically change, the primary financing responsibility for primary and secondary education from the local to the state level. However, the high-profile and well-publicized reform efforts aimed at the finance of public schools should not divert attention from the parallel finance and finance reform crisis facing many private schools. This financing issue has a direct link to the financier role and public education through the various voucher experiments and proposals that have been undertaken or debated in recent years.

With respect to the financing of private education, there is evidence that this is a crucial issue in many areas. The public subsidy of bonds for the Indianapolis Archdiocese is evidence of the financing crisis there. In many inner cities, including Chicago, parochial schools and other private schools are serving large numbers of students as the primary alternative to public schools that many people believe to be inadequate, unsafe, or of poor quality. Many of the students in these areas come from low income families that cannot afford a market-based tuition that would recover the full costs of education. Recognizing the public good nature of education (though often not explicitly), many communities have attempted to finance educational costs through corporate, foundation, and other private donations. For example, in Milwaukee the PAVE (Partners Advancing Values in Education) Scholarship Program that was begun in 1992 provided privately funded half-tuition scholarships to 11,496 low income students to attend private schools, including religiously affiliated schools, in its first four years of operations. "PAVE has been used as a model for similar programs in 21 cities across the nation" (White, Maier, and Cramer 1996, p. 1). One of the motivating factors for PAVE and other similar programs is the legal controversy over the use of publicly financed school vouchers at religiously affiliated schools. As recently as January 1997, a Wisconsin state judge ruled that using state vouchers to send poor children to religious schools violates the Wisconsin Constitution. On June 10, 1998, the Supreme Court of Wisconsin became the first state high court to rule that a voucher program funding private sectarian schools did not violate the establishment clause of the First Amendment to the United States Constitution. On November 9, 1998, the United States Supreme Court decided not to review the Wisconsin Supreme Court's ruling in *Jackson v. Benson*. The Supreme Court did not rule on the Wisconsin case, and therefore its action in not reviewing the case set a precedent for Wisconsin.

On October 12, 1999, the United States Supreme Court dodged the voucher issue again, failing to grant review to an appeal of the practice in Maine of subsidizing private, nonreligious schools while refusing to spend state money for children who go to religious schools. This was a voucher issue because many public school districts in sparsely populated areas of Maine do not operate their own schools but rather pay tuition in order to send local children to the neighboring public or private school of their choice. Since 1981, Maine has prohibited the use of such funds to send students to religious schools. Once again, the Supreme Court set no precedent through its action. However, in 1999, there were indications of growing anti-voucher sentiment. "In the past four months, four courts have outlawed religious voucher programs in six states and Puerto Rico" (Perry and McGraw 1999, p. 1). Yet, fall 1999 also brought the start of the first statewide voucher program, (in Florida), and privately funded programs are thriving in a large number of cities. Furthermore, even though vouchers, even for nonreligious schools, remain controversial, support for vouchers has grown greatly over recent years, with the favor/oppose split now about 50/50 (Billings 1999). Given the magnitude and universality of the legal question in this case, one can expect that the issue will make it to the United States Supreme Court and will be resolved through a ruling by the Justices.

Apart from the issues related to the use of vouchers at religiously affiliated schools, many private schools face other financing issues that often threaten their very existence. In many areas it has been common for private schools, especially religiously affiliated schools, to use a "fair share" approach to charging tuition. Under the fair share approach, a tuition rate is set, a minimum contribution level is set, and each parent or guardian signs a contract to pay some amount at or above the minimum contribution, based upon ability to pay. In recent years many schools have had difficulty in collecting funds from some parents,[44] and in raising adequate sums of money to fund the schools owing to inadequate parent contributions.[45] Furthermore, families with numerous children in school often feel overburdened by having to pay large sums of tuition for each child in school. In an effort to counteract this, many churches have attempted to provide a public subsidy for their schools through a version of tithing in which a portion of an individual's tithe is counted as a payment toward tuition and is tax deductible as a donation to the church. Although the legality of this methodology is questionable, the need to resort to such a financing mechanism is instructive. It is especially instructive to note that financing and finance reform for primary and secondary education is not merely a public sector or public school problem.

From a theoretical point of view, the nature of primary and secondary education means that there will always need to be some level of public involvement as financier. At the same time, the private good attributes of education also mean that some level of private individual finance of education is appropriate and should be expected.

CONCLUSION

Because of the significant positive externalities and the merit good nature of primary and secondary education, market role assessment of the financier role indicates that the government needs to continue to play an active role as financier in the market for primary and secondary education. Government intervention in the financier role in primary and secondary education can be justified under government's functions in a mixed economy. These functions include interventions to mitigate market failures such as those caused by externalities; and paternalistic interventions to promote health and safety, or to promote the consumption or production of goods with high magnitudes and proportions of social benefits. All of these functions can be deemed appropriate in the market for primary and secondary education. However, owing to the significant private benefits associated with primary and secondary education, a private financier role can also be discerned and deemed appropriate.

Given that government must continue to act as a financier of primary and secondary education, one must also evaluate the nature of government's finance role in terms of the level of government most appropriate to play this role, the proportion of finance to be provided by different levels of government in shared finance situations, the nature of the educational activities and/or infrastructure that are appropriately financed by various levels of government, the degree to which government will finance alternative providers of educational services, the basis upon which nonlocally generated funds will be distributed and disbursed, and the means by which the funds to be provided by the various levels of government will be raised and disbursed. Some of these questions have answers that can be firmly grounded in positive analysis through our knowledge of economic theory and behavior, whereas others require normative judgment and analysis.[46] The answers will be more directly analyzed and presented in subsequent chapters as we discuss some specific reform alternatives in terms of their implications for government involvement. At this stage, however, one must recognize the important role that government must play as a financier of primary and secondary education, even if the specifics of role implementation remain somewhat undefined at this point.[47] Our analysis allows some general parameters of the role to be established.

Clearly, government should finance the social benefits of education. Arguably, government should be responsible for paying for the social benefits regardless of whether the provider is publicly or privately financed. At the same time, given the private benefits of education, it is reasonable to expect some payment on the part of students or their families for the private benefit portion of primary and secondary education, with possible provisions made for scholarships for needy students. The obvious problem is that measuring the social and private benefits of education is a difficult, if not impossible, task. Private benefits alone are likely to vary from person to person, and they therefore create a challenge for formulating an equitable tuition structure designed to have individuals, or at least the marginal individual, paying a cost that is a reflection of his or her marginal private valuation of the education.

However, more than any other role, the appropriateness, and maybe even necessity, of both a private sector and a public sector presence as financiers of primary and secondary education argues for a sharing of the financier role between government and private sector entities, including individuals. This explicit sharing of roles would be a fundamental shift from the status quo and may necessitate a network of elaborate school voucher systems whereby government provides vouchers to offset the costs that represent the social benefits of education.

In Chapter 9, the role of the entrepreneur is discussed as our final example of the roles that need to be played by economic actors in a market. The market role of entrepreneur is an especially interesting one given its centrality in a capitalist system like that of the United States. Furthermore, increasing attention is being given to the entrepreneur's role in American business schools. This is evidenced by the fact that the *U.S. News and World Report* annual rankings of the best graduate business programs now include entrepreneurship. In addition, reinvention and reengineering efforts in government have brought new and well-deserved recognition to public sector entrepreneurship. We turn now to the entrepreneur role.

NOTES

[1]Of course, this ignores the target that such a gun might provide for air strikes.

[2]Recall the notion of nonexcludability that was introduced in Chapter 2.

[3]For further discussion of the free rider problem, see Rosen (1992), pp. 75–78.

[4]Justification for this government intervention is provided under government's function of intervening to prevent market failures.

[5]These factors are derived from consideration of the functions of government in a mixed economy.

[6]Positive externalities must be present, otherwise there will not be unpriced social benefits in excess of the private benefits of the good or service. Private benefits can generally be priced and accommodated by the private market. The positive exter-

nalities must be significant, otherwise government intervention may be dismissed on grounds of *de minimis* benefits.

[7]A sufficiently high cost, like that for national defense, may mean that no private production of the good or service is undertaken in the absence of government intervention.

[8]The term *public services* should be broadly interpreted to include all types of goods and services that might be provided by the public sector.

[9]According to the ability to pay principle, an individual's share of the cost of financing government activities should be based on his or her economic circumstances, with individuals of greater means paying a greater share.

[10]According to the benefit principle, individual shares of the cost of financing government activities should be allocated on the basis of benefits received. Those who receive benefits should pay; those who receive greater benefits should pay more.

[11]For example, a real property tax is very difficult to evade and is very stable as a revenue source. Sales taxes tend to be more volatile, because consumption or spending changes with economic conditions and seasons of the year. For a more comprehensive discussion of these revenue tool and revenue management issues, see Hyman (1996) and Mikesell (1995).

[12]For further information on the Wisconsin experience, see Reschovsky (1994).

[13]The San Antonio case was a federal case that ended up in the U.S. Supreme Court; the Edgewood cases were decided at the state level and were the impetus for reform of the Texas school finance system.

[14]Once again, at least to some extent, this raises an empirical question whose answer should become clearer as generalizable evidence is obtained from charter school and voucher experiments.

[15]This is a trend that began to reverse in the early 1990s, according to National Center for Education Statistics data (National Center for Education Statistics 1999).

[16]An individual's willingness to pay is based upon his or her monetary valuation of the individual benefits accruing as a result of that education.

[17]Nothing in our example has indicated a divergence between marginal private cost and marginal social cost, a divergence generally attributable to a negative externality of some sort.

[18]Although the case for intervention has already been made, the option of nonintervention must still be considered as a baseline that enables the improvements that might be expected from government intervention to be identified and evaluated.

[19]Alternatively, a less than efficient amount of education would be produced and consumed. That is, units of education for which marginal social benefit exceeds marginal social cost would remain unproduced and unconsumed.

[20]Courts in at least twenty states have ruled that education is a fundamental constitutional right (Hickrod et al. 1997).

[21]This is a fundamental and important tenet of economics that is easy to prove but hard to get people, especially public policymakers, to believe. See any principles of economics text for an explanation of this concept.

[22]That is, the output level at which marginal social cost and marginal social benefit are equated.

[23]Technically, as in any competitive market, the unit price charged to the consumer will be based upon the marginal valuation of the last unit of education produced, as

opposed to a differential price paid by consumers based upon their individual valuation of each unit of education they consume.

[24]Individuals will only choose to enter the market if the subsidy plus their individual private valuation is greater than or equal to the market price at which they can purchase education services.

[25]There is an entire economic literature that addresses the demand revelation problem. For further discussion, see Varian (1984).

[26]Making subsidies to government education producers would be functionally equivalent to providing tax revenues to fund a portion of their education system, with the remainder of the cost of production paid through market prices. However, recall that monopoly power is a market failure under which market prices may no longer be appropriate allocators of educational resources, and therefore inefficiencies may still remain after subsidization.

[27]Further complicating the issue of voluntary finance is the issue of truthful demand revelation. If one could get individuals to truthfully reveal the benefits (in money terms) they receive from the primary and secondary education of other members of society, one might convert these benefits into individual cost shares. An individual should be willing to pay such a cost share as long as it is less than or equal to the value of the spillover benefits the individual estimates he or she receives. Unfortunately, there is no incentive for individuals to truthfully reveal their benefits valuation if they (1) think that their cost share will be dependent on their answer, and (2) perceive that they can receive the same level of benefits regardless of the answer they give to the valuation question.

[28]Not to mention that all members of society receive benefits from the consumption of primary and secondary education by both themselves and by others.

[29]That is, primary and secondary education has attributes of both a private and public good.

[30]For example, the type of coursework that should be mandatory; whether extracurricular activities should be tax supported; whether government should provide equal educational opportunity for all students or some base level of funding.

[31]That is, the price that buyers are willing and able to pay for a unit of a good or service.

[32]Market equilibrium only requires the market to clear (i.e., there is no excess demand or excess supply) at the equilibrium price. Market clearing at the equilibrium price does not mean that all individuals who have a positive valuation for the good will be satisfied. Rather, all individuals who are willing to pay the market price for the good will be satisfied, whereas those with a lower valuation for the good (i.e., a valuation for which the marginal revenue to the firm would be less than its marginal cost of production, thus making production of the unit unprofitable) will not be satisfied.

[33]It should be noted that this intervention could take a variety of forms that differ in their degree of interference with market forces. Possible interventions would include: requiring those who would remain unsatisfied consumers in the unfettered market to pay the prevailing market price, regardless of the relationship of that price to their individual valuation; subsidizing the unsatisfied consumers for the difference between the market valuation and their private valuation; and requiring that units of education be produced until the demand of all consumers is satisfied, which may require a subsidy to producers.

[34]Typically, this would be the political system.

[35]In contrast, typically the benefits of higher education flow to the individual to a much greater degree than do those of primary and secondary education. The benefits derived from differentiation in training or education are generally achieved as a result of training and education after the high school level, with the individual capturing significant gains in earnings and prestige as a result of his or her post–high school education and training activities.

[36]Some critics might suggest that the free market would be capable of dealing with primary and secondary education finance even in the presence of spillover benefits. They would argue that individual consumption expenditures by students and their families could be supplemented through voluntary contributions by all citizens that would account for the social benefits received from primary and secondary education. Three well-developed strains of economic literature suggest that such reliance on voluntary contributions would be unlikely to work: the literature on charitable giving as an alternative to welfare, the literature on the financing of government through contributions rather than compulsory finance, and the literature on social welfare functions.

[37]One might argue about the ends of this continuum, but recall that the financing is the crucial variable. The continuum attempts to vary only the financing mechanism, not the type or quality of education.

[38]This is especially true with respect to private schools.

[39]For example, differences in the fiscal capacity across municipalities.

[40]For example, the issue and importance of local control of schools.

[41]However, import duties might help circumvent this limit in the short run.

[42]Dillon's Rule, named after Judge John F. Dillon of Iowa, "holds that if state law is silent about a particular local power, the presumption is that the local level lacks the power" (Mikesell 1995, p. 19) This is because local governments are creatures of the state and only have those powers that are explicitly granted to them or are logically implied from the granted powers.

[43]In general, the larger the geographic or political area, the less chance of leakages of economic activity and other benefits to outside the region.

[44]It should be noted that under most payment plans the students are enrolled in school for a long time before the full bill comes due.

[45]Indeed, the author's local parish school just went back to a traditional tuition system after many years of trying unsuccessfully to make a fair share system work.

[46]This is especially true given (1) the merit good nature of primary and secondary education, and (2) the equity issues raised by ability to pay considerations with respect to such goods and other goods whose consumption is in some way legally mandated.

[47]The identification of the need for government involvement in the financier role greatly focuses and narrows the school reform debate. It also gives government policymakers some impetus to establish themselves as leaders in school finance reform.

CHAPTER 9

The Entrepreneur
Who Is the Source of Innovation?
Who Bears the Risk of Innovation?

Entrepreneurs and entrepreneurship have received significant attention in recent years. An increasing number of graduate business schools have entrepreneurship programs, with *U.S. News and World Report* now recognizing such programs in its subranking of programs within America's best business schools. The debate over U.S. industrial policy has included significant discussion of entrepreneurship as it relates to economic productivity, with Robert Reich's *The Work of Nations* (1991) and *Tales of a New America* (1987) but two examples of books touching on the theme. Public sector entrepreneurship discussions received a substantial boost with the publication of David Osborne and Ted Gaebler's 1992 bestseller, *Reinventing Government,* the subtitle of which is "How the entrepreneurial spirit is transforming the public sector from schoolhouse to statehouse, city hall to the Pentagon." Contemporary public administration and the modern public administrator are at the center of the debate over entrepreneurship and at the center of attention in terms of producing results for a nation easily enamored by ideas like those expressed by Osborne and Gaebler.

The entrepreneur plays a very important role in the economy. Even though the term *entrepreneur* is commonly used, the parameters of the entrepreneur's economic role are often not understood or explained. Unfortunately, it is clear that Osborne and Gaebler do not understand the economic concept of entrepreneur and do great harm by attempting to redefine the term to meet their own needs and desires.[1] Thus, it is important to describe a well-established conception of the entrepreneur's economic role that can serve as a starting point for this chapter's discussion.

McConnell and Brue (1990) assign four related functions to the entrepreneur in their categorization of economic resources. They describe these functions as follows:

1. The entrepreneur takes the initiative in combining other economic resources in the production of a good or service.
2. The entrepreneur undertakes the chore of making basic business-policy decisions, that is, those nonroutine decisions which set the course of a business enterprise.
3. The entrepreneur is an innovator—the person who attempts to introduce on a commercial basis new products, new productive techniques, or even new forms of business organization.
4. The entrepreneur is a risk bearer. . . . The entrepreneur . . . has no guarantee of profit . . . In short, the entrepreneur risks not only time, effort, and business reputation, but his or her invested funds and those of associates or stockholders. (p. 23)

It should be noted that McConnell and Brue's definition relates to entrepreneurial ability as an economic resource, differentiating entrepreneurial ability from other forms of labor and from land and capital.[2] This point is significant because of the overlap of some of the just-described functions with other market roles we have already discussed. Specifically, functions 1 and 2 are part of the administrator role that was defined earlier in this book, and function 1 also is related to the producer role. As suggested by the title of this chapter, our interest in the entrepreneur's role is defined by the third and fourth functions offered by McConnell and Brue: the entrepreneur as an innovator and a risk bearer. Peter Eisinger, adapting Schumpeter's view of entrepreneurship, notes: "It is the function of the entrepreneur, a risk-taker, an actor with vision, to animate the economic engine by exploiting an invention or, more generally, an untried technological possibility for producing a new commodity or producing an old one in a new way, or by opening up a new outlet for products" (Eisinger 1988, p. 8). Therefore, our task in this chapter is to answer the following question: in the market for primary and secondary education, what type of economic actor or actors can and/or should play the role of risk bearer and innovator? For the purpose of clarity, we will separate the risk bearer and innovator functions, discussing each in turn beginning with that of the innovator.

One of the primary attributes of an innovator is the ability to generate ideas. An innovator must be imaginative, comfortable with abstraction and ill-structured problems, and persistent. The successful innovator must also be able to communicate his or her ideas in such a way that they can be at first appreciated and then operationalized and utilized. Famous inventors such as Thomas Alva Edison and Alexander Graham Bell could clearly be classified as successful innovators. But reference to such famous inventors triggers another question with respect to the innovator role: Can innovation be institutionalized or be the responsibility of an organization? If so, who bears the ultimate responsibility for innovation? Most likely, many people in their conception of innovation and creativity think of the individual innovator fighting against almost insurmountable odds to invent the next super product or device.[3] At the same time, corporations with a reputation for innovation are easy to identify (e.g., Walt Disney, 3M, Microsoft, AT&T). How can these images be reconciled, and what are the implications of this reconciliation for assignment of the entrepreneurial role?

Innovation and creativity are human attributes that are part of the skills that can be obtained from human resources. Organizations and nonhuman resources cannot be innovators apart from the contribution of the intellectual resources of individual human beings. However, organizations can foster innovation and creativity, and they can provide an environment wherein innovators can maximize their potential and their achievements. This is the kind of environment Osborne and Gaebler (1992) would promote for the public sector. Similarly, the Gore Commission, formally known as the National Performance Review, sought to foster such innovation and creativity at the federal level.

Providing an environment conducive to innovation is important to the institutional entrepreneur. One common characteristic of successful institutional entrepreneurs is their ability to assume and manage the risk inherent in innovation and its commercialization.[4] This is also what sets the institutional entrepreneur apart from its creative or innovative staff. Furthermore, this is a reason why a company like Motorola is still believed by many analysts to be a good stock investment even in the face of maturing and increasingly competitive markets for its current computer chip and cellular telephone businesses. The same can be said for a company like Walt Disney, which has expanded its business lines to follow changes in technology and entertainment media that threatened its original products and services. Companies with an established reputation for innovation, human resource development, and good business decisions tend to be able to adapt to changing market conditions and find a way to continue to prosper in the long run.

The notion of the entrepreneur as a risk taker[5] helps us to differentiate between tinkering inventors like Doc Brown in the movie *Back to the Future* and true entrepreneurs, including institutional entrepreneurs. That is, it should be noted that an entrepreneur is both an innovator *and* a risk taker. Indeed, the entrepreneur may innovate by hiring innovators to produce the ideas he or she will seek to commercialize or utilize.[6] This is typically the way that innovative corporations are operated, and it is especially typical of the computer hardware and software firms of the late twentieth century.[7] For example, video game companies hire creative artists and computer programmers to produce the innovative products that end up as the hottest selling of each year's (each month's?) new generation of entertainment software for home or commercial use. Such a system has likely succeeded at least partially on the merits of its obvious economic benefits. Innovators are provided with the necessary resources and are allowed to engage in creative problem solving and invention of new products, without the burden of direct financial exposure from slowly developing or unsuccessful but well-developed ideas and innovations. In other words, the innovator is rewarded with a steady and reliable income in exchange for the rights to his or her innovations. Furthermore, one might argue that there are significant economies of agglomeration and intellectual benefits to having a group of innovators, each with differing skills and comparative advantage, working in close proximity to one another and for a common end. But who represents the entrepreneur in such an innovative firm, and what are the criteria by which we identify this person or persons?

Recall that an entrepreneur is both a risk taker and an innovator. Just as this definition allowed us to differentiate between some types of inventors and entrepreneurs, the definition also allows us to differentiate between entrepreneurs and investors or venture capitalists.

Although investors and venture capitalists are essential economic actors in a market economy and are typically necessary components to entrepreneurial success, they are not themselves entrepreneurs. In simplest terms, investors and venture capitalists play a risk-taking role in the economy but typically do not play the innovator role that is so essential to entrepreneurship. Thus, generally investors and venture capitalists are better classified as part of the financier role.[8] Furthermore, it should be noted that the entrepreneur need not invest any up-front funds in order to qualify as an entrepreneur or risk taker. The entrepreneur's exposure in terms of risk may be in the form of the opportunity cost of his or her time, a factor payment that is contingent on level of success, business reputation, *or* invested funds.

With this refinement of our conception of the entrepreneur's role, we return to the issue of identifying the entrepreneur in the typical innovative corporation. Entrepreneurs tend to be the founders of corporations, whereas managers and administrators tend to be responsible for their day-to-day operations. This makes identification of the entrepreneur fairly straightforward in relatively new corporations, even those of great size (e.g., Bill Gates and Microsoft, Frank Perdue and Perdue Chicken, Sam Walton and WalMart, Walt Disney and the Disney corporation). What about mature, but still very innovative, corporations? Who, if anyone, plays the role of entrepreneur? Does the performance of this role significantly differ from firm to firm in terms of who performs it and how? Do lines of responsibility offer insight into the identification of entrepreneurs?

Identifying the responsibility for the entrepreneur role in a mature, innovative firm requires much intuition and thought, especially because corporate structure tends to vary from firm to firm and industry to industry. Nevertheless, it seems possible to identify the general nature of the entrepreneur's role in a mature firm.

Most mature innovative firms have long recognized the importance of ongoing innovation and technology commercialization. As a result, the responsibility for innovation and commercialization has often been institutionalized through an executive line in the corporate structure. The executive at the head of this line may have a variety of titles depending on the firm,[9] but that individual has ultimate operational responsibility for innovation in the firm, with his or her professional reputation being dependent on the innovation unit's success or failure. Before leaving the company, Jeffrey Katzenberg was the person who apparently filled this role at Walt Disney.[10] Thus, even in mature firms, the entrepreneurial function remains and can at least theoretically be traced to individuals within the corporate structure. Firms can foster innovation and can be catalysts for innovation, but the ultimate responsibility for and ability to engage in innovation must reside with an individual or individuals. Given our interest in public policy and public administration, this begs the question of whether the notion of innovation and entrepreneurship is compatible with public sector responsibility for the entrepreneur role. As we will explain in the following section, public sector entrepreneurship is alive and well, both in terms of individual entrepreneurs and in terms of organizations and governments that foster entrepreneurial behavior.

PUBLIC SECTOR ENTREPENEURSHIP

Innovation is not something limited to the private sector. Indeed, since 1986 the Ford Foundation, in cooperation with the Kennedy School of Government at Harvard, has had a government awards program designed to reward innovations in government. Until 1994, the program was Innovations in State and Local Government; it provided $100,000 awards to each of ten state and local programs each year. Beginning in 1995, the program was renamed the Innovations in American Government Awards; it was expanded to fifteen winners each year, with federal programs having strong domestic components now being eligible ("Innovations" 1994, p. 36). Reading through the descriptions of any year's award-winning programs should convince even the most staunch skeptic of government and its programs that innovation and entrepreneurship are alive and well in the public sector. "Schumpeter's entrepreneur is a private actor. But there are certain social and economic conditions under which private entrepreneurial activity may not suffice to provide the basis for the sustained and high economic growth that a society may have come to expect" (Eisinger 1988, p. 8). Eisinger argues that under these conditions there is a role for the state to serve an entrepreneurial function. But this begs the question as to how entrepreneurship and innovation in the public sector are to be reconciled with the common criticism that the lack of a profit motive in the public sector leads to waste, inefficiency, and technological inertia.

Perhaps the easiest answer to this difficult question would be to simply write off the criticism as misplaced, uninformed, and inaccurate propaganda from antigovernment critics. However, to do so would ignore important differences between the public and private sector that may be instructive in our consideration of the entrepreneur's role. Understanding these differences will also assist in dividing that role between the public and the private sector in the market for primary and secondary education. In addition, changes in the environment within which the public sector operates have by necessity altered many of the rules by which government does business. But before looking at these changes and their implications, a clearer vision of the criticism of government's lack of a profit motive seems in order.

The lack of a profit motive in the public sector appears to have at least two significant components: (1) the lack of a motive or incentive on the part of government or government enterprises to produce or increase profits through productivity and product improvement; and (2) the inability or lack of necessity in engaging in a shutdown of government or government enterprise operations that are not competitive or profitable in the long run. The combination of these factors can be devastating.

The positive and often substantial rewards from innovation and profit seeking, upon which incentive structures in unfettered private markets are built, are not available or not of interest in the typical government activity. Indeed, taxpayers likely would find it most undesirable to have government charging fees for services that include a profit margin, especially if that profit margin were to be consistent with the monopoly power government possesses in many of the markets in which it operates. At the same time, with compulsory finance tools at its disposal, government's incentive to build a profit margin into its services and operations is reduced or eliminated. Government is expected to finance services on a cost recovery basis. Carrying this point one step further, one can logically argue that this lack of a motive to produce or increase profits leads to a lack of incentive to innovate or to improve services, because the financial benefits of innovation or service improvement cannot be captured by the government. Indeed, for most local governments, capturing such benefits would be illegal.

Most governmental units, including local governments, have broad authority to impose user fees and charges to recover the costs of service provision. However, a user fee or charge must not exceed the cost of providing the good or service; otherwise, the fee or charge must be considered a tax. For local governments, taxes generally require explicit authorization from the state. Otherwise, they are likely to be invalid under Dillon's Rule in the absence of broad local home rule powers. Thus, cost recovery is generally the best a local government can hope for as a fiscal reward for entrepreneurial service provision. Therefore, from this perspective entrepreneurial behavior would be neither rewarded nor encouraged. As we will see shortly, the validity of this point has been reduced in the new public sector environment that has dominated public administration in the late twentieth century, especially as it applies to the federal and state governments, but also to increasingly entrepreneurial local governments.

Not being forced to shut down unprofitable operations can also have a negative incentive effect with respect to government operations. However, the ability to criticize this attribute of government is much more constrained than the criticism of the failure to innovate. This is in part owing to government's role as a provider of last resort for certain types of goods and services. A private market does not exist for all goods and services, despite the fact that some of the goods or services that are not provided privately are socially desirable and can be produced such that marginal social benefit and marginal social cost are equated, or there is an excess of marginal social benefits when compared with costs.[11] Examples of such goods and services with incomplete markets include student loans, flood insurance, and deposit insurance. When measured in terms of traditional accounting profits,[12] none of these services is profitable. However, each is "profitable" in terms of a comparison of marginal social benefit and marginal social cost. One can argue that for such goods and services, government last resort provision at an accounting loss (which only includes private costs and benefits) is appropriate. However, such goods and services only represent a small part of the overall operations of government, none of which generally need to obey the traditional private sector shutdown rules. These other cases are more problematic economically.

Economic principles indicate that in the long run the price that a producer receives for his or her product must be sufficient to cover average production costs, including fixed costs and a normal profit. Otherwise, production will not be profitable, and the economic resources utilized in producing the good or service should be freed up and allocated to more profitable or economically valued uses. That is, the producer should strongly consider leaving the market.[13] Long-term profits drive entry and exit decisions by firms and are a key factor in economically efficient resource allocation decisions.[14] Lack of a profit motive on the part of producers could have the effect of misallocating resources, as signals to enter or exit an industry are not acted upon as a result of this lack of motive. Thus, at least in some cases, the concern about the lack of a profit motive in government operations generating inefficient use of resources and potential waste is well grounded theoretically. However, this point should be tempered by consideration of the general environment within which government services are provided.

Even outside of the last resort provider cases noted previously, many of the goods and services provided by government are by necessity not produced or provided in competitive markets that include private sector firms in competition with one another or with the government. In other words, it may be accurate to note that the operations of government do not ensure efficient outcomes, but this criticism is meaningless without consideration of the available and feasible alternatives to the government involvement that is being criticized. That is, the inefficient government solution may in fact be the *best* of a series of alternative inefficient solutions. Economists call this the theory of the second best. In the absence of an efficient solution, the next best (and inefficient) solution is chosen. It should be noted that this inefficient government solution may be better than any other solution, including unfettered market solutions, on all value dimensions except that of efficiency. Therefore, it may provide not only an acceptable but also a preferred solution. However, having made this point, it should also be noted that a common flaw in the use of collective choice mechanisms and political institutions to produce and allocate goods and services involves failing to give serious consideration to alternatives to the government-based solution, even in terms of considering second-best solutions. Too often, after identifying a potential market failure, government-based solutions are brought to the forefront without considering the possibility of superior, privately based "second best" solutions. Indeed, that is one of the issues that drove this book to be written and structured in the way that it has been.

Nevertheless, the lack of a profit motive on the part of government does create some interesting theoretical issues with respect to the nature of the public sector entrepreneur's role in the market. Recall that one key aspect of the entrepreneur's economic role is risk bearing. As noted earlier, one cannot be an entrepreneur without bearing risk in some way. Although the nature of the risk that is borne by the entrepreneur may vary (e.g., invested capital, professional reputation, job security, or merely time), one would further expect that there must be some type of potential payoff to the entrepreneur in exchange for his or her bearing of risk. Once again, the nature of this potential payoff will vary with the type of risk that is borne by the entrepreneur. The absence of a profit motive in government and the typical nonapplicability of the economic shutdown rules to government enterprises makes it somewhat more difficult in the public sector to define the risk/reward tradeoff that one generally expects to link to entrepreneurial behavior. More bluntly, how does the public sector entrepreneur bear risk, and what rewards are reasonable for him or her to expect in return?

From an institutional perspective, government has historically not operated in any significant risk/reward framework. Generally, the failure of a particular government operation or enterprise does not significantly affect government's ability to operate in the future, either financially or reputationally.[15] Indeed, compulsory finance tools can and have often been used to pass on the burden of failed government enterprises or activities. The well publicized default of the county government in Orange County, California, has not caused the county to dissolve or go out of business. Indeed, ultimately the costs of the default will be widely borne by investors and citizens across the nation. This is quite an operational advantage. Can one imagine the glee with which a private sector firm would treat the news that from now on losses from any failed business endeavor could be financed through the sending of legally enforceable bills to existing customers for their pro rata share of the loss incurred by the company's risk taking, with no responsibility to share profits from past or future successes with these same customers? Although it may sound incredible, for many years governments operated with privileges similar to these!

However, just as the risks for government are hard to define, so are the rewards. It is difficult to identify the gains that government receives institutionally from successful programs or activities. Even though one can rightfully argue that government's successes improve social welfare, these gains are not captured by government, nor can they be measured sufficiently in any objective manner for comparative or evaluative purposes. However, risks and rewards do exist in the public sector and may offer a clue to identifying, demarcating, and interpreting a public sector entrepreneurial role.

At least four aspects of the public sector and its operations should be explored with respect to clues about risk/reward behavior and its link to innovation and entrepreneurship: (1) politicians and their behavior, (2) professional administrators and their behavior, (3) interjurisdictional competition, and (4) taxpayer revolt/fiscal stress issues. Not only are each of these issues central and important to twenty-first century public administrators and public policymakers, but each is also central to our debate over government's role in primary and secondary school reform. We discuss each of these entrepreneurial links in turn.

Most politicians are very interested in being reelected to office or elected/appointed to a higher or more influential position. It seems reasonable that politicians would perceive a linkage between their performance in office and their future political rewards.[16] Thus, a politician could be an entrepreneur in the sense that he or she engages in innovation designed to take advantage of the reward structure while subjecting the politician to discernable downside risk should he or she fail. The rise to power of Newt Gingrich and Dick Armey was certainly entrepreneurial in terms of innovation[17] and bore significant rewards while exposing the former Speaker of the House and the current Majority Leader of the House to significant and continuing downside risk, some of which fell on the Speaker and his party in the midst of his successes. Entrepreneurial opportunities may be even greater at the subnational level where the benefits and costs of governmental activity are more directly measurable and noticeable by taxpayers/voters, and where the accountability of government and politicians is more immediate and direct.[18] Thus, we can preliminarily conclude that politicians, at least in a broad definitional sense, can play an entrepreneurial role in the public sector. It should be noted, however, that the rewards to the politician are typically personal, with little necessity for those rewards to simultaneously benefit government or society—unlike the gains from private sector entrepreneurship, which are by nature generally shared with other economic actors.[19]

Professional administrators can also be public sector entrepreneurs. A simple example of this can be derived through consideration of city managers and their responsibilities. The city manager is the chief operating officer in many municipalities and is directly accountable to the mayor and/or city council. In theory, the city manager is apolitical (in the sense of partisan politics) and responsible for acting as a staffer to the policymakers who make the rules and policies he or she will enforce and execute. In practice, most successful city managers are very actively involved in the policy process and its politics, albeit often in subtle and indirect ways. Indeed, the city manager's involvement in the policy process is the general way in which the manager can play the role of public sector entrepreneur. A brief look at the characteristics of this form of entrepreneurship will help to define the parameters of the administrative entrepreneur in the public sector.

There is little question that a city manager's involvement in the policy process requires the bearing of significant risk. The manager's involvement in policy issues increases the chances of ending up on the opposite side of a debate from some subset of council members. The greater the manager's involvement in the policy process, the greater the opportunity for inducing council member dissatisfaction with one or more of his or her policy initiatives or positions. This is especially true if the manager is perceived to be in the camp of, or under the influence of, a particular policy or political faction in a divided council. Council member dissatisfaction with a manager may result in termination, reduced compensation, harm to one's professional reputation, or a hostile work environment, among other things. Nevertheless, there are also significant reward possibilities attributable to involvement in the policy process.

Successful policy initiatives and active participation in the policy process may result in increased compensation, increased availability of professional resources, and an enhanced professional reputation, not to mention improved delivery of programs and/or services to one's constituents.[20] One economic development professional in northern Illinois had an economic development success early in his career in another part of the state that he has been able to parlay into an entire career of extremely high paying (as compared with his economic development cohort) and relatively secure jobs. However, this experience is still an exception in the administrative arena. Public administrators, including school superintendents, are generally judged on the basis of what they have done lately and are often fired quickly despite a relatively good overall track record. For example, over the past several years, many of the most senior and most respected city managers in Illinois have found themselves in transition. In many cases, these managers have been public sector entrepreneurs who have had to bear the risk of their entrepreneurial behavior.

The issue of interjurisdictional competition also has significant implications for analysis of the role of the entrepreneur in the public sector. However, unlike some other activities of politicians and administrators, interjurisdictional competition generally requires the cooperation and active participation of multiple decisionmakers/actors and involves risk bearing by the community or jurisdiction at large, including the citizenry. Thus, the analogue may be closer to institutional entrepreneurship rather than individual entrepreneurship. The political institutions within which issues of interjurisdictional competition are discussed and endorsed may vary significantly from place to place,[21] but the issues of entrepreneurship tend to be pervasive and universal. A general example should help clarify the nature of possible entrepreneurial behavior with respect to interjurisdictional competition: "bidding for business."

In bidding for business, the community[22] attempts to attract industrial or commercial development in competition with other jurisdictions. Although such policies can be undertaken at national and international levels, for tractability we will concentrate on local economic development policy with little or no loss in the generality of our conclusions. Let's examine how undertaking such a competitive strategy might fit under the realm of entrepreneurial behavior. At the simplest level, undertaking a local economic development program will be costly in terms of the use of community resources. Whether undertaken by an individual or by a government as an institutional effort, good local economic development policy is at the heart of an entrepreneurial approach to bidding for business. Good local economic development policy is grounded in government having a clear sense of the values of the community it represents, as well as a vision for the community that has been cooperatively developed by local stakeholders.[23] With this vision statement in place, a general statement of community economic development policy can be agreed upon and implemented. It is after (and only after) this economic development policy has been agreed upon and implemented that entrepreneurial actions can be used to achieve the ends inherent in the community's vision for economic development.

Eisinger (1988) argues that what guides the entrepreneurial state in bidding for business is an attention to the "demand"[24] side of the economic growth equation. "Underlying the actions of the entrepreneurial state is the assumption that growth comes from exploiting new or expanding markets. The state role is to identify, evaluate, anticipate, and even help to develop and create these markets for private producers to exploit, aided if necessary by government as a subsidizer or coinvestor" (Eisinger 1988, p. 9). Once again, the link to the financier role can be explicitly discerned.

Eisinger contrasts his entrepreneurial state with traditional policy approaches. Whereas the traditional approach has focused on lowering production factor costs for established and potentially mobile capital, the entrepreneurial approach focuses on discovering or expanding new markets for local goods and services, with an emphasis on *new* capital. The entrepreneurial approach means government involvement in more high-risk enterprises and activities, but also involvement only on a more strategic and targeted basis (Eisinger 1988, pp. 10–13). In addition, the demand-side or entrepreneurial approach generally involves less active competition between local jurisdictions than traditional smokestack-chasing behavior. This has great implications for increased levels of regional cooperation and also for greater applicability of the traditional business risk/reward framework. Ultimately, the entrepreneurial state model suggests the possibility for the public sector entrepreneur to receive a larger portion of a larger pie. This type of situation offers great hope for a win/win outcome. Especially in a time of fiscal stress, behavior of government according to the entrepreneurial state model has great prospects for economic growth and fiscal reward, as well as for improvements in quality of life. Similar results also appear to be possible with respect to the issues faced by governments related to taxpayer revolt and fiscal stress.

Although taxpayer revolt and fiscal stress may in fact be reasons why governments seek to increase the levels of economic activity within their jurisdiction, whether through traditional or entrepreneurial means, the response to taxpayer revolt and fiscal stress often takes more general forms, many of which also could be considered entrepreneurial.

Revenue structure is an area over which federal, state, and municipal[25] governments have a reasonably wide range of control and latitude. However, in some sense it is the constraints, political or legal, that create some of the most interesting fiscal issues and greatest opportunities for entrepreneurial behavior. Before discussing some examples of this kind of entrepreneurial fiscal behavior, it is important to eliminate certain forms of potentially creative behavior from our definition of entrepreneurship. Entrepreneurial behavior in revenue generation, according to the definition adopted here, excludes the use of backdoor referenda, creative accounting, and manipulation of administrative rules.[26] Instead, entrepreneurship in the face of fiscal stress includes creative economic development efforts designed to broaden and deepen a jurisdiction's tax base or to reduce its expenditure commitments. Entrepreneurship also includes public investments designed to improve overall quality of life and morale on the part of community stakeholders, and it can involve redesign of revenue structures so as to better reflect community values and attitudes.[27] Public entrepreneurs may also reduce fiscal stress by designing mechanisms whereby the stakeholders of the jurisdiction are asked to contribute to the general well-being through non-financial means (e.g., personnel time or some other in-kind contribution, on top of taxes or in lieu of taxes). The stakes in fiscal debates are high, or at least are perceived to be so, and there are likely to be both winners and losers in any redesign of a jurisdiction's revenue structure. Clearly, the risk/reward and creativity aspects of entrepreneurship are both fulfilled in the fiscal stress case.

GOVERNMENT INTERVENTION AND THE
ENTREPRENEUR ROLE

Based on the preceding exploration of the public sector and its operations, we can say that public sector performance of the entrepreneur role and the performance of the entrepreneur role in public sector operations both seem to be viable concepts. Indeed, meaningful examples of each can be readily provided. Yet, this analysis does little in terms of illuminating the necessity for government to perform the entrepreneur role as part of its functions in a mixed economy. Although there may be a number of ways to justify government intervention as entrepreneur that can be related to government's functions in a mixed economy,[28] compelling evidence of a need for government intervention is more difficult to marshal. Nevertheless, at least one generic situation can be identified wherein government intervention as entrepreneur is likely to be necessary.

In the case of entrepreneurial activity for which the marginal social benefit exceeds the marginal social cost *and* the marginal private cost exceeds the marginal private benefit, private performance of the entrepreneur role is at best highly unlikely. Functionally, this is a case of incomplete markets in which there is no market for entrepreneurial services. This means that in the absence of government intervention as entrepreneur, one would not expect an entrepreneurial function to be performed. The implications of this situation are (1) potential stagnation of complementary economic activities, and (2) sustained inefficiencies in the allocation of resources.

A few examples of situations fitting this description can be identified. One example is that of certain types of redevelopment projects. In cases where the private costs of redevelopment make undertaking a project impossible or very unattractive, government intervention in the market may be required in order for redevelopment to proceed.[29] Intervention in the entrepreneur role[30] may include land assembly, demolition, and retrofitting of infrastructure and physical amenities so as to make an area attractive for redevelopment. The risk element is fulfilled by the outlay of public dollars with no assurance of sufficient returns to offset the initial investment. The reward element is fulfilled by the potential of a significant tax and revenue increment as a result of redevelopment, not to mention quality of life benefits that may occur as well. The innovation element can be fulfilled through unique forms of parcel assembly, provision of special amenities to encourage development, and innovative recapture agreements. In sum, in "but for" (see note 29) redevelopment situations, it is unlikely that the entrepreneur role will be played in the absence of government intervention to perform the role. A similar result was observed in the early space program and has been historically true for the development of advanced weapons systems.[31]

Thus, market role assessment of the entrepreneur role indicates that both private and public sector performance of the role are feasible and that both the private sector and public sector have successfully acted as entrepreneurs in markets. In addition, a set of circumstances were developed under which government performance of the entrepreneur role is likely to be compelled in a given market. Having assessed the role in general, we now turn our attention to the market for primary and secondary education.

EDUCATION AND THE ENTREPRENEUR ROLE

The fiscal stress and taxpayer revolt case is obviously very applicable to primary and secondary schools. In states like Illinois and many others, a substantial portion of the local property tax bill goes to local schools, and school districts tend to be severely constrained in their revenue-generating power when compared with general purpose governments. School districts and/or schools have tended to bear a significant portion of the burden of tax and expenditure limitations (e.g., Massachusetts, California, Illinois). Thus, a clear example of a place where the entrepreneurial role can come to the forefront is in the creative solution of education financing issues. Necessity may be the mother of invention, but invention and entrepreneurship have been the mothers of some successful interventions in the area of school finance reform. The drastic reform in Michigan, discussed in more detail in Chapter 11, is a clear example of entrepreneurial behavior. The voucher experiment in Milwaukee and the school reform in Chicago are further examples of entrepreneurial interventions. In each of these cases, creative solutions to difficult problems were proposed, with significant risk and reward tradeoffs implicit in each decision. It is interesting that the source and nature of public entrepreneurship varies in each of these cases. That in and of itself is one of the most important observations to be made at this point: public sector entrepreneurship is alive and well and living, among other places, in the land of primary and secondary education. Further evidence of this point is provided by early results from an ongoing study regarding the role of urban education advocates and the status of urban education reform issues within state education policy-making regimes. Early results have identified the strong role of activist governors in educational innovation,[32] and their roles as leaders in primary and secondary education policy (Gittell, McKenna et al. 1997). Much of this leadership would fall in the category of entrepreneurship.

In discussing the role of the entrepreneur in primary and secondary education, it would be easy to be further diverted by discussion of the numerous success stories of public and private sector entrepreneurs. However, to do so, at least at this point in the book, would be to fall into one of the traps that has been responsible for delaying school reform: failure to focus on the issue at hand. Furthermore, we return to our initial observation that school reform is a classic example of an ill-structured problem whose solution is dependent upon definition and narrowing. Within our framework, this means placing immediate focus on the relative merits of the public sector and the private sector as entrepreneur in the market for primary and secondary education.

Our conclusion with respect to the division of the entrepreneur's role in primary and secondary education is fundamentally a negative one. First, based upon the information and analysis presented in this chapter, there is no credible evidence to require the entrepreneur's role to be exclusively a public sector function in this market. Indeed, private successes such as Montessori schools, military academies, and other unique private sector educational institutions and experiences clearly indicate that private entrepreneurship is a viable option in the market. At the same time, the evidence of successful public sector entrepreneurial behavior in this market that was cited earlier indicates that public sector entrepreneurship can be successful in the market for primary and secondary education. Therefore, exclusive reliance on private sector entrepreneurship may not be advisable. However, owing to the financing methods of public education, the public sector entrepreneur is generally more financially protected than the private sector entrepreneur in the market for primary and secondary education. Therefore, one can argue that private sector and public sector entrepreneurs are not operating on a level playing field because of the public financing advantage. On the other hand, one can also argue that the private entrepreneur has greater ability to personally, more directly, and more tangibly benefit from successful entrepreneurial ventures than does the typical public sector entrepreneur. To some extent, the latter issue is being addressed through the implementation of bonus systems for some public employees and organizations. However, these programs are highly controversial but do offer some leveling of the otherwise unequal reward structure.[33]

CONCLUSION

In the absence of a compelling rationale favoring private sector or public sector performance of the entrepreneurial role, and given evidence of success on the part of both sectors in performing the role, a solution that allows competition between the sectors may be appropriate. That is, the market itself should be allowed to determine the success and failure of entrepreneurial behavior. With this is mind, there is no reason to expect any particular *a priori* optimal division of the entrepreneur role between the public sector and the private sector. However, in order for this system to work, a certain amount of school reform must first take place in order to provide an appropriate risk/reward tradeoff that will help ensure competition between public sector and private sector entrepreneurs. Some of the possible methods for encouraging such competition will be discussed in Chapter 10. This is where the findings from the market role assessment as to the division of the various market roles between the public sector and the private sector will be reviewed, summarized, analyzed, and evaluated. The entrepreneurial role is a central one in public policy innovation, and it is likely to be one of the most important roles in facilitating quality school reform. The overall evaluation of the market roles that is presented in Chapter 10 provides the foundation upon which the appropriate role for government in primary and secondary education and education reform can be better circumscribed and understood.

NOTES

[1]Specifically, Osborne and Gaebler assert in the preface to *Reinventing Government* that risk taking has no place in the definition of entrepreneurship. Not only is the concept of risk essential to the notion of entrepreneurship, but the concept of being an entrepreneur has no meaning in the absence of the *bearing of risk*. Osborne and Gaebler confuse risk taking with risk bearing and therefore create a hollow definition of entrepreneurship that cannot be differentiated from creativity or innovation. However, this criticism should not be interpreted as fundamental disagreement with the many appropriate and instructive points made by Osborne and Gaebler along many other dimensions (e.g., customer orientation, community empowerment, and marketplace leveraging).

[2]In economics, the four basic economic resources are land, labor, capital, and entrepreneurship.

[3]Indeed, this conception is one of the American myths at the heart of Reich's *Tales of a New America*.

[4]For example, see Young (1998)

[5]Having made the point about the problem with Osborne and Gaebler's understanding of risk taking versus the purer notion of risk bearing, we return to the conventional use of the term *risk taker* to describe this attribute of the entrepreneur. Discussion of the term should help further clarify the misinterpretation of entrepreneurship in *Reinventing Government*.

[6]This situation is actually very common. Although firms may set up bonus systems to reward employees for profitable innovations, the innovations themselves typically remain the exclusive property of the firm. Firms bear the risk of the innovation process but reap the rewards from the fruits of its outcomes.

[7]However, it should be noted that innovative firms are often the product of individual entrepreneurs who, at least in the beginning, were principal innovators responsible for seminal innovations that led to the initial success of the resulting firm. Bill Gates, Walt Disney, and Colonel Sanders are examples of such contributing innovator entrepreneurs. For further examples of entrepreneurship in the technology sector, see Young (1998).

[8]However, the significant risk taker role typically played by those we classify as venture capitalists differentiates them from the run of the mill financier, and they were therefore excluded to simplify the previous discussion of the financier role.

[9]For example, vice president of technology, vice president of research, director of research.

[10]When Katzenberg left Disney he joined with two other well-known entrepreneurs, David Geffen and Steven Spielberg, to form the aptly named entertainment blockbuster DreamWorks. It will be interesting to see the long-term success of this combination of three very talented, but very different and very independent and successful, individual entrepreneurs.

[11]However, the private market solution would result in production of a quantity of the good or service such that at that quantity the marginal social benefit of the good would still exceed the marginal social cost, thereby resulting in a quantity of production and consumption below that which is efficient or socially desired. That is, additional units could be produced for which MSB would exceed MSC.

[12]That is, by comparing marginal private benefits with marginal private costs.

[13]For further explanation of the economic theory of decisions to produce or not produce, including the market entry and exit decisions of firms, consult any principles of economics textbook (e.g., McConnell and Brue 1990, or Thomas 1990).

[14]In general terms, the cost of producing a good or service is composed of the payments that must be made to owners of the economic resources (land, labor, capital, and entrepreneurship) in order to obtain the use of the mix of resources that are required to produce the product. In competitive markets, the price of economic resources (i.e., the payment that must be made to resource owners) is equivalent to their value in their next best alternative economic use, and the price that the producer is able to obtain for his or her product is a reflection of the value consumers place on the product. Thus, if product price is less than average cost in a competitive market, the market value of the product is less than the market value of the resources that were used to produce the product, and those resources should be reallocated to their more valuable alternative use.

[15]One exception to this might be the Washington Public Power System, WPPS. This state power system's bond default is legendary and has severely affected its future market credibility.

[16]However, it should be noted that (1) the risk/reward tradeoff may differ between offices and officeholders, and (2) performance in office is measured by satisfaction of those persons who are in a position to provide the desired rewards (e.g., constituents, party leaders, legislative colleagues, chief executives, contributors). Thus, the behavioral implications of the risk/reward tradeoff may be extremely situational.

[17]For example, the Contract with America and Gingrich's wholesale assault and overturn of the traditional House of Representatives seniority system were both innovative and very risky, with the potential of significant rewards.

[18]Furthermore, at subnational levels there are a greater number of paths for advancement than there are in national politics.

[19]For example, the entrepreneur's successes can provide job security for a firm's production workers.

[20]Professional experience indicates that most public managers are driven significantly by public service. Thus, providing better services to the citizens of the manager's jurisdiction would be expected to be positively valued by the manager.

[21]For example, New England town meetings, referenda by initiative, and public hearings.

[22]*Community* is broadly defined to include any political jurisdiction, not just a municipality or other local area. Although a community need not be a political

jurisdiction, the current analysis is clearer in the context of political jurisdictions with statutory powers.

[23]For example, residents, workers, businesses, schools, churches, civic organizations, social service agencies, and governments.

[24]*Demand* is placed in quotes here to indicate the ongoing disagreement as to whether Eisinger has correctly or incorrectly labeled the demand and supply sides of the market. The outcome of the dispute is irrelevant to Eisinger's argument. Thus, we note the dispute, explain what Eisinger means, and move on in using his arguments as part of our analysis.

[25]Nonmunicipal local governments typically have relatively little control over or latitude in revenue structure.

[26]This has been done by some states to obtain additional Medicare payments from the federal government.

[27]It should be noted that a shift to user charges or fees would better link the costs and benefits of services financed by this method, rather than financing them through general revenues.

[28]For example, interventions might be justified as part of government's role in mitigating market failures such as unemployment, externalities, and imperfect information; or as a means of facilitating voluntary exchanges in the free market.

[29]Cases like this are said to meet the "but for" test—redevelopment would not take place "but for" government intervention. This is the classic justification for tools such as tax increment financing.

[30]The entrepreneur role is only one form of intervention that may be necessary in this type of case.

[31]However, private sector investments in these cases may have also been limited by national security concerns.

[32]However, the authors of the study argue that much of the innovation has not been aimed at urban schools.

[33]For example, a researcher the author once worked with left his public sector job a few years ago to take a new job (doing the same thing for basically the same clients) at a different public sector organization that is allowed to, and does, pay (sometimes quite substantial) bonuses to its employees. Despite no known efforts to hide this system, it seems that this compensation system is not controversial only because few persons are aware of it, and it would not necessarily be easily recognized in looking at the open records of the organization.

CHAPTER 10

Common Ground
An Evaluation of Government's Role in Primary and Secondary Education

What should be government's role in primary and secondary education? The answer to this question has not yet been provided in this book, but some directions have been suggested through the market role assessment conducted thus far. In this chapter, we return to the foundations of our analytical framework and review the findings from preceding chapters. Recalling the ill-structured nature of public policy questions like that of primary and secondary school reform, one needs to remember the importance of circumscribing the problem as an early step toward problem solution. Therefore, the first task in moving toward answers about government's role in school reform is to summarize and illuminate the analytical findings regarding the division of the seven identified market roles between economic actors in the public sector and the private sector. Many of these economic roles overlap and interact; thus, it is important to consider the distribution of the roles as a whole, as well as in the isolated fashion presented in the separate chapters earlier in the book. However, it is appropriate to begin with a general look at the findings made with respect to each of the economic roles. To improve analytical clarity, these economic roles are addressed in a slightly different order from that of the preceding chapters.[1]

GOVERNMENT AS FINANCIER[2]

As long as the United States has a system of mandatory and "free" public primary and secondary education, government will have a role in the market as financier. Furthermore, even in the absence of these considerations, the significant social benefits from primary and secondary education require some level of public sector financier role. Although these are relatively simple statements that constitute a similarly unambiguous conclusion from our preceding analysis, this conclusion goes a long way toward simplifying the school reform debate and helping to define some of its terms. *Government must be a financier in the market for primary and secondary education.*

There is a role for government in primary and secondary education, and government must be involved in primary and secondary education reform. Thus, any primary and secondary education reform that is based solely upon privatization will necessarily have problems—if not in gaining approval, then in terms of implementation and sustainability.

At the same time, the analysis in the financier chapter (Chapter 8) also suggests that there is a greater role for private finance tools and private performance of the financier role than is typical currently in the market for primary and secondary education. This is owing to the mixed good nature of such education. Not only does primary and secondary education have significant societal spillover benefits, but it also has significant private benefits that tend to increase with each year of education that is completed. One could therefore argue that a system of "free" public education represents, in part, a subsidy of private benefits for individuals. This may not seem to be a significant issue; but if one alters the context slightly, the nature of the problem becomes much clearer.

One of the criticisms of many economic development subsidy or tax abatement programs is that government should not be in the business of subsidizing private enterprises. At a national level, the bailout of Chrysler was highly controversial. At the state and local level, stadium bond issues for professional sports teams have been equally or more controversial. Similarly, lucrative incentive packages given to Sears by Illinois, United Airlines by Indiana, Northwest Airlines by Minnesota, and Saturn by Tennessee were controversial for reasons including disagreement over the appropriateness of state government subsidizing private business. Subsidy of the private benefits of education is fundamentally the same type of issue, though rarely is the appropriateness of this subsidy given the national or in-depth attention that any of the aforementioned economic development projects received.

Thus, from a philosophical standpoint one can argue that the financier role should be divided between the public sector and the private sector. Yet, deciding on the appropriate division of the role may be more difficult than deciding that it is appropriate to divide the role. Nevertheless, theoretical if not practical guidance is available.

Given the prior analytical discussions, the appropriate division of roles is easy to state, although not easy to implement. Government should finance that portion of primary and secondary education expenditures that represent the social benefits of the education. In an equivalent manner, the private benefits of primary and secondary education should be privately financed. The problem is in identifying, separating, and measuring the private versus social benefits. Furthermore, the social benefits or externalities must also be classified in terms of their nature and geographic range. That is, one needs to have some understanding of the main beneficiaries of the social benefits of education. Do most of the social benefits remain with the community where the student attends school? Do most of the social benefits accrue to those who live in the same community as the educated person? Do most of the social benefits accrue to the nation as a whole, or even to the global economy? Perhaps more important, one must make the linkage between the nature of the social benefits and the appropriate level or levels of government that should be involved in the primary and secondary education financier role, in order to better match financing costs with the geographic flow of benefits.

Unfortunately, it is unlikely that any of the preceding questions can be answered with any precision or objective accuracy. However, certain assertions can be made that will allow some insight into the financier role. In general, the intensity of social benefits will be greatest as the unit of analysis is reduced. That is, one would expect that the social benefits from a given person's education would be greatest at the local level and decrease as one moved the unit of analysis to the state, national, and international levels. Whether one considers the social benefits from an informed populace, more efficient operation of political and market institutions, or greater economic productivity, the intensity of the benefits are arguably the greatest at the local level. It may be easiest to see this by considering the issue in reverse: the societal effects of lack of education.

Little persuasion should be necessary to gain agreement with the argument that one illiterate person will be less likely to have an effect at the national level than at the local level. Clearly, one thousand illiterate people will make a greater impact on society at the local level than at the national level. One can even argue that the conclusion is appropriate in percentage terms: a given proportion of illiterate people will make a greater social impact at the local rather than the national level. Thus, in the absence of a good counterexample or empirical literature, our central assertion will be that of declining per capita social benefits to education as one moves from local to state to national levels.

Despite this helpful conclusion, the issue of local benefits is somewhat muddied by the recognition that both the community of residence and the community of employment for a given individual reap significant social benefits from the individual's primary and secondary education. Although many people work in the same community in which they live, there is no reason that this need be the case. Furthermore, individuals tend to be most mobile at the local level, with decreasing levels of mobility observed between states and between countries. Indeed, there is significant mobility between local communities in terms of both work and residence. Significant mobility of people also causes one to observe differences between (1) the community in which an individual was educated, (2) and those communities in which the individual lives or works during his or her lifetime. This raises some interesting issues with respect to the appropriate level of government at which the financier role should be performed and implemented.

This analysis of the nature of the social benefits of education still leads to the conclusion that the financier role in the market for primary and secondary education should be shared by the private sector, local government, state government, and national government. Given the flow and intensity of social benefits, it seems reasonable to argue that the national government's performance of the financier role should be the least prominent among the three levels of government. Owing to the spillover effects between local jurisdictions, the more favorable fiscal capacity, and the greater capability for some amount of redistribution of funds, the state level appears to be the most appropriate level at which to finance the majority of primary and secondary education costs. Finally, some amount of local support is appropriate given the significant social benefits that flow to local communities as a result of primary and secondary education. In theory, greater levels of local support would be appropriate in areas where mobility between local communities is the least, and lesser levels of local support would be expected and appropriate in areas or regions of high mobility. These decisions, however, should be left to individual states' discretion. Furthermore, even in areas of low mobility a substantial portion of the benefits of primary and secondary education will flow to adjacent communities and to the state as a whole.[3] Therefore, the range of state involvement remains somewhat narrower than it might appear on the face of the issue.

We move to our conclusion regarding the financier role:

> The financier role in the market for primary and secondary education should be split between the public sector and the private sector. Government should finance the social benefits of education, and the private sector, including students and their families, should be responsible for paying for the private benefits of education.[4] In a world of compulsory education and equal access, it is likely that some government provision of need-based aid will be required, but this should be considered as part of the welfare system rather than the education system. Furthermore, the primary public financier of education should be the state government, generally followed by local government and then the federal government. In the typical state, this might mean a division of the public share of education finance as follows: 50–80% state share, 10–35% local share, and 5–15% federal share.[5]

As mentioned in Chapter 8, many states are funding education in a manner that does not fit this mix of responsibilities, largely as a result of greater reliance on local sources. Yet, the most controversial part of this analysis is likely to be the call for greater private sector funds for education. Part of the reason for this controversy is likely to be a misunderstanding that is easily cleared up: the public sector financier role just outlined should apply to *all* students, not just public school students. Although there may still be screening of educational providers under a regulatory or auditing role to ensure health and safety, there will be no difference between eligible schools in terms of government financing of operational costs.[6] Furthermore, government assistance for low income students could be used at any eligible school, although tuition differences between schools might not be covered by the financial aid from the government. Based on the tuition for private schools in the northern Illinois area and the recent definition of a foundation funding level in Illinois, both of which are probably higher than in many other areas, under the proposed system one might expect parents to be required to pay several hundred dollars in tuition for each student in the primary grades, and perhaps as much as double that amount for a student in the secondary grades.[7]

Given the current controversy over publicly supported vouchers for primary and secondary education, this finance system may be difficult to sell. When the private component of the finance system is added to the mix, opposition may increase. However, there is also likely to be a perception that the system is more equitable, especially if adequate access is provided for low income families and open enrollment policies are required in order for a private school to receive "social benefit" funding.

With this basis, let us move on to the evaluation of the other market functions.

GOVERNMENT AS REGULATOR[8]

Government needs to be a regulator in the market for primary and secondary education. However, government also needs to substantially cut back the parameters of its role in regulating primary and secondary education. In general, government's role as regulator in this market is strongly justified only in terms of government's universal roles as a regulator that aids the workings of the competitive market and intervenes for the protection of health and safety. Because the main consumers of primary and secondary education are children, it is not appropriate or desirable to depend upon market forces to weed out unhealthy or unsafe providers.

Therefore, our conclusions with respect to the regulator role are fairly straightforward:

> Government should play an important regulatory role in the market for primary and secondary education. However, the appropriate regulatory role is one that is much narrower than that played currently by the government in primary and secondary education. The federal government has the primary responsibility for upholding the constitutional guarantees of

equal opportunity and nondiscrimination in primary and secondary education, in the same way as it does in any market. In addition, government's role in promoting competition also applies to the market for primary and secondary education.[9] Furthermore, government's responsibility for regulating workplace and schoolplace health and safety is a legitimate function of government in a mixed economy and is important in the market for primary and secondary education. Beyond these major areas, government should generally discontinue its regulatory intervention in the market for primary and secondary education. That is, government regulations relating to length of school day, curriculum, capital facilities (apart from aspects related to health and safety), and other operational regulations should be eliminated. The market should be allowed to determine the value of competition and differentiation on the basis of operational variations.

This would be a major change in the role of government in primary and secondary education. It is a change that is central to the charter school reform effort, and some idea of the likelihood of its ultimate success will be provided by the experiences of the charter school experiments. However, a systematic change in government's regulatory role is likely to have a different effect from that of the limited experimental experience of charter schools. Nevertheless, the reduction of the government regulatory role in school operations is likely to be popular, and those remaining regulatory functions would not represent an increase in the exercise of regulatory power by government. Thus, one might expect that the allocation of the regulator role is not likely to be unpopular or highly controversial. It should also be noted that the regulatory role is not the most central to the debate over school standards and outcome-based education. The most central role is that of auditor.

GOVERNMENT AS AUDITOR[10]

As long as government is involved in a financier role in the market for primary and secondary education, it will also have an auditor role in the market. Indeed, in general any entity having finance responsibilities in a market will likely also perform some type of auditor role. Especially in the case of government, which finances activities with public dollars, the performer of the financier role will require some type of accountability in exchange for the dollars it puts into the market. One significant means of accountability is provided by the process and results of independent audits. It should be noted that the audit or audits performed as part of the audit function often will not be conducted by the economic actor playing the auditor role in a given market. Rather, performance of the auditor role indicates responsibility for having the audit conducted and examining its results.

Increasingly, government has been asked to cede much of the regulatory authority it has traditionally exercised over primary and secondary education. Whether through charter school legislation, implementation of outcome-based funding reforms, or legislation allowing districts to seek waivers of certain state regulations, much of today's school reform is linked to reduced government regulation combined with an increased government audit function.[11] Internal audits are also an important elemant of the auditor role. Obviously, the actor responsible for internal audits will be the same as the actor responsible for the function (e.g., administration, production, distribution). The actor or actors responsible for conducting independent or other external audits will also generally be a function of the actor playing the regulatory and financing roles,[12] as well as the stakeholders for the relevant part of the educational experience.

Thus, our brief summary conclusion about government's performance of the auditor role in the market for primary and secondary education is as follows:

> Government has an important auditor role in the market for primary and secondary education. This role includes responsibility for financial audits to help ensure appropriate and efficacious use of public funds. This responsibility takes on heightened importance when government is the educational provider, and it includes both an internal audit function and an independent audit function.[13]

> To the extent that performance-based measures are implemented or required in exchange for regulatory relief, government is likely to have audit responsibilities to ensure that outcome standards[14] are being met and that compliance with regulations is taking place.

> Although other stakeholders will likely simultaneously be performing the audit function in the market for primary and secondary education, government's role as auditor will be of increasing importance as accountability for outcomes is substituted for government regulation of the educational process and its inputs.

> It should be noted once again that the responsibility for the audit function is not equivalent to the performance of the audit itself or audits themselves. Indeed, the credibility of the attestation function comes from a level of independence that is often incompatible with responsibility for and performance of an audit residing with the same economic actor or actors.

Other economic actors should play a major auditor role with respect to primary and secondary education, but government still has an important and likely perpetual role as an auditor in this market. As noted, educational reform has and will likely continue to expand this role, as well as government's performance of the role. Government's role in financial audits of recipients of public funds is incontrovertible. Similarly, government audits of health and safety issues should not be controversial, especially if performed by independent auditors. If a set of agreeable outcome measures were to be developed, government audit of those measures would not likely be controversial, especially if carried out by independent auditors unaffiliated with the government. Thus, the audit role is unlikely, in and of itself, to be a major flash point in the debate over primary and secondary school reform.

GOVERNMENT AS ADMINISTRATOR

As noted in Chapter 4 devoted to the assessment of the administrator role, the administrator is responsible for the day-to-day management of the economic endeavor, for the execution of policy, and for directing the enterprise toward the achievement of its goals and objectives. Clearly, this is an economic role that has been successfully played by both private and public sector actors, given the success of private schools. Thus, an exclusive role for government as administrator is not necessary. A more precise question might be: Does government have a special claim to the role of administrator of today's *public* schools?[15]

The answer to this question is much more complex than it might have appeared prior to our market role assessment of the administrator role. There remains no theoretical reason why the public sector should have a special claim to the administrator role for public schools. Yet, private administration of public schools has generally been a failure. Some have blamed this failure on teachers' unions; others have blamed it on unrealistic expectations on the part of both contract parties. The degree of freedom accorded the private firms in these experiments is also subject to some dispute. Regardless of the reason, these failures promote concern about the sustainability of private administration of public schools.

However, the failure of these large administrative experiments draws attention away from the widespread success of public school districts in privatizing many of the support services that were previously part of their administrative function. These support services include transportation, maintenance, school lunches, accounting services, and payroll. There has also been limited success with privatizing special education and at-risk services in some urban areas (Bushweller 1997).[16]

Furthermore, numerous school reforms in recent years have pushed administrative responsibilities down to the local school level. This has enabled significant administrative reform to take place without the disruption of outside contracting. Such efforts have often had positive effects on educational outcomes and local student, teacher, administration, and parent morale (Ferguson and Nochelski 1996). Similarly, site-based reporting has improved accountability for dollars and allowed locally based financial problem areas to be more quickly identified and rectified. Charter school reform experiments may also provide useful information on the appropriate division of administrative responsibility.

For now, our brief summary conclusion about the administrator market role is as follows:

> The administrator role is regularly played by both private sector and public sector actors in the market for primary and secondary education. Such a division is likely to continue in the midst of ongoing school reform efforts. Nevertheless, it is likely and appropriate that support services for primary and secondary education will be increasingly provided by private firms, even in traditional public schools. Even with respect to instructional administration in public schools, there is no rationale based on government's role in a mixed economy as to why government needs to perform the administrator role in primary and secondary education. However, educational administration will likely continue to be provided by the same sector that acts as the producer of the education, as no sustainable success has yet been experienced in the private administration of public schools.

Even though the failure of privatization of administrative services remains perplexing, clearly the overall role of government as administrator in primary and secondary education has diminished, and it will continue to diminish as reform efforts increase the viability of private educational alternatives and the feasibility of privatizing support services. One question that remains for study is whether government has a comparative advantage in administering public education. Even some of the fiercest critics of government have suggested this as a possible explanation for the empirical evidence reported regarding the administrator role. Unfortunately, such an investigation is too large and diversionary a task to be undertaken in this book.

GOVERNMENT AS DISTRIBUTOR/ALLOCATOR

Recall that the role of distributor involves performing the marketing and delivery functions for the good or service, including information flows between producer and consumer, whereas the role of allocator involves performing the resource allocation function. The allocator determines (1) what resources will be made available for production of which goods and services, and (2) to whom the goods and services will be made available once they are produced. Considering the increased attention to customer satisfaction and customer service by government, the distributor and allocator roles should be of special interest to the contemporary public administrator. Not only do these roles ultimately determine who gets what from government, but they also determine the communication lines available between constituents and their government. These functions are central to service delivery and customer service, especially at local levels of government, where most public goods and services are produced and delivered.

In private markets the distributor and allocator functions are generally played by the price system itself. These markets are characterized by little external intervention or explicit performance of the allocation role, but by relatively active performance of the marketing functions associated with the distributor role, at least in imperfectly competitive markets where product differentiation is important.

In the market for primary and secondary education, the allocator/distributor role varies significantly between public sector and private sector providers. The major difference between providers in the status quo is the open enrollment requirements that apply to most public schools and public school systems. This means that the allocation function has less meaning and is much more passively performed in public education. Similarly, the need to market public education is reduced by the general pricing advantage that public schools have in most markets.[17] As school reform efforts increase competition in the market for primary and secondary education, more active performance of the allocator/distributor role by the public sector and in public schools can be expected.

Our brief summary conclusion about the performance of the allocator/ distributor role(s) is as follows:

> Although access to education is essential, especially under a system of mandatory education, there is no compelling reason why government needs to be the allocator in the market for primary and secondary education. Open and unbiased access to educational opportunities can be provided through a regulator that is supported by an auditor. Even though government will likely need to ensure that a last resort allocation mechanism is available, government need not necessarily perform directly as that last resort allocator. This is especially true under the more market-based performance of the financier role suggested in our earlier analysis. Once an adequate number of education slots are made available in a local market,[18] those slots could be allocated among students based on a market or quasi market allocation system.[19] Government can still act to provide universal access but use differentiated market prices to allocate educational opportunities within the universal access system. In any case, even under the status quo, nonmarket, government allocation of education through geographic attendance zones will become increasingly a thing of the past.

As competition in primary and secondary education becomes ever more important, so does the role of distributor. Regardless of whether educational opportunities are publicly or privately provided, the provider needs to market its programs and services to prospective clients, and information should flow freely with respect to the availability, content, and quality of educational programs. This role includes the use of innovative delivery mechanisms to reach out to placebound and special needs students. Yet, neither sector needs to have a monopoly on the performance of the distributor role. For example, government could make the allocation rules and the allocation decisions, but the distributor function could in theory be contracted out to a private firm. In any case, to the extent that greater competition moves into the market, public schools will need to much more actively pay attention to the distributor role.

Throughout the book we assumed the continuation of mandatory and free education. In such a context, the role of last resort allocator is essential. Even in the more competitive model suggested by the financier analysis and others, the need for providing educational opportunities to those persons who are unable to afford them remains undeniable and in need of attention. Thus, though reforms are unlikely to be primarily grounded in the allocator or distributor role, these roles remain essential to the ultimate success of any reform of primary and secondary education.

GOVERNMENT AS PRODUCER

Recall the definition of the producer from Chapter 6: "The producer is that economic entity that brings a product into existence through mental and physical effort involving the combination of economic resources." Education is typically produced by a combination of teachers, parents, school-based administrators, local central administration, local school boards, and state school boards and administrators. The role of producer has been effectively played by private sector actors, with early childhood education dominated in most areas by private and nonprofit sector actors. However, the track record of previous administrative privatization experiments shows little evidence that privatization of the production function for traditional public schools is currently sustainable. However, given the multifaceted nature of primary and secondary education, including the need for active parent and student involvement in producing desirable outcomes in the portion of the educational experience that occurs outside the classroom and outside the school, it is equally clear that the production function cannot be borne exclusively by government at any level.

In general, the role of producer should be played by the entity that can achieve the greatest educational results with the least consumption of resources. Reforms designed to increase competition in the market for primary and secondary education, including the type of price-based competition suggested under the financier recommendations made previously, will increase the chances of appropriate division of the producer role. However, once again, in a system of compulsory education government will likely need to play the role of producer of last resort. Unfortunately, if the Education Alternatives experiences are typical, profitability considerations may result in government acting as the producer in a much wider range of circumstances than might otherwise be expected. This result would do little to alleviate concerns about private sector creaming, concerns that are often an issue in reforms that involve increased competition and reduced regulation. However, when bundled with other roles, profitability possibilities for the private sector producer may increase. Once again, charter school experiment results may provide some guidance as to the likelihood of success and positive outcomes.

Therefore, our brief summary conclusions with respect to the producer's role in the market for primary and secondary education include the following:

> There is no reason, based on the functions of government in a mixed economy, that the public sector must play the producer role in the market for primary and secondary education. However, mainly as a result of mandatory education laws, there is likely to always be a role for government as a producer of primary and secondary education,[20] if only as a producer of last resort. At another level, the production of primary and secondary education is so complex and multifaceted as to require production assistance from parents, teachers, school boards, and others. Thus, even for publicly produced education, private sector actors are likely to play an important producer role. Private sector producers are an important part of the market even under the status quo, especially in early childhood education. However, reliable and generalizable empirical evidence has not yet been developed to indicate the feasibility and sustainability of private production of public primary and secondary education. If anything, the evidence is to the contrary. Although charter school experiments may indicate the possibility of future increased private sector presence in the production of public education, it is more likely that any inroads in private sector production will occur as a natural result of reforms designed to increase competition in the market, with private producers producing larger quantities of privately based educational services that will be purchased by an increasingly broader market segment.

The producer role, in and of itself, does not appear to offer significant hope for substantial reform efforts or a substantial change in government's role in the market. Although it is likely that the private sector's production role in the market for primary and secondary education will increase and change the balance of power in the market, this is likely to be incidental to reform efforts grounded in other market roles.

GOVERNMENT AS ENTREPRENEUR

The role of entrepreneur may very well be the most important in determining the course of school reform. Our discussion in Chapter 9 indicates that no sector need have any monopoly on the performance of this role in the market for primary and secondary education. To the extent that entrepreneurship in primary and secondary education can be rewarded by traditional profit-based returns, the likelihood of a strong private sector interest in the entrepreneur role increases. The current experience in the market for early childhood education is not encouraging in this regard. Early childhood providers indicate that significant wages and profit returns are simply not available in the market; most argue that one can earn more as a classroom teacher at the primary levels than as an entrepreneur at the early childhood level (Peddle and Bennett 1997). Some anecdotal evidence suggests that this observation may even hold for private entrepreneurship in the typical primary and secondary educational institution. To the extent that such observations about the lack of profit potential in primary and secondary education are accurate perceptions, the role of the public sector entrepreneur becomes that much more important. This point is of grave importance in terms of the source of and impetus for education reform.

With these points in mind, our summary conclusion with respect to the entrepreneur's role is as follows:

> In theory, both private and public sector entrepreneurship should play important roles in primary and secondary school reform. There appears to be no obvious and compelling reason for government to be the sole entrepreneur in the market for primary and secondary education. However, there is increasing evidence, much of it anecdotal and circumstantial, that the profit potential in primary and secondary education may not be sufficient to reward private entrepreneurial behavior. This may be indicative of an incomplete market for entrepreneurship in primary and secondary education, and it may require government intervention as entrepreneur or to facilitate private entrepreneurship. Combined with the current state and structure of primary and secondary education, it seems reasonable to expect that government or public sector performance of the entrepreneur role will be a crucial factor in successful primary and secondary education reform. The impetus for reform may ultimately be provided by private sector interest groups or even by private sector entrepreneurs (especially those who are driven by entrepreneurial rewards beyond profits), but it seems likely that the success of primary and secondary education reform will depend in good measure upon public sector entrepreneurial behavior, at least in the short term.

Given the nature of entrepreneurial behavior, a significant challenge will be to simultaneously encourage a more entrepreneurial public sector presence and also encourage the public sector to increase efforts to facilitate more competition among entrepreneurs in the market. This is especially difficult when the success of some public entrepreneurial efforts is adversely affected by increased private sector competition. Nevertheless, such steps likely have great social merit that should outweigh the potential negative effects on the public sector and its entrepreneurs. A further challenge is in taking appropriate steps to encourage entrepreneurial public sector activities in the area of primary and secondary school reform.

Putting the conclusions together to evaluate government's role in the market for primary and secondary education.
Government has a substantial role to play in school reform. Although this conclusion is hardly earthshaking given the analysis in this book, the statement significantly defines the terms of the debate over school reform. Even though government's record in primary and secondary education is far from perfect, market role assessment indicates that removing government from the market is neither feasible nor appropriate. However, the analysis points to substantial opportunities for change, some of which include significant redefinition of the government's role in the market, and hence in the reform of primary and secondary education.

The analysis in the first nine chapters of the book presented a look at the fundamental market roles that come together to support a viable market for a given good or service. On the basis of these roles, a concise market role assessment was conducted for the primary and secondary education market. By analyzing the need and desirability of government's performance of each of these roles in the market, we made an effort to considerably narrow the terms of the school reform debate. Careful review of the analysis indicates a significant level of success in achieving this narrowing of the ill-structured problem. The terms of the debate are redefined in the next section.

A POSSIBLE MARKET-BASED VISION OF GOVERNMENT'S ROLE IN SCHOOL REFORM

As the next step in market role assessment, the analysis conducted with respect to each role needs to be reevaluated to identify priority roles for policy-making attention. These priority roles may be ones that are particularly important from the perspective of acting as catalysts in the treatment of ill-structured problems, or they may be roles of importance from the perspective of requiring significant change in the nature or level of government activity in the market. Categorization of the market roles allows further circumscription of the policy issue to take place. For example, effective progress in school reform may be more probable if greater focus is given to those areas in which government's role in the market is most in need of adjustment or is essential to the success of any reform effort. Within this context, let us return to the conclusions regarding the seven market roles analyzed in this book. Each role will be placed in one of three categories based on the market role assessment:[21] market roles where the need for government's performance of the role in the market for primary and secondary education has been established with reference to conditions that are likely to prevail in the market; market roles where the need for government performance has not been established and open competition appears feasible; and roles whose performance is highly dependent on the allocation and quality of the performance of other market roles.

Category 1 Roles: High priority market roles with an established need for government performance of the role:

• financier
• regulator
• auditor
• entrepreneur

This set of four roles constitutes what will be called Category 1 roles. They represent the highest priority in terms of attention in the public policy process. Although analysis of these roles may indicate, as in the case of primary and secondary education, that these roles should not be the exclusive province of the public sector, for each of these roles a compelling need for public sector performance has been established through market role assessment. It should be noted that one additional, plausible type of Category 1 role has not been identified in the market for primary and secondary education. This type of role is one in which its market performance under the status quo has been one of exclusive public sector province, but for which market role assessment indicates the need for total government divestment of the role. In other words, this would be a case in which no government performance of the role can be justified, but because of the nature of the division of the role under the status quo, divestment of the role would involve a significant change in public policy.

In the case of each of the Category 1 roles in primary and secondary education, government performance of the role is compelled by a factor such as the assumption of mandatory, "free" education (e.g., the financier role) or by the likely existence of an incomplete market (e.g., the entrepreneur role). However, private sector performance of each of these roles is expected and desired to continue. Indeed, in the case of the regulator role, government will continue to play an important role in regulating health and safety, but market role assessment indicates that government divestment of the regulator role related to the operational aspects of education is appropriate. Thus, despite being in Category 1 as a role in which government performance is compelled, it is recommended that government's role as regulator be reduced as compared with the status quo. Market role assessment also led to a call for increased *private* performance of portions of the financier role, whereas government was charged to take a greater role in financing the social benefits of education across *all* providers. Although private performance of the entrepreneur role was felt to be desirable, incomplete market concerns suggested that short-term leadership by government may be necessary to facilitate private entrepreneurship. Finally, as government divests itself from more and more roles, and reduces its performance of others, the auditor role becomes increasingly important to government as a means of providing accountability for the expenditure of public funds and for the reduction in operational regulations.

Each of the Category 1 roles in primary and secondary education involves a significant alteration of government's responsibility for performance of the role. Some these changes are likely to be more controversial than others, as is often noted in the assessment of the individual roles. For example, government finance of private education is likely to be very controversial, as is the intent to have individuals pay for the private benefit share of primary and secondary education. On the other hand, reductions in government regulation of school operations are likely to be immensely popular.

Each of the Category 1 roles is also very important to the prospects for primary and secondary education reform, as is the group of Category 1 roles considered in aggregate. Changes in the financier role are likely to provide the impetus for a more level playing field that can promote vigorous competition in primary and secondary education. Changes in the regulator role would be expected to have the same type of procompetitive effect. The changing role of the auditor is a necessary outcome of deregulation and will be crucial in monitoring the success of reform efforts and ensuring quality outcomes in the market. Ultimately, entrepreneurship is at the heart of innovation and market progress, and primary and secondary education is no exception in this regard.

Category 2 Roles: Market roles with greatest probability for open competition between the public and private sectors:

- producer
- administrator

These Category 2 roles are ones that will involve the greatest amount of divestment on the part of government, but also the roles in which open competition is most likely to produce a mix of government and private sector performance of the roles. Producers and administrators are essential day-to-day operators in a market. These are the performers that will most benefit from deregulation and be most affected by the increased use of auditors to evaluate outcomes. Government is deeply involved in the performance of these roles under the status quo, and there is a lack of a sustainable track record of private production and administration of public education. However, in a newly formulated market for primary and secondary education that is designed to foster competition, one would expect to observe increased private performance of these roles as time passes and the market goes through normal adjustment processes. Although they are very important, the producer and administrator roles are less central in terms of fundamental changes in education policy. Nevertheless, increased private production and administration of public schools is likely to be controversial. However, fundamental policy changes above the local level are less essential to privatizing these roles than some of the others, such as that of financier or regulator.

Category 3 Roles: Market roles with dependent performance characteristics:

• allocator/distributor

Allocator/distributor is the sole Category 3 role identified in the current market role assessment. Category 3 roles are described as market roles, without regard to importance in the market,[22] whose performance is determined primarily through decisions regarding the performance of other, higher priority roles. In the case of primary and secondary education, the allocator/distributor role is greatly constrained and defined by the financier, regulator, and entrepreneur roles. Although the allocator role in particular is essential to the ultimate outcomes in the market, the choices of the actors and rules for performance of these other market roles seem to be much more crucial and to have temporal priority over the allocator in the policy process.

CONCLUSION

Market role assessment enables roles to be prioritized for attention in the public policy process. This prioritization is based on (1) the relative need for fundamental changes in government's performance of each role, and (2) the relative centrality of each market role as a catalyst in reform efforts carried out through a public policy process. In the market for primary and secondary education, the highest priority, or Category 1, roles were identified as financier, regulator, auditor, and entrepreneur.

Most of the successful reform efforts in primary and secondary education appear to have occurred in areas related to these Category 1 roles. Although the decisions motivating these reforms were certainly not based directly on the type of analysis[23] conducted in this book, it is extremely interesting to note the potential support for the end prioritization developed through our market role assessment. In Chapters 11 and 12, two different general categories of reform efforts are examined to try to gain information about potentially successful means of implementing school reform in the framework identified through our market role assessment.

In Chapter 11, finance-related reform is explored. In Chapter 12, some nonfinance-related reforms are described. A look at these reforms also offers insight into a few of the methodologies used, and barriers encountered, in past efforts to make progress in primary and secondary education reform. Attention now turns to cases involving school finance.

NOTES

[1]The ordering of the roles for the initial analysis was chosen to best elucidate an introduction to market role assessment as it applied to individual roles. However, as the analysis moves toward conclusions regarding the set of roles and the market as a whole, the ordering presented in this chapter seems more appropriate to building a conception of the overall division of roles in the market.

[2]The analysis of each role is built from the analysis contained in the corresponding preceding chapter. The reader is referred back to these chapters should further justification of this chapter's summary analysis be desired.

[3]It should be again noted that our focus is on primary and secondary education. Even if an individual completes higher education, the primary societal benefits accrue through the individual's primary and secondary education. Therefore, the fact that higher education provides significant private benefits is not relevant to our current discussion.

[4]Technically, this would violate the assumption of "free" public education, but as long as provisions are made to ensure access for those who cannot afford to pay the (full) tuition, the general spirit of free education could be maintained, at least in part.

[5]According to the Consortium for Policy Research in Education at the University of Wisconsin—Madison (<www.wcer.wisc.edu>) in 1995–1996, the sources of public school revenues were estimated to average 7.0% federal, 47.7% state, and 45.3% local, but there is a great variation from area to area.

[6]The issue of capital expenditures may be ticklish. For now, one could argue that capital expenditures could be amortized as part of the tuition paid by students and their families. This avoids getting into the argument of an unfair public subsidy that would be given to public schools for capital costs. Furthermore, it is the operational costs that provide the ultimate societal benefits of education. The implementation problem that occurs as a result of the presence of existing public schools could be addressed by putting all of the schools up for auction (for sale or rent), with new public school corporations and private or nonprofit entities involved in the bidding. Successful bidders would be required (1) to make payments to the "owner" government for the use of the building, or (2) to purchase the building.

[7]For example, in 1997 Illinois policymakers agreed on a definition of $4,225 as the foundation per-pupil operating expenditures for primary and secondary education. This figure is used as a base in the following example. In the early grades, the primary beneficiary of education is society, with private benefits increasing with each year of

education. As a plausible example, assume that the benefits of kindergarten education are 95% social and 5% private, and that for every two years of education the proportion of private benefit increases by five percentage points. That means that for grades K–8, the average private benefit will be a little over 10% of the total. For grades 9–12, this figure jumps to 27.5%. Using simple mathematics, paying for the private benefits would require tuition of about $450 per student for K–8, and $1,150 for 9–12. In many states these figures will be less, whereas in some states these figures will be more. If one disagrees with any of the example parameters, a recalculation can be easily performed to produce revised estimates using a different set of parameters.

[8]Recall that the regulator is the maker and enforcer of rules.

[9]However, the need to intervene to maintain competition in the market for primary and secondary education has not been established in our analysis.

[10]Recall that in simple terms, the auditor is responsible for examining and verifying results.

[11]This is as well as (presumably) increased performance of audits by private and non-profit sector entities.

[12]However, it should be noted that this point offers little in the way of guidance in allocating the audit function between the public sector and the private sector, because an external audit function need not be performed by an actor from outside the *sector* of the actor being audited.

[13]A given government would have the responsibility of hiring an independent auditor if the government were to simultaneously be the financier and the provider in a given market. However, if another government were the provider, the financier government might perform the independent audit of the provider's operations.

[14]However, the outcome standards need not be developed or enforced by government.

[15]Given the topics discussed in this book, one might inquire as to the definition of a "public" school. The easiest way to answer this question is to note whether the ultimate source of educational policy is a public sector board or agency. If it is, then the school qualifies as a public school.

[16]It should be noted that some of these private providers are actually quasi public organizations representing a consortium of school districts that share these special services and fund them on a capitation basis.

[17]To the extent that a multischool public education system allows parents and students to choose their school of attendance, or has magnet schools, the marketing function becomes more important.

[18]Providing an adequate total number of education slots in some markets may require government to perform the allocator role in the resource market, so as to stimulate production of an adequate quantity of primary and secondary education.

[19]As an example of such a scheme, recall the suggestion of a quasi market solution to the transportation and allocation questions raised in our analysis in Chapter 5.

[20]It should be noted, however, that effective government performance of the financier and allocator roles could ensure sufficient levels of access so as to render the notion of last resort production meaningless in practice.

[21]The categories into which the roles are divided may vary across market role assessments, but in all cases the categories should be formulated in such a way as to focus priority and temporal ordering in policy debates. Thus, categories in general

should focus on the relative need for government intervention and the relative importance to possible reform efforts of the changes in the particular market role.

[22]That is, a market role may be an essential role in the market but is not an important factor in reform because of its dependence on other higher priority market roles, or because there will be no change in its performance as a result of any reform effort.

[23]However, it should be noted that market role assessment merely formalizes an analytical structure whose different elements have been used to one degree or another as part of many different incarnations of public policy analysis.

CHAPTER 11

School Finance Reform in Practice
What Can We Learn from Recent Experience?

.

One of the thorniest and most pervasive problems in primary and secondary school reform is school *finance* reform. The problem of school finance has received national attention and has been taken up in one form or another by nearly every state. Based upon market role assessment, the financier role is one of high priority in public policy making related to school reform. In this chapter we briefly examine some of the general trends in school finance reform, recent and prominent school finance reform efforts that have taken place in Michigan and Wisconsin, and a case study related to school finance reform in Illinois.

"Between 1971 and 1992, plaintiffs in 23 states alleged that funding and management [of primary and secondary schools] was inequitable. Courts in eleven states overturned school funding systems" (Davare 1994, p. 8). By 1997, forty-one states had seen school finance lawsuits filed, with fifteen state supreme courts ruling in favor of plaintiffs. The main issue in most cases has been the reliance on land-related (i.e., real property) taxation to fund public schools (Youngman 1995). As with many public finance issues, California provided the major impetus for the switch away from real property tax funding of local schools. The 1971 *Serrano v. Priest* case found the California school finance system to be unconstitutional under the state constitution. In 1978, Proposition 13 severely restricted the use of property tax revenues for any purpose. When the two events were combined, necessity became the mother of invention and a new system of school funding emerged. This was but the tip of a movement in the 1970s toward lesser reliance on the property tax for the financing of schools. "Back in the 1970s, there was widespread agreement that schools needed to be less dependent upon the property tax. States began a major push to boost state aid for elementary and secondary schools" (Mackey 1994, p. 23). Mackey notes that in 1972 President Nixon asked federal agencies to study whether a federal value added tax could be

used as a substitute for local residential property taxes to fund schools.
"While the federal financing role never did expand significantly, the state
share of K–12 funding grew from 40 percent in 1970 to 47 percent in 1979"
(Mackey 1994, p. 23). It should be noted that the state share stayed at about
47% through the 1980s but declined to about 43% by 1994, according to the
National Center for Education Statistics (National Center for Education Statistics 1999).

Thus, it may not be surprising that the 1990s brought renewed interest in
finding alternatives to the local property tax for funding education, with
numerous new court challenges filed, primarily in states left behind in the
reform efforts of the 1970s. Despite many favorable court rulings, little
progress was made in the reform of school finance as a result of these rulings.
This is because, as noted earlier, most court decisions have referred the issue
to the state legislature for action.[1] Such referrals have generally resulted in
great delays and little significant action. Over the past several years, at least
two states have made aggressive efforts to reform their methods of school
funding and have succeeded in overhauling their previous system. These
notable cases are Michigan and Wisconsin, each of which will be briefly discussed.

RADICAL REFORM IN MICHIGAN

School finance reform in Michigan was especially notable, owing not only to
its radical nature but also to its swiftness and the political process by which it
was carried out. For many years, Michigan had among the highest property
taxes in the nation. In 1992, it ranked tenth among all states in property taxes
per $1,000 of personal income, nearly 50% above the national average and
nearly 33% above the Great Lakes average (Wortley 1997, p. 2). In addition,
Michigan ranked third among states in 1991 in terms of the share of school
spending (65.2%)[2] that was financed locally (Courant, Gramlich, and Loeb
1995, p. 6). Furthermore, great disparities existed in the total level of operating revenues available for individual school districts. "Seven ballot[3] proposals from 1980 to 1992 attempted to provide a combination of property tax
relief, sales tax increases and school spending reform. All seven ballot proposals failed to get voter approval" (Wortley 1997, p. 4). As suggested in our
analysis of the financier role, a major issue in the debate over reform was
local control of K–12 schools. The policy jam was swiftly and suddenly broken in the summer of 1993, with reform following quickly and radically.

Perhaps the most key piece of the reform puzzle came unexpectedly and
drastically. In the summer of 1993 the legislature in Michigan, with little
debate and no hearings, passed a bill that "simply abolished, with no source
of revenue replacement specified, all use of local property taxes for school
operating expenditures" (Courant, Gramlich, and Loeb 1995, p. 6). The law

took effect with the 1994-1995 fiscal year (FY). For all intents and purposes, the state had imposed a local tax cut of $6 billion with no offsetting tax increase. In addition, the state no longer had a means of financing public schools in the absence of new legislation. In the end, the legislature put together a financing bill that contained two options between which voters would be able to choose.

On the last day of the legislative session in December 1993, both houses passed and the governor signed "a financing bill that contained two options, either of which would have radically changed the system of school finance in Michigan and either of which would have replaced approximately all of the lost revenue" (Courant, Gramlich, and Loeb 1995 p. 6). The main difference between the two options was that under one proposal the state sales tax would be increased, and under the other the state income tax would be increased. The state sales tax plan was presented to voters as a referendum in March 1994. Defeat of the sales tax plan would have required the income tax plan, also known as the back-up plan, to be implemented. Therefore, though voters only made a decision regarding the sales tax plan, in effect they voted between two alternative reform measures. It should be noted that the status quo was never an option after the radical vote in the summer of 1993 to elim-inate the local property tax as a source of education funding. Michigan voters approved the sales tax plan by a more than 2 to 1 margin in mid-March 1994. "The increase in the sales tax put in place various other tax changes previ-ously approved by the legislature" (Wortley 1997, p. 8). Among the tax reform elements of the Michigan school finance reform were the following:

- a limitation on the annual growth of property tax assessments to the lesser of 5% or inflation
- a sales and use tax rate increase from 4% to 6%
- an income tax rate decrease from 4.6% to 4.4%
- imposition of a real estate transfer tax at 0.75%
- a cigarette tax increase from 25 to 75 cents per pack
- imposition of state property tax at a rate of 6 mills on all property
- imposition of a local school property tax at a rate of 18 mills on non-homestead property (Wortley 1997, pp. 8–9)

The net effect of this tax reform was to bring the property tax burden in Michigan to a little below the national average when measured in burden per $1,000 of personal income (a drop of about one-third) and to bring the sales tax burden (measured in the same fashion) up to approximately the national average (Wortley 1997). Under the new school finance system, approxi-mately 80% of the revenue is raised by the state as compared with 31% under the previous system (Courant, Gramlich, and Loeb 1995, pp. 6–7). However, the Michigan reform was much more than a reform of the revenue structure for financing schools. It also dealt with aggressive reform of state school aid, accountability requirements, and provisions for charter schools.[4]

According to Wortley, in FY 1993–1994, the last year under the former system, the base revenue available to school districts varied from $2,200 to $10,294 per pupil. Thus, some form of statewide program to better ensure funding equity across school districts was believed to be needed. "Michigan's former tax-based equalizing school aid formula and categorical spending were replaced with a foundation allowance per pupil" (Wortley 1997, p. 13). A system of state foundation grants was thus begun. These grants are based upon eligible revenues in 1993–1994 plus a growth factor. When fully implemented, all school districts in the state will have reached the basic foundation allowance, which was $5,308 per pupil in 1996–1997 (Wortley 1997). The foundation allowance is financed by a combination of state and local revenue. The local share comes from the local property tax on nonhomestead property, and the state makes up the difference between the guaranteed foundation allowance and local revenues.[5] One of the unique features of the Michigan reform is its handling of districts that were near or above the basic foundation allowance. In effect, the Michigan reform was implemented by dividing school districts into three groups and applying a slightly different revenue policy to each group.

"The 365[6] districts . . . that spent less than $4,772 per student in 1993–1994 will be brought up to the basic foundation allowance over the next few years under a formula that allows these districts to 'catch up' " (Courant, Gramlich, and Loeb 1995, p. 8). The 122 districts spending between $4,772 and $6,500 per student in 1993–1994 received small real increases in spending per pupil in 1994–1995. "After 1994–1995, per pupil spending in these districts will increase by the same dollar amount as the basic foundation grant" (Courant, Gramlich, and Loeb 1995, p. 8). From figures provided in Courant, Gramlich, and Loeb, one can calculate that more than 90% of public school students in Michigan in 1993–1994 attended school in a district in one of the first two categories.

About 9.7% of students attended school in one of the thirty-seven districts spending more than $6,500 per pupil in 1993–1994. For these districts, their guaranteed foundation allowance level was set at $6,500 for 1994–1995 and increased by the same absolute amount as the basic foundation grant in subsequent years. "However, these high-spending districts are allowed to supplement their foundation grant by levying local taxes on *homestead property*[7] [emphasis added], provided that their revenue per pupil does not exceed the 1993–1994 level, plus $160 for 1994–1995, plus the dollar increase in the basis foundation grant in future years" (Courant, Gramlich, and Loeb 1995, pp. 8–9). Thus, no school district was forced to cut spending under the Michigan reform (in this way the reform plan avoids one of the major criticisms often leveled at school finance reform efforts designed to improve the lot of poorer school districts). However, the ability of higher spending districts to increase spending was greatly constrained by the reform. Furthermore, the Michigan law places the major burden on residential property for the financing of educational spending that is significantly above the basic foundation allowance level. It should be noted that although Michigan did greatly reduce its reliance on the local property tax for the financing of primary and secondary education, it substituted a statewide property tax on homestead property and retained a local property tax on nonhomestead property. A significant, though reduced, portion of Michigan primary and secondary education remains funded by the property tax. It should also be noted that the tax on nonhomestead property (18 mills) is at least partially aimed at shifting the tax burden to nonresidents of Michigan who have vacation homes that do not qualify as principal residences. There is some early evidence that the school finance reform has begun to have an effect.

As of FY 1996–1997, only the third year of the new financing structure, Wortley (1997) states that forty-eight lower revenue school districts had reached the basic foundation allowance and that the allowance varied from $4,816 to $10,762 per pupil in 1996–1997.[8] This represents a considerable narrowing of the financing gap present in FY 1993–1994. In the first year of the program, 1994–1995, schools in Michigan saw a 4.8% increase in their overall level of funding.

As mentioned, the success of Michigan's passage of school reform may also be grounded in the nonfinancial reform measures included as part of the package. Though not the primary focus of this chapter, these additional reform provisions included: strengthened requirements for an academic core curriculum, pupil performance standards, and minimum numbers of school days (Courant, Gramlich, and Loeb 1995, p. 7). In addition, the law made provisions for charter schools, authorized and sponsored by four different eligible groups: the state department of education, local school boards, intermediate (regional) school districts, and state public universities. Initially, state universities were the main authorizing body for charter schools, though few state universities opted to participate in sponsoring such schools (Courant, Gramlich, and Loeb 1995). In Michigan, charter school funding was linked to the school finance reform by providing a state per-pupil grant of the lesser of $5,500 or the foundation allowance of the district in which the school is located. The public school would then lose the per-pupil state revenue for those pupils opting to attend a charter school.[9]

The long-term effects of Michigan's reform cannot yet be discerned. A study of California, a state that preceded Michigan by fifteen years in moving to foundation level funding, observed that per-pupil education spending rose much less rapidly there than in the rest of the country over the same period (Courant, Gramlich, and Loeb 1995, p. 25). Because the Michigan reform preserves a great deal of disparity between local districts, Courant and his co-authors argue that the downward push in school funding experienced in California will be much less intense and less consequential in Michigan. This is especially true because "under the current Michigan formula, all districts receive, dollar for dollar, any increases in the basic foundation allowance" (Courant, Gramlich, and Loeb, 1995 p. 26). However, in the longer term the authors see the potential for unraveling of the foundation funding method: "there will be immediate pressure . . . for districts to have some flexibility at the margin. . . . Over time, as some districts get richer and others get poorer, this pressure will get stronger. . . . This will lead to pressure for changing the formula. To the extent that these pressures induce the legislature to permit local financing at the margin, the basic foundation system itself could tend to unravel" (Courant, Gramlich, and Loeb 1995, p. 26). This will be a further long-term counterweight to the kind of reduced state spending experienced in California. In the short term, the hope of providing a system of school finance that improves equity outcomes seems to have become a reality with the Michigan radical reform.

Wisconsin's reform, although much less radical, has also received a great deal of attention in terms of the methods used to achieve a greater financier role for state government. What the reform lacks in substance, it makes up for in political rhetoric and spin control.

REFORM IN WISCONSIN: IS IT REALLY A SOLUTION?

As in Michigan, the impetus for reform was provided by a fairly radical and somewhat undefined piece of legislation. "In the spring of 1994, in an effort to 'get schools off the property tax,' the legislature passed and the governor signed Wisconsin Act 437. This bill commits the state to fund 66.7 percent of total public spending on K–12 education for the 1996–1997 academic year and thereafter" (Reschovsky 1994, p. 1). The "two-thirds commitment," as the initiative has been popularly known, simultaneously increased the state's share of school funding from 48.4% to 66.7% and restricted the increase in school spending to the rate of inflation. This was expected to mean substantial property tax relief for the average Wisconsin taxpayer. "Estimates by the Legislative Research Bureau suggest that the school property tax rate will decline from $17.80 per $1000 of equalized value in 1993–1994 to $10.80 by 1999–2000, a reduction of nearly 40% [in the school portion of the tax rate][10]" (Reschovsky 1994, p. 1). As in Michigan, the funding solution was not provided by the initial legislation. The original charge of the two-thirds solution required the state to identify $975 million in increased revenues to meet the increased state financing role for primary and secondary education. Unfortunately, Wisconsin's response to this challenge does not pass the infamous "smell test" (i.e., if something does not "smell" or seem right, something is probably amiss): a major portion of the increased state commitment was and is funded through natural revenue growth. As one of Governor Tommy Thompson's aides freely admitted in a 1997 speech to Illinois business leaders, "Our system of school finance is deeply dependent upon not having an economic downturn. We are back nearly to square one if we experience a recession" (Wood 1997). Such a financing system is at best irresponsible and fiscally unsound; at worst it may be reckless. Nevertheless, the Wisconsin experience demands a deeper look.

The apparent impetus for reform in Wisconsin was much like that in Michigan: property tax reform in a high property tax state. "In fiscal year 1991, property taxes in Wisconsin as a proportion of personal income were 31 percent above the national average. Wisconsin ranks 11th from the top across all 50 states in property taxes as a proportion of personal income" (Reschovsky and Wiseman 1995, p. 44). The beginning of reform actually came with the 1993–1995 biennial budget passed by the Wisconsin legislature that not only aggressively attacked increasing property tax bills but also put constraints on the collective bargaining rights of teachers. Wisconsin has placed controls on the arbitration and mediation process, putting limits on teacher compensation that are not linked to the rate of inflation (Reschovsky and Wiseman 1995).

Unfortunately, the much-ballyhooed Wisconsin reform appears to be very little reform and lots of political rhetoric. The basis of the reform is lasting property tax relief to all taxpayers in Wisconsin, with property taxes now at their lowest levels in thirty years. Simultaneously, the state restricted the rate of increase in school spending to the rate of inflation and greatly constrained collective bargaining. In addition, the governor took the position that no new state general tax increases would be imposed and that the state's needs would be met within existing tax resources (State of Wisconsin 1997, p. 3). "The state is committed to providing property tax relief by maintaining the state share of school costs at two-thirds, which will require state assistance to K–12 schools to increase by about $400 million over the next two years" (State of Wisconsin 1997, p. 5). It is interesting that projected revenue growth figures in the same document are about $900 million over the same time frame.

Wisconsin, in effect, has attacked the school reform issue from the perspective of property tax relief and strict cost controls, combined with some level of increase in the state share of education funding. However, Wisconsin's approach to financing the spending with what amounts to uncommitted revenue growth seems dangerous and fiscally unsound.[11] Furthermore, property tax relief in Wisconsin has not been as widespread or deep as the governor and his staff have tried to claim, at least in terms of having a noticeable effect on one's property tax bill.

It is hard to describe the Wisconsin legislation as school finance reform. Ultimately, it is better described as a revenue and expenditure limitation whereby, in good times, the state replaces a portion of the lost revenue through a statutory commitment. In fairness, it should be noted that much of the rhetoric in the governor's 1997–1999 biennial budget proposal paid some attention to gubernatorial initiatives to implement educational standards, a high school graduation test, and strengthened school-to-work programs. Unfortunately, there appears to be little permanence in the funding mechanism or little substantive improvement that can be pointed to as a result of the changes in Wisconsin. Despite the attention it has received, insights into school finance reform are few and far between (if at all existent) in the Wisconsin experience.

However, if we broaden our look at Wisconsin to include its innovative voucher experiments, this conclusion of lack of insight is far from applicable. Indeed, Wisconsin has *two* ongoing major voucher experiments that have received national attention. The Milwaukee Parental Choice Program was the first operative private school voucher program in the United States. The 1999–2000 school year is its tenth year of operation. This program began relatively small (742 students in 1993–1994), but owing to its uniqueness it has received great attention and has exploded in size. The program currently permits up to 15,000 students, or about 15% of students in the city system, to attend private schools with vouchers. In 1998–1999, about 6,000 students took advantage of this opportunity ("Supreme Court" 1998). Since its inception in the fall of 1992, a privately funded scholarship program already has provided half-tuition scholarships to over 11,000 low income students (4,303 for the 1995–1996 school year) who, as under the state program, almost all are residents of the City of Milwaukee. This private program is known as PAVE, Partners Advancing Values in Education. A further look at these programs may be instructive, especially because in many ways they represent the type of adjustment in the financier role that was suggested by our market role assessment.

The Milwaukee Parental Choice Program was enacted as part of the state budget process in the summer of 1990. The main impetus for the program was the energy of an African-American state assembly Representative, Annette "Polly" Williams, who had fought with the Milwaukee Public Schools (MPS) for years over general school reform and the education of her four children. She finally withdrew her children and enrolled them in an independent, almost all African-American private school. "Her argument was that MPS was failing and that many of her constituents did not have the alternative choices of more affluent families. She also vehemently opposed busing African-American children solely for integration purposes" (Witte and Thorn 1995, p. 129). Although the program was enacted without a direct, separate vote in either chamber of the legislature, the battle over the program only began with the legislative action. An initial lawsuit filed by the state Department of Public Instruction, the state teachers' union, the Milwaukee chapter of the NAACP (National Assocation for the Advancement of Colored People), and several parents challenged the enactment procedure and the constitutionality of the law, and raised several other issues as well (e.g., equal protection for other poor families in the state). "A Dane County Circuit Court (Madison) found the law constitutional in August 1990 and students were allowed to enroll in the program pending appeal. The State Appeals Court reversed the lower court ruling in November 1990, but the Wisconsin Supreme Court upheld the statute in March 1992, by a 4 to 3 margin" (Witte and Thorn 1995, p. 129). Yet, this was only the beginning of the fun, because federal courts then became involved in the issue.

When the program first began, religious private schools were not allowed in the program; therefore, it was not clear that any relevant federal court questions were involved. The issue was placed on the table in two fashions. In 1993, "a federal lawsuit was filed on behalf of parents who applied for vouchers, but were denied admission because there was not space in the private schools. The claim is that the program discriminates against religion by limiting vouchers to secular school" (Witte and Thorn 1995, p. 153). In addition, Governor Tommy Thompson desired to expand the voucher program to religious schools.

The rulings on this issue were fairly consistent in the beginning. In March 1995, a federal district court judge ruled that the expansion sought by the parents in their 1993 suit would be unconstitutional. "U.S. District Court Judge John Reynolds said that state education payments to religious schools would violate the clause in the First Amendment that bars laws 'respecting an establishment of religion' " (Worthington 1995, p. 3). Governor Thompson argued that because his proposal deals with giving the vouchers to parents rather than schools, the ruling would not apply to his proposed expansion of the state program. However, in January 1997 a Wisconsin court took a very different view from that of the governor. "In a school-choice case that is expected to reach the U.S. Supreme Court, a state judge . . . struck down a plan to use taxpayer money to send poor Milwaukee children to religious schools" ("Voucher Plan" 1997). The state's plan would have expanded student participation from 1,650 students to 15,000. This also played into the judge's decision. The state Supreme Court blocked the expansion in March 1996 but became deadlocked on the constitutionality of religious school choice, sending the case to the judge who made the January 1997 ruling. However, Judge Paul Higginbotham struck down the law on different constitutional grounds as well. "He said that because of the expansion, school choice was no longer an experiment with a statewide purpose, . . . but instead amounted to an unconstitutional local or private bill" ("Voucher Plan" 1997). The fortunes of the Milwaukee voucher proponents took a significant turn for the better in 1998. On June 10, 1998, the Supreme Court of Wisconsin became the first state high court to rule that a voucher program funding private sectarian schools did not violate the establishment clause of the First Amendment. The U.S. Supreme Court refused to review the case in November 1998. This leaves the Wisconsin ruling intact but leaves unsettled the question of the constitutionality of vouchers that can be used at religious schools. According to many legal experts, the U.S. Supreme Court's 1973 ruling in *Committee for Public Education v. Nyquist* remains the national precedent. In that case, the high court invalidated a New York program under which parents were given public funds to send their children to religious schools.

Early unfavorable court rulings were one reason given for the founding of PAVE, the other private school choice option program in Milwaukee. Most of the participating schools in PAVE are parochial schools. Indeed, of the 101 participating schools listed for 1995–1996, more than 80% are easily identifiable as religious schools. The PAVE program, owing to its private funding, provided a voucher type option even in the presence of any unfavorable court rulings about expansion of the Milwaukee Parental Choice Program.

Under the Parental Choice Program, the state pays schools up to $5,000 per student in money that would normally go to the public schools that they would otherwise attend. "Eligibility for the choice program is limited to families with incomes 175 percent of the poverty line or less, and to students not enrolled in private schools or in public schools other than MPS in the prior year" (Witte and Thorn 1995, p. 129). The income requirement, as noted by Witte and Thorn, is higher than the income required to qualify for a free lunch but lower than that required to qualify for a reduced price lunch.

In general, schools in the program have limited ability to reject students for reasons other than space limitations. "Schools cannot discriminate in selection based on race, religion, gender, prior achievement, or prior behavioral records. A court ruling stipulated, however, that the schools do not have to accept students with disabilities for which they cannot provide necessary services" (Witte and Thorn 1995, p. 129). Students must be randomly selected if there are more applications than seats in a given grade.

It should be noted that the participation in the program is very limited. The program had a cap of 1.5% of the MPS student population originally. Now, with the support of the favorable court rulings, vouchers could be provided to as many as 15% of the MPS students, whereas Witte and Thorn estimated that about two-thirds of MPS students meet the eligibility criteria. The PAVE program picks up a small portion of this void.

In terms of annual enrollment, the PAVE program had historically provided assistance to about four times as many students as the state program in Wisconsin before the recent expansion of the Parental Choice Program was made possible through more favorable rulings. PAVE has the same eligibility requirements as the state-funded program. It should be noted, however, that PAVE requires students' families to pay half-tuition and provides the other half in the form of a scholarship.[12] This may have created some differences between Choice and PAVE families, as is borne out somewhat in the PAVE data. "Some 5% of those children who were granted PAVE scholarships in the fall of 1995 declined to use them. The most important reason was an inability to pay the rest of the tuition. This was especially true of those who had initially applied for Choice: they were five times more likely to cite financial reasons for their non-participation than families which had applied directly for PAVE" (White, Maier, and Cramer 1996, p. 2).

What can be learned from the Milwaukee voucher experiments? Clearly, the nation has watched Milwaukee carefully and is extremely interested in every study relating relative performance of students in the program. Furthermore, "PAVE has been used as a model for similar programs in 21 cities across the nation" (White, Maier, and Cramer 1996, p. 1).

From the perspective of interest in government's role in the market for primary and secondary education, it appears that the message from Milwaukee is somewhat mixed. On the one hand, it appears from all accounts that the voucher system has not lead to the demise of the Milwaukee public schools. However, there may be a great difference once such a program is expanded to the general population. On the other hand, the experience with PAVE may indicate that government vouchers are not required; the private sector has done an admirable job of funding its own voucher system in Milwaukee. The PAVE program's partial payment method helps to split the costs of education between the voucher and the family and more accurately distinguishes social benefits from private benefits. Such a system may work in the long run but would likely be doomed to failure on a large-scale basis owing to free rider problems in gaining adequate finance for the system. This may be why a shared system of compulsory finance and private contribution such as that suggested in the market role assessment may be a viable and preferred option.

Studies on the outcome results of the Choice program have been mixed in their findings (Saks 1997). A series of studies conducted by John Witte and his colleagues at the University of Wisconsin—Madison for five years after inception of the program found no significant differences in achievement between voucher and general public school students in Milwaukee. A more recent (1996) study by Jay Greene of the University of Houston and Paul E. Peterson of Harvard University compared 1,034 voucher students with 407 students who applied but were turned down for lack of space. This study found that voucher students in their third and fourth years did show higher test scores than their control group counterparts. Both studies have received criticism, and the jury is still out on outcome improvements resulting from school choice in Milwaukee (Saks 1997). What is clear is that the results have not been immediate, nor do they yet appear to be particularly earth shattering.

Both the Michigan and Wisconsin experiences are predicated on a greater responsibility for state government in the financing of education, and both have provided notable successes in this regard. Wisconsin's voucher experiments suggest a further refinement of the financier role along the lines of the reforms suggested by our market role assessment. A brief overview of some school finance reform efforts in Illinois will offer further insight into the political process and political difficulties likely to be encountered in implementing school finance reform. The reform considered in the Illinois case is generally less radical than that suggested in this book's market role assessment, or in the Wisconsin or Michigan cases that have just been discussed.

SCHOOL FINANCE REFORM 1999 STYLE: AN EXPERIENCE IN ILLINOIS

The path to school reform in Illinois has been extremely arduous and was an ongoing process as of late 1999. This section of the chapter recounts some of the author's experiences as a participant observer in one part of the Illinois school finance debate.

The issue of school reform and school finance reform in Illinois has a long and complex history. The story recounted here begins in early 1992. At that time, numerous local governments in high growth areas of Illinois were struggling with growth management issues and other problems related to fiscal stress. At the same time, there was increasing dissatisfaction among Illinois citizens about rising property tax bills, diminishing quality of services, and the need for government accountability. Based on the author's experiences in assisting municipalities and nonmunicipal local governments, including school districts, with growth management plans and revenue analyses, it became clear that government concerns and citizen concerns were inextricably intertwined. In particular, property tax reform and school finances were issues that permeated the debate over growth management, and impact fees in particular. In November 1992, a proposed state constitutional amendment to require the state to provide the majority of funds for primary and secondary education was supported by slightly short of the 60% of voters needed to approve the amendment. Thus, there was evidence that a great, but not overwhelming, majority of citizens supported school finance reform in Illinois.

In January 1993, the first[13] Illinois Task Force on School Finance made its long and eagerly awaited report (see Task Force 1993). The report suggested some significant changes in the state's role in funding education and was well received publicly in light of the narrow defeat of the proposed constitutional amendment just a few months earlier. The committee recommended a system of financing primary and secondary education that would be "at a level sufficient to fund an adequate education program." In simple terms, the task force recommended adequate funding for general state aid; a cost-based definition of an adequate level of financing that would have raised the guaranteed level of per-pupil support from state and local sources from $2,600 to $3,898; regional cost adjustments; and a "leveling up" approach to equity whereby the per-pupil expenditure/revenue would be raised at the lower end of the distribution. In addition, the task force (1) recommended property tax relief for taxpayers in school districts with high Education Fund tax rates, and (2) made recommendations designed to increase school district consolidations. Although the task force's recommendations were greeted with interest, no substantive progress toward reform was made as a result of the report.

Shortly after the task force made its report, a group of business leaders, under the impetus of the Illinois Manufacturers' Association, formed the Illinois Business Education Coalition. Early meetings of the coalition indicated a strong interest in objective research of options in school reform and school finance reform. Soon thereafter, however, the agenda turned much more one-sided. The business members of the coalition held a hard core "no new money" approach to education finance reform. That is, they believed that new money should not be provided to primary and secondary schools until intense accountability standards were imposed, fully implemented, and evaluated. On this point, there was to be no compromise. Those members of the coalition who did not agree with this view soon found themselves no longer on the invitation list when future meetings were called. The Illinois Business Education Coalition was a behind-the-scenes participant in the early 1990s and resurfaced in a new configuration during the school finance debate that began anew in 1997.

Pressures for school finance reform intensified with the passage by the state legislature of a property tax extension limitation law in late 1991 that applied to non–home rule local governments, including all school districts, in the five counties surrounding Chicago.[14] The property tax limitation was extended to Cook County in 1995, and provisions followed in 1996 for the other counties in the state to impose a similar limitation by referendum.[15]

In 1994, school finance reform was unsuccessfully staked out as the primary issue in the gubernatorial campaign by the Democratic candidate. Illinois comptroller Dawn Clark Netsch, the Democratic nominee, advocated a funding change under which the state would undertake both an increased level and an increased share of the funding for primary and secondary education. The increased state funding was to have been paid for through an increase in the Illinois income tax. In exchange for the statewide income tax increase, taxpayers would receive a decrease in local property taxes. Even though the Illinois income tax is one of the lowest in the nation, any talk of a tax increase was rudely welcomed in political circles, despite the fact that numerous state polls indicated that the public was willing to accept increased state income taxes to pay for increased funding of education. Trading the increase in income taxes for a reduction in property taxes made the proposal even more publicly popular, but not enough so as to overcome the inertia of other political considerations, including the reelection power of an incumbent governor. Furthermore, some interests were concerned about the loss of local control that might occur with an increased state funding role.

As debate over school finance reform in Illinois continued, the lines of the battle increasingly and more distinctly divided participants into one of several camps based on their priority reform issue: those who insisted on property tax relief; those who were interested in increased funding for poorer school districts; those whose priority was increased accountability; those who simply wanted increased funding for schools; those who focused on collective bargaining and teacher tenure issues; those whose concern was with the state's share of education funding and the means by which to increase this share; those who were concerned about capital bonding issues; and those who were primarily concerned with increased competition for public schools. This laundry list is indicative of the degree of fragmentation among supporters of school reform in Illinois. Unfortunately, the debate made very little progress toward reform, in part owing to the very parochial approaches of many of the participants in the debate. This point will be revisited shortly.

In early 1994, State Representative David Wirsing (R-Sycamore) called together a group of four of his constituents for a conversation about school finance reform. The first-term representative was interested in getting guidance about the potential for reducing reliance on the property tax for the funding of primary and secondary education. The group that was called together consisted of a school superintendent, an economist who was also a local school board member, an economist and accountant who taught public finance at the local university, and a local education consultant who spent time as a staff member at the Illinois State Board of Education. Representative Wirsing called together this disparate[16] group of people with the intent of creating what he called a "brain trust" on the issue of school finance reform. The representative set clear parameters for the initial discussion and acted as a moderator/mediator for nearly three years of closed door discussions that hammered away at the problem of school finance reform.

At the first meeting, the charge was given to the group to offer counsel on how to eliminate the property tax as a source of primary and secondary education funding in Illinois. At least three, if not all four, members of the committee argued against wholesale elimination of the property tax as a financing tool for education. Although all in the room recognized the need for reduced reliance on the property tax, elimination was not seen as a desirable or feasible option.[17] With the impending threat of the extension of property tax caps to the entire state, the time for some kind of reform seemed pressing. Nevertheless, agreement on the appropriate course of action was slow in coming. After the Republicans took control of both chambers of the General Assembly in November 1994, the committee further heated up its discussions in anticipation of taking advantage of the greater control of the policy agenda that was now in the hands of Wirsing's political party. Unfortunately for Wirsing, his party again lost control (though only by one seat) of the House (but retained control of the Senate) in November 1996. By this time, agreement on the appropriate direction for school finance reform was crystallizing in the group but had not yet been formalized.

The key to any progress was Representative Wirsing's tireless devotion to seeing something happen and his willingness to all opinions to be fully explored and exercised.[18] The result of this tenacity was the drafting of a piece of legislation that was a joint effort of the committee and Representative Wirsing. This piece of legislation was one that at least three members of the committee strongly supported. Yet, it was a policy proposal that represented a vision of school finance reform that was a long way from the point at which the committee members began the process. Before discussing the legislation in brief, it is important to share an understanding of the school reform and school finance reform debate in Illinois that was developed through active participation in the process.

As mentioned earlier, stakeholders in the education reform debate were divided along the following lines: property tax relief, increased funding for poorer school districts, increased accountability, collective bargaining and teacher tenure issues, the need for additional funds for schools, the means for increasing the state's share of education financing and the degree by which to increase the state's share, capital bonding issues, and increased competition for public schools. Some of these issues are easier to deal with than others, and some are of lower priority than others, but over time reform has generally been held hostage by an unwillingness in Illinois to attack each piece of the puzzle in turn.[19] In Michigan, the impetus for successful reform may have been the ability to deal with the system through comprehensive legislation that was built piece by piece. Unfortunately, in Illinois too many interest groups have been taking an "all or nothing" approach to their preferred method for school reform. This has had the effect of stifling many meaningful efforts at reform.

The problem becomes especially clear when considered in terms of the legislation emanating from the Wirsing advisory committee. The legislation, in simple terms, provides for a local option local income tax that allows local school districts, upon referendum approval by voters, to levy a local income tax that replaces, dollar for dollar, 50% of the school district's residential property tax levy for operating purposes. The legislation would provide quick and substantial property tax relief, allow local communities to choose their mix of funding sources, neither increase nor decrease school tax levies, and reduce the need for artificial interventions such as property tax caps. This legislation would not, in and of itself, provide school finance reform from an equity or accountability standpoint. Nor would it alter the current structure of local property tax revenues from commercial and industrial property. It is, however, still the only piece of legislation pending in Illinois that would absolutely guarantee the property tax relief that many are calling for as part of school finance reform. The legislative history of the bill from January 1997 to September 1999 provides an interesting example of the strange workings of legislative politics on major issues.

In January 1997, Illinois governor Jim Edgar made an about-face on school finance reform. In his State of the State address, the governor called for renewed efforts for school finance reform and advocated an increase in the state income tax, coupled with a reduction in property taxes, as a means to increase the state's share of education funding. Many members of Edgar's party were appalled at his support of a plan that he had condemned when it was put forth by Dawn Clark Netsch in the 1994 election. With school finance reform back on the front burner, Representative Wirsing decided the time was ripe to put his committee's ideas into the policy process.

Representative Wirsing had to make several decisions crucial to the life of his bill. Among these decisions were: whether to file the bill, whether to call the bill before committee, and whether to put the bill to a subcommittee vote. Given the number of places a bill can die in a legislative body (e.g., the rules committee never assigns the bill out), each of these decisions was crucial. To make a very long story short, Representative Wirsing filed and called his bill, then known as HB 549, for testimony before the House Revenue Committee's income tax subcommittee (nominally three members—two Democrats, one Republican) but did not put the bill to a vote in the subcommittee. According to the rules of the committee, all testimony is taken at the subcommittee level, and therefore HB 549 had its on-the-record hearing before the committee as a result of this process. By not calling for a vote, which certainly would have gone against the bill, Wirsing was allowed to keep the bill alive. A defeat in the subcommittee would have made the bill unresurrectable for the 1997–1998 legislative session.

At the subcommittee hearing, staff of the Illinois Department of Revenue testified against the bill, and the Illinois Taxpayers Federation, Illinois Federation of Teachers, and a large unit school district association filed as opponents of the bill but did not orally testify.[20] Later investigation and analysis indicated that none of the nontestifying organizations opposed the bill on any grounds other than the fact that it was not their particular solution to school finance reform in Illinois.[21] The Department of Revenue opposed every other tax bill that was before the subcommittee on the same day as Wirsing's bill and it opposed Wirsing's bill on the grounds that (1) it would cost the department large sums of money to administer,[22] and (2) the department could not administer a local income tax with varying rates (even though it already administers a much larger local sales tax program with varying rates). From a public administration standpoint, it was especially interesting to observe the

Department of Revenue staff testifying about revenue policy, given that revenue policy is outside of their mission or responsibility as a state agency. The politics faced even with the simple reform idea put forth in HB 549 is only a slight indication of the difficult road to meaningful school finance reform in Illinois.

As it turns out, Representative Wirsing's policy decisions on the bill were masterful. The bill was brought before the House Republican Caucus's task force on school reform in April 1997 and was approved as a part of the package it would be seeking to get through the state legislature. The House Minority Leader has also signed on as a supporter of HB 549 as part of a compromise designed to achieve meaningful school reform in a timely fashion. Achieving the other parts of that compromise is likely to be much more difficult than choosing a clear route to property tax relief through a local option decision.

Some of the inertia preventing school reform and school finance reform in Illinois finally broke in mid and late 1997. Governor Edgar continued to push hard for progress on school finance, and the typical barriers to progress remained. However, as the end of the spring session of the legislature approached at the end of May 1997, progress began to come more quickly. By the end of the summer in 1997, the Illinois State Board of Education had approved the Illinois Learning Standards program. The new outcomes-based program provides for ninety-eight statewide goals in seven subjects: English language arts, mathematics, science, social science, physical development, fine arts, and foreign language. Achievement of the goals is to be measured by a new statewide Illinois Standards Achievement Test that was piloted in 1999. Eventually, schools' and students' scores will be categorized as having exceeded, met, or not met state standards.

In addition to the approval of the Illinois Learning Standards for public schools, the teacher certification system in Illinois was revamped. The new system provides for a three-tiered certification system and the requirement that teachers have individual development plans that are monitored by school districts ("Teachers Are the Key" 1999). This was another type of accountability reform that seemed to provide some impetus for reform of school finance in the state.

Governor Edgar continued to push for school finance reform and for an increase in the state income tax to pay for increased funding of primary and secondary education. With some progress being made through actions that increased the accountability of teachers and students, the ball was back in the court of the state legislature to deal with the funding issues. After the legislature narrowly missed approving a school funding bill in the November 1997 veto session, the governor called legislators back to Springfield in early December 1997 for a special session devoted to school finance. This time, a bill was passed by the required supermajority necessary to provide immediate implementation. The bill ensured that at least $4,225 would be spent in budget year 1999 on each student in the state. The increased state spending is to be financed by increases in cigarette taxes, telephone taxes, gaming taxes, and allocations from other tax sources. The bill also funded a $1.4 billion matching program for school district construction and repairs, as well as a loan program for the acquisition of technology resources. It also incorporated the learning standards and teacher certification reforms approved by the Illinois State Board of Education. However, "for all the latest proposal's benefits, including student and teacher accountability reforms, it does nothing to address the bigger problem: Schools are financed through property taxes and, as such, are the victims of vast inequities throughout the state. Many predicted that the passage of the measure would take the contentious issue of overhauling school funding off the table for the foreseeable future" (Pearson 1997, p. 28).

Contrary to the governor's promise a month earlier, Governor Edgar, now a lame duck governor, continued in his 1998 State of the State address to push for a school funding tax swap whereby the state income tax would be increased in exchange for lower property taxes. He also appointed a blue ribbon panel to investigate such a swap. Ultimately, the panel was unable to agree on a plan for such a swap.

With the issue of school funding, and property tax funding of education in particular, back on the public policy agenda, Representative Wirsing filed his legislation again in January 1998, and an identical bill was filed in the Illinois Senate. Nearly two years later the bill remains mired in the legislative process, though hearings on the bill were held in the summer of 1999 before the Senate Revenue Committee, and no further substantive progress has been made on school finance reform. Although it is probably fair to say that the grassroots concern over school funding has somewhat quieted since the 1997 legislation, there still remain serious concerns over high property tax bills and the heavy reliance on the property tax for school funding. New governor George Ryan has made a pledge to devote 51% of all new revenues to education, but he has broadly defined education to include initiatives such as training and school to work programs. It appears that the three-year experiment with increased state foundation funding of local schools, the state construction program, and loans for technology have been sufficiently successful[23] to merit renewal.[24] Nevertheless, no sustained and sufficient financing for the program has been committed. In general, the plan is being funded through revenues that are available primarily owing to favorable economic conditions in the state. Similar to the situation in Wisconsin, in the absence of new revenue growth the Illinois plan is unlikely to be sustainable as presently structured.

Although much of the lesson in this review of the Illinois experience is simply related to the ways to play good, hard-nosed politics, the other message is the need to break up the issue into understandable pieces that enable debate to take place in a meaningful and productive fashion. The ill-structured problem framework outlined in this book has led us to redefine the issue of government's role in primary and secondary school reform such that debates like the one in Illinois can be more productive. Efforts in Michigan and Wisconsin have both shown that property tax relief can be achieved and a greater role for state financing can be defined.[25] This book has endorsed a greater role for most states in the financing of schools, but also a greater contribution on the part of parents and the private sector. The Milwaukee voucher experiments indicate that increased competition, while retaining significant outside funding, public or private, is not only possible but workable in a large city, albeit on a small scale. Thus, with the exception of tuition payments from all students, elements of the reforms we have suggested with respect to the financier role have some history and probability of limited success. In Chapter 12, we explore some of the experiences with non–finance related reform efforts.

NOTES

[1]Indeed, in Illinois the supreme court refused to overturn the system in *Committee for Educational Rights v. Edgar* (1996), arguing that the school finance system was a legislative matter outside the jurisdiction of the court. Similar analysis led to the referral of court decisions to legislatures for ultimate action in other states.

[2]Recall that the average state share was about 47% at that time.

[3]Proposals went to the voters because of the Michigan constitutional limit on the sales tax of 4.0% (Wortley 1997).

[4]This may be *prima facie* evidence of the ability for changes in the financier role to be a catalyst for more wide ranging types of school reform efforts.

[5]Until the system is fully implemented, the gap will not be totally funded. However, those districts below the basic foundation level will have their state funding increase more rapidly than those districts whose guaranteed foundation allowance is above the minimum.

[6]Courant, Gramlich, and Loeb's numbers differ slightly from those in Wortley (1997), but not in any material or meaningful sense given our emphasis on understanding the general structure and nature of the Michigan reform.

[7]Technically, the law requires homestead property to bear the full burden until the nonhomestead mill rate of 18 mills is reached. If additional revenue is still required and permitted, the additional funds may be raised with a uniform rate across all types of property, but no district is allowed to spend more than twice the basic foundation allowance.

[8]Figures provided by Wortley indicate that in FY 1993–1994 there were 385 school districts below the estimated $5,000 floor level. Of these, 242 were below $4,500 per pupil in revenues. Therefore, great progress appears to have been made, but there also appear to be many districts that yet need to be brought up to the revenue floor (Wortley 1997, p. 3).

[9]These nonfinancial reforms appear to be the tradeoff for improved financing of public schools. All of these reforms are consistent with our market role assessment of primary and secondary education, with the notable exception of regulation of the minimum numbers of school days. The latter reform is incompatible with the more deregulated approach to school operations suggested by market role assessment.

[10]Reschovsky states that in Wisconsin, school property taxes are on average about 55% of the total property tax bill.

[11]One of the criteria by which a government revenue system is measured is its ability to provide reliable revenues for essential services. One element of providing reliable revenues is for the revenue source to be relatively insensitive to economic downturns (Mikesell 1995).

[12]This sharing of costs is closer to the reconstruction of the financier role suggested by our market role assessment.

[13]A second task force was appointed by the governor and began work about three years later. Neither task force's report was influential in the policy process, although both helped keep the issue on the policy agenda.

[14]That is, Lake, McHenry, Kane, DuPage, and Will Counties, also known as the collar counties.

[15]It should be noted that the provisions for the balance of the state were somewhat less onerous than those imposed on the collar counties. The collar county tax cap was imposed by the state legislature. In the realm of tax and expenditure limitations in the United States, this was highly unusual. The balance of state counties were authorized to impose a property tax extension limitation through referendum approval by voters. This approach is much more in line with the referenda- and initiative-based limitations imposed in other states. Furthermore, those limitations in Illinois that are imposed by referendum set the base year for the limitation as the tax year following passage of the referendum. What this means is that unlike the collar counties, downstate non–home rule local governments subjected to an extension limitation are given one tax year in which to adjust their base extension prior to the limitation taking effect.

[16]Most of the group would likely classify themselves as Democrats, and most had very different views from Representative Wirsing on many major issues, including, as it turned out, approaches to school finance reform. This was especially relevant given the position staked out by Dawn Clark Netsch.

[17]Elimination of local property tax revenues for schools would have required the identification of such a large amount of revenue (a sum that was more than half of the total income and sales tax revenues of the state under the status quo) that the infeasibility of that option was evident through simple calculations. The option was therefore soon eliminated from the menu of reform possibilities.

[18]These traits are uncommon in today's society and perhaps even less common among legislators whose time horizon rarely allows for such patience in the policy process.

[19]Given this perception, one can understand at least one of the author's interests in promoting the tool of market role assessment as a means of simplifying and focusing policy debates of this type.

[20]Legislative hearings in Illinois require every person or organization wishing to be heard or recorded as present at the hearing to file a testimony slip. On the testimony

slip, the person or organization indicates their position on the bill (including a no position option) and whether they wish to provide oral testimony, written testimony, or merely have their position recorded.

[21]In a view that was shared to great degree by one of the Wirsing committee members, it was felt by some opponents that anything short of a single, comprehensive school finance, property tax, and school reform bill would take the onus off the state legislature to make any progress on overall larger issues. Supporters of the bill argued that by offering a means of property tax relief without altering other elements of the system, one reduced the likelihood of the legislature being drawn into making hasty, ill-conceived decisions that the citizens of Illinois and the education community would have to live with and pay for. Unfortunately, the Illinois legislature had a history of making those types of bad decisions during times of crisis. Notable examples include the bailout of the Chicago White Sox and the passage of an ill-conceived (administratively, not politically) property tax extension limitation law, both of which happened in the rush of the wee final hours of legislative sessions.

[22]This was despite a 2% administrative fee that the Department wrote into the bill in the process of preparing it for introduction.

[23]The Metropolitan Planning Council in Chicago reported that, when calculated, the state's share of funding for schools in 1999–2000 was expected to be in the range of 38%, up from a state share of 32% in 1996–1997 (the last year before the new influx of state money).

[24]One of the compromises in the December 1997 legislation was a sunset clause.

[25]It should be noted that there are many critics of the move to increased state financing of primary and secondary education. For example, William Fischel has argued that the shift in responsibilities has been ineffective and ill advised (Fischel 1997).

CHAPTER 12

Regulatory and Other Nonfinancial School Reforms
Has a Change in Government's Role Been for the Better?

Given the complex and multifaceted nature of primary and secondary school reform, it is hardly a surprise that reform efforts have come in every shape, size, and variety. The task in this chapter is to explore some of the more prominent examples of nonfinancial school reforms. This exploration is intended to produce information regarding the relative efficacy of different types of reform, particularly in terms of government's changing role in the market for primary and secondary education. In order to make our task more manageable, we focus on two generically broad types of reform: outcomes- or standards-based education, and general administrative-type reforms.[1] Within the scope of these broad categories are other types of reforms such as charter schools, which will also be mentioned and briefly analyzed.

OUTCOMES AND STANDARDS

In recent years, great attention has been given to the outcomes of the educational system in the United States. National education standards received considerable attention in the early 1990s. "The movement for national standards and assessments began after an agreement in 1989 between President George Bush and the nations' governors to set national education goals" (Ravitch 1995, p. 2). In March 1994 President Bill Clinton signed into law legislation known as Goals 2000. This law was intended to advance national education standards and the use of assessments.

There are a number of reasons for the increased interest in standards and assessments. On the one hand, it is a reflection of continuing general interest in managerial efficiency: how to get more output with fewer inputs, especially fewer tax dollars. On the other hand, many people believe that the state of primary and secondary education itself encourages attention to outcomes. "Many people believe that the K–12 system of education is not adequately preparing students, at reasonable cost, for the challenges of the global economy. . . . Today, the global economy increases the demand for workers who are sufficiently well educated to have the flexibility to move from one job to another as opportunities change job demands" (Ladd 1996, p. 1). The value of education continues to rise. Yet, as reported widely even in the popular press, American students continue to lag behind their peers from around the world in science and math skills[2] (Ravitch 1995).

Interest in outcomes-based education is also a simple matter of resources. Indeed, resources to improve K–12 education are expected to be especially limited throughout the first decade or so of the twenty-first century. This is partially a function of rising enrollments. For example, it was widely reported in the fall of 1999 that U.S. primary and secondary enrollments had reached their all-time peak and would continue to rise for another eight to ten years (Illinois Association of School Boards 1999). Using 1994 as a base, "by 2004, enrollments are projected to rise by 13 percent at the K–8 level and by 24 percent at the high school level" (Ladd 1996, p. 2). For state and local governments, declining federal aid combined with increased fiscal stress and taxpayer scrutiny mean that resources for increasing education spending, especially spending per pupil, will be difficult to obtain. Outcomes-based education is regarded as an additional means of making difficult resource allocation decisions.

Furthermore, Ladd (1996) points out that education in the United States has come under increasingly close scrutiny for not efficiently turning resources into quality educational outcomes. Despite increased real levels of per-pupil spending,[3] test scores have remained relatively flat or declined (Ladd 1996, p. 2). "Given that resources are not likely to increase much in the future, and there is a need for a better-educated work force, most people agree that schools need to become more productive in the future" (Ladd 1996, p. 3).

Outcomes-based reform "begins with ambitious academic goals or standards for all children and curriculum frameworks that describe what all children should know and be able to do" (Ladd 1996, p. 4). Reform of this type requires a fundamental change in the role of government in the market for primary and secondary education. This change is very much along the lines suggested in our analysis. States would shift their regulation efforts for accreditation purposes *away* from a preoccupation with educational inputs[4] and *toward* the educational outcomes of students attending a particular school or school system. At the same time, local school boards would change their oversight role. Greater responsibility would have to be taken for (1) the development of educational goals for the schools, and (2) the auditing of student outcomes and school performance in terms of achievement of those goals. At the same time, all levels of government will need to aggressively play an evaluator role as part of their internal audits; that is, not only must development of educational goals and auditing of student outcomes take place, but an evaluation of the appropriateness of the goals and the quality of programs must also take place.[5] Thus, though not explicitly defined in our previous market role assessment, the evaluator function is especially important to define and take notice of as we move toward school reform in the twenty-first century.

The great attention given to outcomes-based education and educational standards offers a wealth of material for discussion. Because our focus is on government's role in school reform and on the role of the contemporary public administrator, it is appropriate to discuss a few of the outcomes-based reform efforts that have been approved and/or implemented, especially at the subnational level.

Corpus Christi, Texas, is a school district that is ahead of the pack when it comes to implementing academic standards. Twenty-three schools in the city tested the academic standards in 1995–1996, and in 1996–1997 all sixty-one of the city's schools adopted the academic standards "and every student was immediately accountable" (Ritter 1997, p. 4A). Students in Corpus Christi are required to master standards in every grade and subject, beginning with prekindergarten. The Corpus Christi system is based upon both content and performance standards. "Content standards specify what is to be learned, and performance standards specify how students show that they've learned the content" (Ritter 1997, p. 4A). In reading about these standards, one is impressed by the change in content standards with grade level. For example, kindergarten has nine content standards that focus on behavioral skills, language and vocabulary development, learning about order and sequence, and using information. Second grade science focuses on three content standards related to change in the physical world, whereas one year later in third grade the science content standards relate to plant and animal life, planetary bodies, and basic physics (Ritter 1997, p. 4A).

Corpus Christi's standards are too new to assess in great detail or to yield substantive conclusions. However, the success of this particular set of standards is less important to the current analysis than (1) the process by which the standards were successfully integrated into the schools, and (2) other elements of the initiative that increased the probability of implementation and success. The implementation of standards moves one toward the kind of changes in government's role that our market role assessment identified as being appropriate in the market for primary and secondary education. Yet, such moves have not been as popular as one might expect given the public outcry for accountability in government and education.

It is interesting that "the hue and cry for higher standards has gained momentum in the last decade behind corporate leaders, education reformers, and politicians, including President Clinton. But the pace of school reform and the move to curriculums based on standards have been slow" (Ritter 1997, p. 4A). Anecdotal evidence supports the notion of a slow bandwagon.

In a course on economic restructuring, I have twice introduced the notion of outcomes-based education into extensive discussion of efforts to improve the American workforce and have found little support for such a notion among my heavily conservative mix of students. Although this was somewhat surprising, it seems consistent with the experience of selling outcomes- and standards-based education to the general public. Standards come under fire from both ends of the political spectrum.

Despite the common linkage between standards and reduced day-to-day regulation, conservatives often oppose standards as a governmental attempt to dictate what is taught in the schools (an issue that is even more acute among the religious right). Conservative candidates railed against Goals 2000 in the 1994 election, and the Republican landslide that year represented a change in the political mood of the country that resulted in no appointments being made to the National Education Standards and Improvement Council (NESIC) that was provided for under Goals 2000 (Ravitch 1995, p. xvii). The release of national history standards in late 1994 and a proposal for national English standards in March 1996 met with vigorous outcry, including a 99 to 1 condemnation of the history standards by the U.S. Senate in January 1995. In opposing standards, traditional liberals often worry about potential cultural bias and the well-being of underserved minorities or special needs students under such a system. According to Ritter, "the public seems to have no appetite for national standards. A Bush administration proposal to set national standards bombed. President Clinton is trying to jawbone the states, but progress is fitful" (Ritter 1997, p.4A). Diane Ravitch (1995) attempted to popularize the debate through her book *National Standards in American Education: A Citizen's Guide.* Although it is a very good book, it never threatened those on the popular bestseller lists.

However, experiences with standards like those of Corpus Christi have given hope to some education reformers. Corpus Christi is a relatively large city with large numbers of poor and minority students.[6] It has set standards for all of its 42,000 students and demanded that teachers teach them and students learn them. Yet, Corpus Christi's path to those standards is particularly notable. In the midst of a labor market in which employers were complaining about the lack of basic skills among high school graduates, and a higher education system that found more than half of the high school graduates enrolling at the local community college in need of remedial coursework in one or more subjects, the foundation for action was built. One immediate problem was identified: the lack of consistency in what was being taught to students in different sections of the same course.

"The realization touched off a two-year crusade that brought together parents, teachers, and experts. The final product: *Real World Academic Standards*—50 pages of the stuff students must know and how they are to show they know it, from pre-kindergarten through 12th grade" (Ritter 1997, p. 4A).

When the district's overall course failure rate dropped during the first year of the fully implemented standards programs, educators in the district argued that students had risen to the heightened expectations. It will be interesting to investigate the programs' continued success.

Success in Corpus Christi has also been facilitated by other elements of the standards initiative:

- a discipline code that strips away disruptions to learning;
- regular testing to determine whether the standards are being taught;
- programs that kick in quickly to help students who are falling behind, including a summer school program that students only are required to attend long enough to pass standards they have failed; and
- a ban on the "social promotion" of students whereby they would advance grades even in the absence of meeting the standards for the lower grade. (Ritter 1997)

The ban on social promotion is exceedingly popular with the teachers' union and may provide the best insurance that students meet standards. But, as Ritter also points out, few districts have the stomach or tenacity (including the willingness to actively litigate against angry parents) necessary to ensure that such a system works. One of the positive aspects has been "a level of cooperation that outsiders say is rare in an education bureaucracy. A key to success is that teachers had a central role in drafting the standards" (Ritter 1997, p. 4A). One can easily see the importance of the auditor and newly defined evaluator function to the ultimate success of a program like that undertaken in Corpus Christi. The initial success with standards in Corpus Christi has promoted (1) more radical approaches to teaching in an effort to further enhance the number of students that are being reached, and (2) broadly based and significant improvements in student achievement. Corpus Christi is certainly not the only district that has experimented with standards, but they have yet to catch on in a widespread way elsewhere.

The American Federation of Teachers (AFT) has longed pushed for standards. Indeed, it conducts an annual review of progress toward that end. According to Ritter (1997), the 1996 annual review found that only fifteen states have standards in math, English, social studies, and science that are "clear, specific, and well grounded in content." Two states have no standards at all; twelve states have standards that fail the outlined AFT standards test in all four core subject areas; and the remaining twenty-one states have standards in one or more subject areas that fail the "clear, specific, and well-grounded" test. However, "most states that have set standards . . . don't take the critical extra step of requiring students to pass tests based on them. So there's no guarantee that schools will use the standards" (Ritter 1997, p. 4A). Unlike the city-based reform of Corpus Christi, schools in Oregon have recently faced a wide-ranging school reform effort that includes an attempt at establishing standards.

"Starting this year [1996–1997], pupils in the 3rd, 5th, 8th and 10th grades will be given a battery of tests to determine whether they can meet Oregon's new academic standards, the linchpin in a five-year experiment to overhaul instruction from kindergarten through college" (Haynes 1996, p. 13). Unlike other states that formulated general academic guidelines, and then allowed districts to customize their own learning goals to meet their own students' needs, "Oregon's 1991 school reform law mandated that all districts follow the state's prescribed formula for improving instruction" (Haynes 1996, p. 13). In the long term, proponents of the system in Oregon envisioned the awarding of "certificates of mastery" in place of traditional high school diplomas, as well as numerical scales of objective levels of standardized achievement in place of traditional letter-based grading. Ultimately, the legislature extended the implementation date to 1999 and chose not to make the program a requirement for high school graduation (Smith and Sherrell 1997). However, some results are available from Lake Oswego, Oregon,[7] one of the school districts that has designed and piloted a performance-based certification program. The Certificate of Initial Mastery (CIM) is at the center of Oregon's program and was the center of the program in Lake Oswego. Information about Lake Oswego is based on its four-year experience in piloting a CIM style program. At the time of the report, the district was two years away from issuing its first CIM (Smith and Sherrell 1997). Thus, one lesson to be learned is that the introduction and refinement of an outcomes- or standards-based education system takes time and patience.

To earn a CIM, "a student must accumulate a sufficient body of evidence displaying a high level of achievement toward each of several learning goals developed by the state. Students begin accumulating evidence in elementary school and continue until they have met all of the requirements for the certificate" (Smith and Sherrell 1997, p. 46). Lake Oswego has instituted a "continuous progress" approach whereby the certificate is awarded when all of the requirements have been met, regardless of the student's age or grade level. This differs somewhat from the law's expectation of completion by the end of tenth grade.

The body of evidence required for the CIM has two parts. The first part directly addresses content standards. "In Oregon, a content standard describes the knowledge and skills a student should master in a discipline" (Smith and Sherrell 1997, p. 46). Typically, students will demonstrate mastery through examinations that are broad tests of recall and comprehension.

The second part focuses on a student's ability to apply knowledge and skills to a variety of tough problems.[8] "This is where performance assessments will play a major role. Some of the evidence will come from on-demand performance assessments that are part of the statewide assessment program, and other pieces will come from performance assessments developed at the district level and embedded in the local curriculum" (Smith and Sherrell 1997, p. 47). The same discipline-based scoring guides will be used for all performance assessments, whether state or locally developed. Guides for reading/literature, writing, speaking, math, science, and social studies are being developed at the state level and will be used uniformly by all districts in Oregon. Scoring guides and performance standards for the arts and foreign languages will be developed and administered locally (Smith and Sherrell 1997, p. 47).

It should be noted that "in addition to scores from performance assessments, Oregon law also requires that actual scored samples of student work be included in the body of evidence, so that the quality of student work becomes public" (Smith and Sherrell 1997, p. 47). As one might imagine, formulating methods by which such records can be organized and maintained is one of the challenges noted in Lake Oswego's four years of piloting the program. Other lessons learned include the following:

- "Continuous progress" is a better approach than mandated benchmark reviews. The expectations under mandatory benchmarks ensure a "winners and losers" dichotomy and the emergence of constituencies to defend the "losers." "The political viability of a certification system depends on *not* adopting a grade-level approach" (Smith and Sherrell 1997, p. 47).
- Curriculum agreements are essential to conduct performance assessments and to foster the collaboration needed among teachers to more uniformly judge the quality of student work.
- Performance assessments need to be developed collaboratively rather than by individual teachers. "The high-quality performance assessments needed for certification must include clear specifications, standard expectations for documentation, careful field testing, and adequate security measures" (Smith and Sherrell 1997, p. 48).
- Because of the broad scope of the CIM learning goals, the assessment demands for teachers in self-contained classrooms[9] were overwhelming. Therefore, assessments in lower grades were reduced by phasing in the areas in which evidence was to be gathered and reducing the amount of evidence to be gathered at any one time. "These somewhat reduced expectations are justified at the elementary level because monitoring, not certification, is the focus at this level. The key is to collect just enough information to make sound remediation decisions" (Smith and Sherrell 1997, p. 48).
- In many constituencies, the top-down nature of the enactment of reform legislation heightened the political unpopularity of standards. Lake Oswego tried to build support for the certifications system

through efforts to deliberately connect the goals and elements of the legislation with local values presented in strategic documents. But, "the job of monitoring and cultivating support for significant changes is never ending" (Smith and Sherrell 1997, p. 49).

- In an effort to better manage record keeping, students in Lake Oswego are given the responsibility for being custodians of their own collections of evidence once they reach the secondary level. In addition, the CIM certification records are maintained in a "rolling" fashion whereby old evidence is removed as newer evidence becomes available. Furthermore, on the small scale of one local district, Lake Oswego has found it feasible to store each student's data on a recordable compact disk in an organized presentation format (Smith and Sherrell 1997, p. 49). Much remains to be learned as the Lake Oswego and Oregon programs continue through the implementation stage. At present, the system seems ready for widely based testing and evaluation.

At the policymaking level, and in the discussions of educational reformers, the notion of standards- or outcomes-based education continues to burn brightly. Whether through the grassroots efforts of places like Corpus Christi or the statewide efforts of a place like Oregon, the attempt to develop a workable system of standards is unlikely to fade anytime soon even in the absence of broad public involvement or support. The business community is generally very supportive of efforts such as CIM programs that are based upon a standards- or outcomes-judged curriculum. Similarly, as programs like that in Corpus Christi demonstrate the feasibility of a certain level of cultural, political, and economic neutrality in standards implementation, it is likely that some of the opposition to standards will begin to disappear. Furthermore, the economic incentives that can be produced through linking outcomes-based performance with supplemental school aid appropriations can go a long way to producing potential buy-in to a standards program. Variations of such school incentive programs are already in place in South Carolina, Georgia, Indiana, Kentucky, Tennessee, and Texas (Clotfelter and Ladd 1996, pp. 28–29).

Once again, the role of the evaluation function must be noted. This role is extremely important and is acknowledged to a great degree in Clotfelter and Ladd's discussion. The evaluation role extends considerably beyond the auditor role of determining whether standards have been met. The evaluator must also rank schools or districts according to (1) how well they met the standards, and (2) whether the degree to which the standards were met was appropriate to the amount and quality of the resources available and used to achieve the educational outcomes. Furthermore, given the great controversy and relative inexperience with standards, the evaluator must also assess the quality, appropriateness, and delineation of the standards themselves. In simple parlance, it is the auditor's job to find out if standards are being met, whereas it is the evaluator's job to assess how well the standards are being met.[10] Performance of the evaluation role will be central to the long-term efficacy and success of standards-based reform.

Although standards-based reforms have received great attention in recent years, especially with the president's support for the Goals 2000 initiative, many other notable nonfinancial reforms have also taken place. Such reforms include the Chicago School Reform Act, charter school experiments, and regulatory waiver legislation, as well as the experiences with school-based management and privatized administration discussed in some detail earlier in this book. Each of these reforms was based on the alteration of government's role in the market for primary and secondary education. Some have been linked with the kind of standards-based reforms discussed in the previous section of this chapter. We therefore look briefly at the Chicago school reform and some charter school experiences.

THE CHICAGO REFORM EXPERIENCE

Reform of the Chicago Public Schools occured in two waves. The first wave came with the Chicago School Reform Act. "The Chicago School Reform Act passed in December 1988. . . . It created the eleven-member local school council (LSC).[11] . . . The LSCs have the power to hire and fire principals based on how well the principal meets standards in a four-year performance contract drawn up by the council" (Wong and Sunderman 1995, p. 163). The system essentially involved school-based management under which principals were given greater authority in hiring staff, filling nonprofessional positions within the school, and allocating funds. "Resources were reallocated within the system, with each school receiving a lump sum allocation based on the school enrollment and number of special needs of the student body. . . . Finally, the law sets specific graduation, attendance, promotion, and achievement test levels for schools to meet as a measure of reform implementation" (Wong and Sunderman 1995, p. 163).[12]

The second wave came in 1995 "when the Illinois General Assembly abolished the old school board, eliminated the superintendent, and authorized Mayor Richard M. Daley to appoint a five member 'super-board' and a chief executive officer to run the city's schools for four years. For the latter position, Daley chose his own chief of staff and budget director, Paul Vallas" (Jones, July 1997, p. 24). As one might expect, given Vallas's background, he concentrated first on the finances of the schools. Vallas brought much of his administrative team from the budget office with him to the school administration. This meant that the financial team was now comprised of accountants and public finance specialists who were primarily trained in MPA programs. Applying basic public administration techniques and processes to the management of the public schools was one of the factors that led to a very rapid and successful turnaround in the Chicago Public Schools' finances. Specifically, a $1.3 billion shortfall in the schools' projected four-year budget was eliminated in less than two years of management. "With the solid financial footing, Vallas and his management team turned their attention to the low academic achievement of Chicago's students" (Jones, July 1997, p. 24). During Vallas's tenure, principals have been fired, numerous schools have been taken over, and local school councils have been abolished or reconstituted owing to failure to meet the established standards. In September 1996, nearly 20% of Chicago's schools were officially placed on probation. This meant that the schools had to improve or face reconstitution, a process in which the school's entire staff could be replaced. "Individual students, schools, and administrators are being held accountable for low academic achievement" (Jones, July 1997, p. 24).

The schools that were placed on probation in September 1996 were chosen because only 15% or fewer of their students were reading above their grade level; moreover, all the high schools placed on probation had dropout rates that ranged from 36% to 67%. Indeed, "Vallas would have liked to have put even more schools on probation. But if the probation plan had included all of the schools where only 30 percent of students read at or above their grade level, that would have meant putting three times as many schools on probation" (Jones, July 1997, p. 25). The feeling was that the original probation list of 109 schools was about the maximum number that the management team could work with responsibly at any given time. This is because schools on probation are given extra attention. The extra attention includes a business or operations manager who administers the non-education aspects of the school, to free up the principal to provide instructional leadership. The schools also are provided with advisory "external partners" and probation managers who are principals or former principals at successful schools—public or private, city or suburban. Although some principals have complained about being labeled by probation status, especially at schools that have been making progress, the assistance and extra attention given to schools on probation has generally been viewed as a positive development. Also, "schools will continue to receive assistance when they go off probation and move on to the next step, remediation" (Jones, July 1997, p. 25). Other measures are being taken to hold students accountable for their own performance. One of Vallas's early reforms was to end social promotion in the schools. Also, a six-week "summer bridge program" was required attendance for students who had low reading scores on the Iowa Tests of Basic Skills. Teachers have spoken of increased attentiveness on the part of students that they attribute to these accountability measures.

Although the evidence from Chicago is somewhat mixed and seems to change with the passage of each day,[13] in general decentralization has appeared to have the desired effects. Local communities seem to have taken greater interest in and ownership of their schools. The emphasis on standards and local control has also led to substantial cost savings as principals begin to find alternative means of acquiring and maintaining ancillary services such as maintenance. The loosening of regulatory controls in exchange for compliance with standards and outcomes improvement has seemed to work reasonably well even in a deeply troubled school district like Chicago. The success in beginning to turn around the Chicago schools in terms of both outcomes and finances has somewhat changed the terms of the school reform fight in Illinois, as there is now less credibility to the argument that any reform will merely be a means of funding a bailout of the Chicago Public Schools with little benefit to the rest of the state. At the same time, recent problems with isolated cases of abuses of power and authority on the part of LSC's have given unwanted attention to the schools at a time when there are many positive things to be said about the progress of the Chicago Public Schools.[14] It is not surprising that the tenure of the reform board and of Mr. Vallas have been extended indefinitely.

The experience in Chicago represents a significant reform in the performance of the administrator, regulator, and auditor roles. Most of the reforms left these roles solely in the public sector, but with significant changes in the level and nature of responsibility.

CHARTER SCHOOLS

As suggested numerous times during our market role assessment, charter schools appear to have substantial promise as proving grounds for administrative reforms and as a means of increasing competition in publicly accessible education. "Charter schools are the hottest trend in American education reform. . . . Though they were nonexistent five years ago, public charter schools rapidly are increasing in number. According to the U.S. Education Department, almost 500 charter schools are operating in the 25 states that allow them" (Jouzaitis 1997, pp. 1, Back Page). It has been widely noted that charter schools are one of the few widespread points of agreement between Republicans and Democrats who are anxious for meaningful school reform. As implemented in most states, charter schools have many desirable features:[15] They are essentially limited-enrollment public schools;[16] they provide an easy and low-cost method for exploring the possible gains from regulatory relief and from alternative educational approaches or delivery mechanisms; and they have proven to be an especially positive means of providing alternative educational opportunities for students who have failed to achieve or attend school under the status quo. "An August 1995 survey of charter schools found that . . . about half were intended to serve at-risk students" (Molnar 1996, p. 11). Indeed, the first charter school in operation in

Illinois was the Peoria Alternative Charter School, a school for the most troublesome of Peoria's school-aged population[17] (Chen 1997, pp. 1–2). In general, the long-term effectiveness of charter schools cannot yet be judged owing to their relative newness[18] (Saks 1999). The report card thus far is at best a mixed one. The most recent test scores from Minnesota, Michigan, and Chicago indicate that charter school students do not perform better than public school students overall (Saks 1999). However, there are many success stories, and there is some evidence that charter school students have higher and faster rates of improvement than students at large.[19] Furthermore, to the extent that charter schools are enrolling at-risk and disadvantaged students, scores that keep up with overall norms may actually correspond to a relatively high level of achievement.

There seems to be substantial evidence that alternative approaches to education can be immensely successful and that the relaxation of day-to-day regulation of schools is unlikely to lead to anarchy or poor student outcomes (especially in a true standards-based system). As suggested, the charter schools have also apparently increased student retention through their seemingly unique ability or willingness to provide last-resort alternative educational services for problem students. Similarly, legislation to allow school districts to request waivers of certain state regulations has been successful in returning school district focus to education and its outcomes, rather than the restrictions on the inputs they are allowed to use to produce what they deem to be effective education. Unfortunately, the jury is still out on the case of charter schools, especially in terms of their ability to sustain results when reform moves to a larger scale. This is disappointing, given our hope for guidance from the results of charter school experiments. Considering the tremendous insights that charter school experiments can offer with respect to many of the issues raised[20] through our market role assessment, evaluation of these programs should be watched closely.

CONCLUSION

In summary, there appears to be considerable evidence of successful nonfinancial reform efforts.[21] These efforts share some commonalities in terms of changes in government's role in the market for primary and secondary education.

The successful reforms discussed in this chapter for the most part feature a reduced and redefined regulatory role for government, along with an increased role for government as auditor and evaluator. The function of evaluator is probably of greatest importance in the context of nonfinancial reforms. In fact, it is fair to conclude that the success of nonfinancial reforms is likely to be significantly related to government's ability to appropriately define, pay attention to, and implement an evaluator function in the market for primary and secondary education. Given the nature of primary and secondary education distribution, much of this responsibility for leadership and reform must be borne locally.

It should be noted that reforms of the type discussed in this chapter have not been easy politically and that reform will continue to be a political challenge for policymakers. All of the discussed reforms require a willingness to relinquish control on the one hand, and to increase accountability on the other. Neither type of change is desirable to all of the powerful stakeholders in primary and secondary education.

The characterization of the high priority role changes and redefinitions summarized in Chapter 10 is supported by the analysis we have just concluded. Indeed, the present paths of some of the most prominent school reform efforts appear to include an important place for government performance of the revised roles of auditor and regulator. However, few efforts have taken the extra step in defining and committing to the importance and centrality of the evaluator function.

The final chapters of this book bring closure to two important remaining analytical issues: the prospects for and nature of primary and secondary school reform in the United States in the twenty-first century, and the role of the contemporary public administrator in such reform, especially in terms of the suggested adjustments in government's roles in the market and in school reform.

NOTES

[1]*Administrative reforms* uses the word *administrative* in a generic sense rather than in terms of the administrator role defined earlier in the book.

[2]It should be noted that these reports also acknowledge that American students have the highest self-image regarding their math and science skills. Apparently, "feel good" education is succeeding!

[3]Ladd argues that the increase in resources for primary and secondary education is significantly overstated and that, in effect, resources have remained quite constant over the past twenty to twenty-five years when cost considerations, special needs programs, and societal changes creating changes in required resources (e.g., security) are factored out.

[4]For example, classroom space, teacher education, and length of class day and school year.

[5]Recall that the auditor function involves examining outcomes based upon a set of predetermined rules and functions. Evaluation involves assessing the predetermined rules and functions themselves. Evaluation represents a final feedback stage to the internal portion of the audit function. An often overlooked role, evaluation is rarely explicitly undertaken in the traditional market setting. In today's competitive environment, successful firms are giving increasing attention to the evaluation function. Indeed, any form of quality management is intimately involved with the evaluation function. As government continues to be pressed for greater accountability, the evaluator function becomes that much more important and useful.

⁶Corpus Christi has a Hispanic majority.

⁷Lake Oswego is a school district with 7,000 students in suburban Portland.

⁸The link to the problem-based learning discussion in the prologue of this book should be noted.

⁹That is, classrooms in which a single teacher teaches the students multiple subjects.

¹⁰I owe an intellectual debt to Pete Trott, a nationally recognized expert on workforce evaluation and skills standards, for initially raising the evaluation issue and engaging in thought-provoking conversations about its implications for markets and the role of government in an era of quality management and accountability.

¹¹The LSC is made up of six parents, two other community members, two teachers, and the principal. The LSC is responsible for setting school policy and making key educational decisions, including budgetary decisions.

¹²The focus of Wong and Sunderman (1995) is on the effects of school reform in Chicago based upon systemwide administrative and other more macro concerns. Although numerous studies and anecdotal renderings had offered evidence of the power and success of decentralization and local control, the systemwide concerns and issues addressed by Wong and Sunderman ultimately led to the demise of the old form of central administration, with legislation in 1995 turning over control of the schools to the mayor.

¹³For example, the Chicago Public Schools' test scores showed great improvement in 1998 and slight gains in 1999, but the vast majority of students remain well behind grade level norms, especially in reading.

¹⁴One of the problems that received considerable attention involved the accusation that (1) a local high school's LSC and its administration were associated with a radical terrorist group, and (2) these radical beliefs and support of the group were being integrated into the school's curriculum, with nonbelievers being punished in a variety of ways. Furthermore, there were accusations of money laundering to help fund the group's activities. Needless to say, the central administration's move to take control was swift and complete. The case has yet to be fully resolved, and it resurfaced as recently as 1999.

¹⁵According to Molnar (1996), one of the most significant differences among the various charter school laws is the degree of autonomy granted to the schools. "Strong" charter school laws (e.g., those in Arizona, California, Colorado, Massachusetts, Michigan, and Minnesota) allow the schools to operate as legally independent entities with a high degree of autonomy. "Weak" laws (e.g., those in Georgia, Hawaii, Kansas, New Mexico, and Wyoming) grant charter schools little more autonomy than other public schools have.

¹⁶This alleviates the concerns of those who oppose subsidies to private or exclusive schools.

¹⁷It should be noted that the Peoria alternative school was already in existence prior to the charter school legislation in Illinois; the community decided to convert the school to charter status in order to give it further flexibility and freedom from regulations. As of 1999, there were twenty charter schools in the state that were open or ready to open.

¹⁸For example, nearly one-half of the charter schools as of fall 1996 were in two states: Arizona and Michigan.

[19]For example, see Nathan (1996).

[20]For example, the merits of engaging in deregulation in exchange for outcome standards.

[21]However, one has to wonder how successful school reform would have been in Chicago had the financial problems not been solved first.

CHAPTER 13

School Reform for the Twenty-First Century
Can We Find the Path to Success?

Primary and secondary education reform is an ill-structured problem. Answers to such problems tend to come only with much effort and much discomfort. Market role assessment, an analytical tool introduced in this book, can be used to organize and carry out analysis of ill-structured public policy problems such as primary and secondary education reform.

The analysis in this book was built on a framework of market role assessment whereby a set of candidate market roles was identified; parameters for the roles were defined; presumption rules for the analysis were established; private sector benchmarks for individual roles were considered; analysis of each role was conducted in the general context of government's functions in a mixed economy; each role was assessed in terms of the market for primary and secondary education; and conclusions were drawn about the need for government performance of each role, as well as the relative responsibility for performance of each role that should be expected to remain with the private sector. This analysis enabled roles to be prioritized for attention in the public policy process. In the market for primary and secondary education, the Category 1, or high priority, roles were identified as those of financier, regulator, auditor (with its evaluator subfunction), and entrepreneur.

A look at some recent financial and nonfinancial reform efforts indicated promise for future efforts grounded in the Category 1 roles. Yet idiosyncracies, market imperfections, and political realities, among other things, can get in the way of the best laid plans. In this context our final chapter speculates about the prospects for successful primary and secondary education reform in the early twenty-first century, especially reform of the type envisioned as a result of our market role assessment.[1]

Successful reform of primary and secondary education is much more than a dream, as the success stories of Chapters 11 and 12 indicate. Nevertheless, the success stories related in this book are incomplete and have yet to be generalized. The path to success in primary and secondary school reform for the twenty-first century has only recently begun to be cleared. The path still needs to be leveled, smoothed, paved, and permanently maintained. This is an immense task but one that is far from impossible, especially with the commitment of time, energy, and other resources by parents, students, private businesses, not-for-profit organizations, interest groups, and governments.[2] The analysis of the market for primary and secondary education as framed by our market role assessment should convince the reader that school reform is a reasonable goal for the early twenty-first century.

THE ROLE OF GOVERNMENT IN EDUCATION AND EDUCATION REFORM

Market role assessment confirms that government has an important role to play in helping to make school reform possible and in helping to ensure the success of the chosen reform efforts. However, success in these endeavors is likely to come only with the kind of redefinition of government's role in the market for primary and secondary education that was suggested in the extensive preceding analysis. Indeed, this is the core message of that analysis. Our analysis of government's role in this market indicates that the roles of financier, regulator, auditor, and entrepreneur are the highest priority for attention in debates over the appropriate path and implementation strategies for reform efforts. In addition, analysis indicates the need to give greater commitment to evaluation as an integral function in any reform efforts, especially those with a performance-based component. Given the likely increase in the importance of the auditor role that was established in the analysis of the market for primary and secondary education, it is reasonable to expect government to have important responsibilities for performance evaluations related to reform efforts in this market.

Yet, redefinition of government's role and relationships in the market also means that the private sector and nonprofit sector must adapt to new roles and relationships as the mutual stakeholders, along with government, in the primary and secondary education system. The entrepreneurial government movement has in part meant that the private sector and the public sector are beginning to speak the same language when it comes to management and administration. The private sector and government also seem to be discovering that they are common stakeholders in the outcome of many important issues, of which primary and secondary school reform is only one. As a result, the private sector and the public sector are undergoing a blossoming of their potential for utilizing partnership approaches to the solution of difficult problems. As an example, the advantages of public-private partnerships in local economic development are well established.

CHALLENGES TO REFORM: THE ENTREPRENEUR ROLE

An entrepreneurial spirit is a key to the success of any public policy endeavor, especially those requiring major changes in government's role in the economy. Although it may be unfair to suggest that primary and secondary education reform is a matter of trial and error, it is fair to expect some measure of failure along the path to success. Entrepreneurs are not scared off by the prospect of failure or risk in general, but they do expect some measure of compensation for the risk they bear in undertaking a given activity. The potential rewards or profits from success must be sufficient to offset the losses from inevitable failures, as well as to compensate the entrepreneur for bearing the risk.

One initial concern related to the prospects for primary and secondary education reform in the early twenty-first century is that sufficient financial profits to attract traditional private sector entrepreneurs may not exist in the market for primary and secondary education, at least in terms of administration and production. Indeed, the lack of financial support and start-up funds are among the factors consistently cited as barriers for charter schools (Molnar 1996). Thus, it seems appropriate to look further at the entrepreneur role, as well as the changes in the performance of the role suggested by our market role assessment, as clues to the prospects for primary and secondary education reform.

Although there are nonfinancial rewards that might help to compensate the entrepreneur in the market for primary and secondary education, these rewards are unlikely to be of a type that will promote a long-term and diverse entrepreneurial effort on the part of the private sector.[3] Therefore, at least in the short term, the public sector must be prepared to create an environment that rewards public and nonprofit sector entrepreneurs who can be attracted by the existing nontraditional rewards available for success in primary and secondary school reform.[4] In the long term, even the prospects for private entrepreneurship in the market may be improved by creating this type of fostering environment.

There is ample anecdotal and empirical evidence to indicate that entrepreneurs exist and increasingly are being rewarded in the public and nonprofit sectors. However, further encouragement of entrepreneurial behavior on the part of the public and nonprofit sectors will require an open mind on the part of citizen constituents. This is because most persons are not used to the aggressive and innovative behavior that often accompanies entrepreneurship, especially on the part of the public sector. Furthermore, there will likely be notable and prominent failures as part of the risk taking inherent in the risk/reward framework of entrepreneurship. This requires that a much longer term and broader evaluation of the overall success of programs be conducted, rather than focusing on the success or failure of individual projects. A general rule of thumb for evaluating the results of government entrepreneurship might be provided by answering a question like the following: "How would I react if a private firm in which I owned stock made a similar strategic decision under similar circumstances, or had the overall track record of success and failure that my government does?" In most cases, one can expect public entrepreneurial activities to be well evaluated on these investment-type criteria. Thus, a first step in moving down the path to success in primary and secondary education reform is to encourage and reward public and nonprofit sector entrepreneurial behavior with respect to primary and secondary education, with the intention of seeding increased private entrepreneurship in the long run.

Entrepreneurial activities often push the envelope through their attributes of innovation and assumption of risk. Such activities can provoke intense responses owing to the changes they necessitate and incorporate. Although all stakeholders in primary and secondary education should expect to have input in the reform process, it is unlikely that reform will provide unmitigated gains to all stakeholders, nor is it likely that any reform effort will be supported enthusiastically by an overwhelming majority. Successful change often means undergoing a period of (often significant) discomfort and pain.

A good example of this kind of process and experience is standards-based education, a reform that remains entrepreneurial in nature. Much of standards-based education is grounded in reduced barriers to entry into the teaching profession and reduced regulations about the educational process, both of which may be threats or perceived threats to teachers and teachers' unions. At the same time, standards place a structure on the content of learning that may make parents or other interest groups uncomfortable. Unfortunately, such discomfort over details and change often gets in the way of taking the first step toward reform. Inertia acts against even small changes. This is why some of the most prominent reforms in recent years were swift, preemptive, and radical.

The finance reforms in Wisconsin and Michigan, as well as school reform in Chicago, began with radical first steps by state legislatures that broke the inertia of details-oriented debates. In each case, public entrepreneurship was at the heart of the bold first step. Development of an environment that fosters entrepreneurial behavior can improve the chances of overcoming policy inertia. Once inertia has been overcome, progress on related policy issues can follow quickly and furiously. As the old adage goes, "the journey of a lifetime begins with a single step." The difficulty of this first step is dependent on the amount of inertia to be overcome. Some sense of the strength of relevant inertia can be discerned from recent results of surveys related to attitudes toward primary and secondary education reform, and from perceptions regarding general attitudes toward government and government intervention. The strength of the inertia can best be gauged in the context of the high priority roles identified in our market role assessment, possible reform strategies identified in the market role assessment, or the examples discussed in Chapters 11 and 12.

BARRIERS TO REFORM: THE FINANCIER ROLE

Recall again that the four Category 1 roles we identified were entrepreneur, financier, regulator, and auditor. Some of the potential barriers to private entrepreneurship in primary and secondary education have already been discussed. Yet, even if primary and secondary education were to become a profitable venture, private entrepreneurship still might not be a viable commodity in the market. In a 1995 survey of school board presidents and chamber of commerce executives, DeSpain and Livingston reported that only 35% of chamber executives and 10% of school board presidents felt that public funds should be used to educate students at for-profit schools, and only 55% of chamber executives and 28% of school board presidents approved of the use of public funds to pay for the education of students in not-for-profit schools (DeSpain and Livingston 1996, pp. 17–18). Although we will discuss the attitudes toward voucher programs in more detail under the financier role, it should be noted that voucher programs also do not enjoy widespread support from the public, especially when religious schools are involved. However, support for vouchers has increased substantially over the past few years, with the level of support approaching 50% in recent polls (Billings 1999).

In general, the public remains skeptical and wary about using public dollars for the benefit of private businesses. Buying services from for-profit firms when not-for-profit providers exist or could be developed appears to be a heretical thought for many people.[5] Similarly, rewarding public entrepreneurs seems to be a difficult concept for many people to swallow. Publicly funded bonuses, extraordinary raises, "profit"-sharing plans, and other rewards for entrepreneurial behavior are very controversial even in the face of widely accepted private sector counterparts. Furthermore, despite widespread calls for government to be more businesslike in its operations, the thought of a government operating at a "profit" is untenable to many people.[6]

Public sector entrepreneurship has great potential for providing leadership in the move toward primary and secondary school reform, but the constraints imposed on entrepreneurial behavior through limits on potential reward structures, uses of public funds, and narrow visions of appropriate public sector leadership may create significant barriers to creating the kind of environment that is necessary to foster an entrepreneurial spirit. However, with the growing success and recognition of public entrepreneurship, attitudinal barriers may be somewhat easier to overcome. Also, the impetus for reform is likely to come from small pockets at first, and the possibilities for effective entrepreneurship increase markedly in local politics where accountability and rewards are more tangible and direct.

It should be noted that the already discussed reforms in Chicago, Michigan, and Wisconsin all began with a revision of the financier role. Our market role assessment indicated the need for government to continue to perform the financier role but noted that revisions in government's role might be appropriate. The basic conclusion of the analysis was that government and the private sector should share the performance of the financier role, with government funding the social benefits of education and the private sector funding the private benefits of education. From an efficiency standpoint, the private benefits of education would be best financed by the individuals receiving the education. It should be noted that this conclusion included the proviso that the social benefits of education should be financed by government, regardless of whether the producer of that education was government or the private sector. Perhaps more than any other reform idea mentioned during the market role assessment, this one is likely to be highly controversial.

There are at least three different elements of the idea that are likely to be of concern to some people: (1) public funds flowing to private education, (2) public funds flowing to religious schools, and (3) requiring payments from individuals for the private benefits of education. Voucher programs remain controversial. In a 1998 Gallup poll, "respondents were asked if they favored allowing parents to choose a private school for their children at public expense: the number who favored such a plan has increased to 44 percent, up from 24 percent in 1993" (Billings 1999, p.15). By 1999, support in the annual Phi Delta Kappa/Gallup poll had climbed further to 47%, with 48% of respondents still opposing vouchers, as reported in the October 1999 issue of *The American School Board Journal.* Support for vouchers seems to be inversely related to satisfaction with one's own public schools.[7] This is one reason why there is growing support for vouchers among some low income minority parents (Saks 1997). In general, support for vouchers that include religious schools has typically been less than that for programs limited to nonsectarian schools. It is interesting that "not all churches favor vouchers. Following the Wisconsin ruling, the National Council of Churches, representing the nation's mainline Protestant Churches, presented a strong resolution stating that public money should go only to public schools. The group represents an estimated 52 million Christians in America" (Billings 1999, p. 16). Thus, public dollars for private schools, religious or not, is likely to remain a controversial idea, but one that seems to be growing in acceptance given the well-publicized voucher program in Cleveland, the first statewide voucher program in Florida,[8] and the expansion of private voucher programs in many cities. Even as voucher programs expand, the issue of vouchers for religious schools remains thorny. The Cleveland voucher system was in court in late 1999 because of this very issue. The other part of the reform suggestion, private dollars for public education, is also likely to be controversial.

The meaning of a "free" public education has long been debated. In general, the most common interpretation appears to be that no tuition is charged. The appropriateness of fees is less clear. Even though mandatory book fees, lock fees, towel fees, laboratory fees, and parking fees have been on the scene for many years and are firmly entrenched, schools are increasingly turning to fees for sports and activities in the face of severe revenue shortages. "A 1991 survey by Roger W. Hamm, a former associate professor of education at Ohio Northern University, and Sandra Crosser, an associate professor there, found that 34 states permitted some type of student fees, 15 states and the District of Columbia permitted no fees, and one state, Nebraska, has no statute addressing the issue" (Hardy 1997, p. 26). Increased use of fundraising, booster clubs, and local education foundations has also been seen as schools try to make up for revenues lost to changes in state funding, tax limitations, and economic conditions. These alternatives have been particularly popular in states that have banned fees. "Pay-to-play," as these fee systems have been termed, has been a controversial topic. Many people have considered such fees to undermine the American notion of free public education (Hardy 1997). With so much outcry over relatively affordable fees, typically in the range of $30 per sport or activity, one wonders about the intensity of the potential outcry over a proposal to, in effect, begin charging some level of tuition for all primary and secondary education. No doubt the outcry would be substantial.

Therefore, prospects for reform of the financier role in the way suggested ·in our market role assessment seem rather dim. However, the notion of public funding for education regardless of the provider is likely to continue to grow in popularity as a means of providing competition for public schools. Even though true competition would also require market-based tuition for public schools, that sort of change is unlikely to happen as long as an entitlement view of tuition-free public education is widespread.

BRIGHTER PROSPECTS: THE REGULATOR ROLE

Prospects for reform of the regulator role may be the brightest among all of the Category 1 roles. The most popular aspect of reform is likely to be reduced regulation of educational inputs and processes. Giving public schools the freedom to alter inputs and processes to fit local needs and the local environment will likely result in improved efficiency and effectiveness of public schools (Hanushek 1994). Furthermore, subjecting all schools to the same health and safety regulations and requirements will help ensure a level and competitive playing field for public schools, charter schools, and private schools. There is widespread support for demanding the same degree of accountability from private and church-related schools that receive public dollars as is demanded from public schools. "Three-fourths said private or church-related schools that get public money should be accountable to the state as public schools are" (Billings 1999, p. 15). This accountability is implemented through both the regulator and the auditor roles.

Although some people would object to government remaining in the regulatory role at all, even for purposes of protecting the health and safety of children, health and safety regulation is a well-established role for government in a mixed economy. The retention of a government regulatory role related to the prevention of discrimination and the assurance of equal opportunity may seem controversial owing to a perceived linkage to controversial past implementation strategies such as affirmative action. The government regulatory role justified under market role assessment involves enforcement of civil rights laws against unfair discrimination, not remedies for past discrimination.

It will be difficult for many legislatures to give up broad regulatory control over public schools, but the reasonable *quid pro quo* for relaxing regulation is a move to the increased use of performance standards and the monitoring of educational outcomes. For example, Illinois, like many other states, has already broadened its granting of regulatory waivers to school districts on a case-by-case basis. In December 1997, Illinois also approved implementation of a set of standards, the Illinois Learning Standards, as part of overall changes in the state's role in education and education funding. As a result of growing experiences with charter schools that have been relieved of much regulation as part of the legislation constituting them, and the increased authorization of charter schools by state legislatures,[9] the environment has greatly improved for broader regulatory relief. The prospects for reform of the regulatory role seem particularly good in the early twenty-first century.

In sum, government's role as regulator will likely change in implementing favored types of school reform for the twenty-first century. In simple terms, government's role as regulator is likely to be greatly reduced in the education environment of the future. Indeed, government's primary regulatory function will likely shrink to that which it generically plays in nearly all markets: enforcer of civil rights and equal opportunity, health and safety, and pro-competition laws and regulations. No longer should (or will!) government be responsible for regulating the day-to-day operation of the educational process; rather, government will take new responsibility for the review of educational outcomes through increased performance of auditor and evaluator roles and functions.

ASSESSING REFORM: THE AUDITOR ROLE AND EVALUATION

In its role as auditor, government in the twenty-first century ultimately will be responsible for ensuring compliance with outcomes and standards that have been established as benchmarks for performance of students and the education system as a whole. This auditing function is part of the tradeoff under which local schools are to be freed of much regulation and oversight in operations, in exchange for increased scrutiny with respect to student achievement and other measures of educational outcomes. Such a move toward regulatory relief and outcomes-based education is likely to be a cornerstone of successful school reform, and it will be consistent with the appropriate role of government established through market role assessment of primary and secondary education.

Acknowledgment of school reform as a process places further emphasis on the importance of the evaluator role in the market. If reform is to be process based, the effectiveness and appropriateness of any reform effort must be assessed regularly and objectively. Although a portion of this assessment will be conducted as part of the audit function, where questions of compliance and achievement of goals are answered, arguably the more important part of the assessment will be evaluative. The results of evaluations will be used by public administrators to make policy decisions that can change the direction of reform or the methods relied upon for such reform. Performance measurement and evaluation of outcomes-based standards have been popular topics in recent public administration and practice. Increased emphasis on accountability through the auditor role and evaluation function in the market for primary and secondary education is likely to be well received by both the public and policymakers. Even though the degree of intrusion that will be accepted through the government performance of the auditor function may be debatable, the notion of established outcomes-based performance measurement should continue to hold great promise as a successful reform tool to be implemented in the early twenty-first century.

Evaluation involves assessing not only how well goals are being met but also the appropriateness and articulation of the goals themselves, and issues related to productivity and organizational capacity. The evaluator role will also be an important means of judging the appropriateness of entrepreneurial activities and the means used to foster such activities. In addition, the evaluator role is crucial to the ongoing examination of the appropriate division of economic roles between the public sector and the private sector. To some extent, this entire book has been grounded in the performance of such an evaluation of government's role in the market for primary and secondary education, with the goal of providing insight into government's role in reform of that system.

The prospects for reform of the remaining market roles assessed in this book are somewhat dependent on the success in implementing reforms in the Category 1 roles. Without reforms in the regulator role, the ability for greater performance of the producer or administrator roles in public education may be stifled by the statutes and regulations of the status quo. Although there is not yet evidence of sustainable private administration of public schools, the recent rejuvenation of the Edison Project (Billings 1999) may provide hope of additional progress in this regard. Furthermore, to the extent that private administration has been stifled by the constraints heretofore placed on public school administration outside of charter schools, the prospects for reform may further improve once the private administrator has fewer constraints on its operations.

Should reforms be successful in producing a more competitive market for the production and consumption of elementary and secondary education, reform of the allocator/distributor role is likely to occur naturally and automatically.

CONCLUSION

The prospects for reform of primary and secondary education in the early twenty-first century seem relatively good, but there is much inertia to overcome. Concentrating initial reform efforts on areas affecting the targeted, Category 1 roles of government in the market are likely to have the most immediate and lasting effect, as well as probabilities of success on a relatively universal level. Although it is unlikely that reform of any particular type will be successful in all areas or be noncontroversial, fitting reform efforts into the targeted clusters is likely to increase the chances of success in any given situation. In some cases, however, greater attention may need to be given to reform in areas we identified as important but of lower priority. For example, contracting out support services in some school districts may result in sufficient cost savings so as to make other reform efforts feasible when they would not have been affordable otherwise. Furthermore, some type of administrative reforms, particularly like those that increased accountability in Chicago, may be a prerequisite to an increased state role in the funding of local schools.

Based upon our analysis and the historical record with different reform efforts, it seems reasonable that certain types of reform efforts, in generic form, are likely to be popular in the twenty-first century. These include: voucher programs; outcomes- or standards-based education; regulatory waivers, including further expansion of charter school experiments; contracting out of support services; increased state responsibility for education combined with a reduced reliance on local property taxes for education; and increased emphasis on evaluation with an aim toward both accountability and improved quality. It is also possible, though less likely, that we will begin to see direct financial rewards to public sector entrepreneurs for innovations that improve the quality as well as the efficiency of primary and secondary education. An improved entrepreneurial environment in the market for primary and secondary education would be a major step toward sustained improvement in public education and its administration, as well as the attraction of private entrepreneurial efforts.

The attention given to primary and secondary school reform clearly indicates that a variety of constituencies are interested in making progress; these include parents, teachers, employers, and students. Given the level of interest in school reform, it would not be unreasonable to expect the process to become self-perpetuating, once placed in motion with some level of measurable success to point to as an incentive for further action.[10]

The message is simple: Have an open and honest discussion about the proposed path for reform, but then *give reform a chance*. Reform is a process, not a place. It is highly unlikely that one's first reform effort will be perfect or that it will be one's last chance to make a difference. Overcoming the inertia opposing change is like breaking a writer's block: the ideas begin to flow freely and openly.

A flexible and innovative attitude, combined with a willingness to experiment, evaluate, and make changes, will go a long way toward providing an environment that is likely to foster meaningful primary and secondary school reform in the twenty-first century. School reform in the twenty-first century will include a significant role for government. Thus, leadership from public administrators is likely to be an important factor in the success of school reform efforts. We explore the role of the contemporary public administrator in school reform in the epilogue of this book.

NOTES

[1]The results of the market role assessment contained in this book may be disputed by persons of good faith who are informed in their judgments. Nevertheless, market role assessment can allow such disputes to focus on specific market roles, as well as on underlying values that influence decision paths. Therefore, market role assessment still performs its advertised role of circumscription and narrowing of the policy debate.

[2]Murphy (1996) indicates that there is a growing interest in privatization as a means of transforming education. However, Murphy identifies no fewer than *ten* options for privatization (e.g., load-shedding, asset sales, user fees, franchises, contracting, and subsidies) that need to be considered and evaluated by policymakers. The market role assessment presented in this book has evaluated all of Murphy's options at one level or another, and it provides a starting point for the difficult task of moving toward reform efforts, including those based in the various types of privatization

[3]However, traditional entrepreneurial opportunities appear to be available in certain segments of the market. For example, there may be significant remaining entrepreneurial opportunities for the provision of support services and education services for at-risk students (Hardy 1999).

[4]It should be noted that a public sector entrepreneur could be rewarded financially through promotion or increased compensation. However, such financial rewards are often controversial despite their private sector analogues. Great outcry, ultimately resulting in a disavowal of the agreement by the legislative body, was heard when a public administrator in the author's area was given a contract that allowed him to share in the "profits" of the governmental unit that resulted from his immensely successful

economic development efforts. Although he had clearly earned his incentive bonus the board chose to terminate the administrator on unrelated personal behavior grounds, and denied him the bonus he had already earned, while disavowing the original agreement itself.

[5]Indeed, many state constitutions and state statutes are very strict about the structure and operations of local school districts, including their ability to use public funds to contract out services, develop financial incentive programs, or engage in other entrepreneurial behavior (e.g., see Hanushek 1994). This is part of the reason why voucher programs and charter schools have required state legislative involvement apart from the financial aspects of their programs.

[6]Although individuals do prefer government to run at a surplus, there is a perception that services should be priced on a cost recovery basis, where cost generally includes no compensation for entrepreneurship in the public sector.

[7]An interesting result from the 1999 survey was that 54% of public school parents favored vouchers, whereas only 42% opposed them. This supports the notion of the linkage of support for vouchers to satisfaction with one's own public schools.

[8]It should be noted that under the Florida law, only children in schools deemed as failures are eligible for the state vouchers of $3,389 (*The American School Board Journal*, October 1999, p. 13).

[9]Over thirty states now have authorized charter schools.

[10]As noted by many members of the Corpus Christi community, reform is likely to produce results only over time. Thus, one must be careful to evaluate the program on an ongoing basis so as to fully appreciate the small gains being made and to ensure continued commitment in the face of slow progress that might even be occasionally interrupted by a temporary setback.

Epilogue
School Reform and the Twenty-First Century Public Administrator

Government has important roles to play in the market for and the reform of primary and secondary education. Public administrators must manage or actually perform all of government's roles, not only in the market for primary and secondary education but in the markets for all goods and services. This is a tremendous responsibility, and in most cases it means that public administrators have a great deal of influence over the path and ultimate success of reform efforts involving government's role in the economy. The public administrator's influence often extends to all three branches of government. A brief example will illustrate this point.

A planning director for a municipality is involved in and influences the legislative, executive, and judicial functions of local government. As a city staff member, the director has responsibility for producing studies and opinions that the legislative body can use to make policy decisions. After policy decisions are made, the director and other city staff have the responsibility of implementing and administering the policy. In cases of challenges to policy or its interpretation, the director and city staff are often asked to appear at hearings and trials as expert witnesses. Furthermore, public administrators often write the administrative regulations that courts are asked to enforce in disputes.

Under the status quo, administrators in primary and secondary school systems are asked to perform a similar set of roles. They act as staff on policy issues for the board of education, enforce board and other regulatory policies, and interact with the judicial system with respect to disciplinary, health and safety, and other issues.

Administration of organizations is a genuinely human endeavor, and public administrators are the significant human element of the management of public and nonprofit sector agencies, organizations, and governments. As such, the contemporary public administrator is likely to play a key role in guaranteeing movement down the path to successful primary and secondary school reform. As the financially based 1995 Chicago school reform has shown, administration and effective management can make a great difference in the viability of an organization and in the public perception of that organization.

The public perception of government agencies and of government itself is an important wild card in today's environment of continuing skepticism toward government, increased calls for accountability, demand for higher quality services, and cries for more cost efficiencies. Isolated incidents of official misconduct, or agency inefficiencies and lack of accountability, can be difficult for public sector entities—most uninvolved with such problems—to overcome. In the midst of school reform efforts in Illinois, the State Board of Education there has come under tremendous fire.

"Everything from employee conduct to the accountability of state Schools Supt. Joseph Spagnolo will come under scrutiny as the embattled agency tries to clean house" (Bils 1997, p. 6) This agency oversees approximately one-third of the total spending in Illinois schools. Historically, not only has its poor control over access to items in its warehouse (including new computers) been poor, but its central administration has been accused of reckless spending and making poor internal management decisions at the same time that the state has been pushing for greater accountability and fiscal soundness from local school districts. This has raised credibility problems within some constituencies. As might be expected, Illinois got a new state schools superintendent in mid-1998. Glenn "Max" McGee, the new superintendent, was well known in Illinois, as he had been superintendent in Lake County. McGee's reputation as a straight shooter, a talented administrator, and a reformer made him an excellent choice for the embattled department. He has been strongly supported in his brief tenure, despite massive reforms being undertaken in his short time on the job.

The State Board of Education, under the previous superintendent, played a leadership role in developing and approving the accountability measures for students and teachers that helped to make limited school finance reform possible in Illinois in late 1997. Although somewhat overwhelming, McGee's leadership has resulted in these reform measures being effectively implemented and fairly well received. This has also helped restore confidence in the Illinois State Board of Education.

Public administrators are generally the contact point with government for constituents.[1] The actions of public administrators often have a great deal to do with the image and credibility of government as seen through the eyes of the general public. On an issue as divisive and controversial as school reform, the public administrator's role in providing a good image for government and its programs is important and must be aggressively but honestly performed. The importance of this role is further enhanced to the extent that the government undertakes entrepreneurial activities.

Contemporary public administrators are a prime source of public sector entrepreneurial resources. Furthermore, the same public administrators are likely to have primary responsibility for creating and managing an environment in which entrepreneurship is encouraged and allowed to flourish. Many traditional public administration topics find application here: merit and incentive pay, performance measurement, risk management, and worker empowerment, just to mention a few. Public managers/entrepreneurs are likely to be challenged to apply all that they have learned about management and to experiment with many techniques and methods with which they have much less experience than mainstream methods. As traditional public administrators are increasingly asked to take responsibility for educational administration (or share in such responsibilities), a flexibility in techniques and a willingness to learn are likely to be attributes of the most successful managers. It seems reasonable to expect that contemporary public administrators will have primary responsibility for the success of the need to shift entrepreneurial responsibility to the public sector in the early stages of primary and secondary school reform. However, it will also likely be primarily public administrators that are responsible for implementing partnerships between the private sector and the public sector to share entrepreneurial interventions designed to further school reform.[2] The public administrator is also likely to have significant responsibility in carrying out government's roles as auditor and evaluator.

In the case of the auditor role, public administrators are likely to have primary responsibility for any internal audit functions in the public sector, in the same way that private managers take responsibility for this function in businesses. Even in the case of external or contracted audits, public administrators will have an extremely important role in the audit function. This will include service on, staffing for, and/or management of the audit committee; development of audit policy that places parameters on what is to be audited and by whom; and responsibilities for suggesting and implementing policy or procedural changes in the face of adverse or qualified audit findings.[3] In some cases the public administrator's actual training and job description may be as an auditor, but in many cases the auditor role will be merely one of the general responsibilities that a public administrator is expected to assume.[4] Such audit responsibilities are more likely to be required of a public administrator than a private administrator in a comparable position. There are a few reasons for this.

First, the nature of public sector activities means that more auditing is required than in the typical private sector business. Although financial audits of various types can be conducted and can provide useful information in the private sector, government and nonprofit programs rarely have the same ability to be measured in financial terms and have outputs that are much more difficult to define and measure than those of private sector firms. Second, the fact that public dollars are used in the finance of government activities means that in many cases greater scrutiny is given to governmental activities than if they were undertaken by a private firm. The same is often true of nonprofit organizations.[5] Thus, given the growing expectation of and demand for public sector accountability, auditing becomes that much more important. Third, for a given size of enterprise, the public sector generally has fewer administrative resources than many private sector firms, and requires more general skills of its administrators. For example, city managers have a great deal of financial management and policy responsibility, whereas the typical finance director must also be actively involved in the management of economic development policy, and the planning director must also have policy responsibilities in the fiscal effects of growth management.

Whether the difference between the public sector and the private sector on these points is large or small, public administrators clearly have significant responsibilities in carrying out the audit role. To the extent that this role is increased as suggested in our analysis, the public administrator will be that much closer to the heart of the reform effort. This is probably even more true of the evaluator function.

The evaluator function fundamentally asks "how well" rather than merely "did you." In an era of increasing attention to quality and to customer responsiveness, asking how well we do things and analyzing how we can do things better has great merit and support. In the private sector, evaluation in many ways comes easily. In terms of manufacturing, spoilage rates, purity of output, accuracy standards, and customer retention can all be used to measure how well a job is being done without a great deal of independent evaluation effort (at least in relative terms). In the case of the public sector and outputs like primary and secondary education, such objective means of quality mea- surement or satisfaction are typically not readily available and need to be developed. Evaluation is one of the core subjects taught in MPA programs owing to its importance and applicability in public administration.

As already noted, evaluation will be especially important in the dynamic and amorphous world of twenty-first century school reform. Given environ- mental idiosyncracies, as well as problems in fairly and objectively measuring outcomes, change and adjustment will be important components of primary and secondary school reform. For example, if standards are poorly defined or hard to measure, evaluation can help to point the appropriate direction and means for change. Public administrators are likely to play an important role on both sides of the reform equation: as evaluators on behalf of economic actors like the financier or auditor, and as evaluators and administrators on the front lines of education production who must ensure the implementation of the reform and respond to requested changes in the path of reform.

The training and familiarity of public administrators with evaluation, either from on the job experiences or through their academic training, is likely to make these managers a principal resource in the performance of the evaluation function. This may mean actual performance of evaluations or management of the evaluation process. In any case, the ball falls back into public administrators' laps when it comes to establishing the appropriate policy response to the findings from evaluations. Public administrators will have the responsibility for summarizing and interpreting the findings for their elected and appointed officials, recommending policy directions, and then implementing the legislative body's chosen direction. In the case of internal evaluations and those related to the administrator role, the public administrator may be responsible for managing a staff-level, rather than legislative body–level, response. Again, displaying responsiveness and overcoming the inertia against change remain the responsibility of the contemporary public administrator.

Even in the midst of a redefined and reduced regulatory role for government, the public administrator will still have the primary responsibility for the promulgation and enforcement of administrative guidelines. In many cases, this will be as a cooperative venture with the judicial system and its officers who have great interest in defending the Constitution's guarantees of equal protection and due process, as well as ensuring equal opportunity. Health and safety regulation is generally carried out on a day-to-day basis by governmental agencies and their public administrator employees. Such will continue to be the case under the path for school reform envisioned in this book.

Government can be expected to have a significant and meaningful role in school reform in the twenty-first century. The contemporary public administrator will have the primary responsibility for managing and implementing the newly defined roles for government in primary and secondary education and its reform.

NOTES

[1]Recall our discussion of the distributor role and the important customer service function inherent in this role.

[2]Even in the presence of possible partnerships, it will be the responsibility of the public sector to ensure the health of the entrepreneurial spirit in primary and secondary education until adequate opportunities and rewards can be identified so as to create a self-sustaining flow of private sector entrepreneurial activities in the market.

[3]At the same time, it is likely that public administrators rather than elected officials or appointed officials will be held primarily responsible for the existence of any adverse or qualified findings by an external auditor.

[4]In general, the auditor role is most likely to be a responsibility beginning with mid-management (e.g., supervisors and ancillary department heads) and continuing in some form to the highest administrative level in the organization.

[5]Consider the relative scrutiny given to chief executives in the public sector with respect to their travel budgets, as opposed to the chief executive officer of a similar sized business. The scrutiny is probably much higher in the public sector. Similarly, consider the relative debate over the level of compensation of the executives.

Bibliography

Aronson, J. Richard, and Eli Schwartz (eds.). *Management Policies in Local Government Finance,* 4th ed. Washington DC: ICMA, 1996.

Augenblick, John. "The Current Status of School Financing Reform in the States." In Van D. Mueller and Mary P. McKeown (eds.), *The Fiscal, Legal, and Political Aspects of State Reform of Elementary and Secondary Education,* pp. 3–20. Cambridge, MA: Ballinger Publishing, 1986.

Barlett, Donald L., and James B. Steele. *America: Who Stole the Dream?* Kansas City: Andrews and McMeel, 1996.

Barrows, Henry. *Problem-Based Instruction.* Presentation at the Illinois Mathematics and Science Academy Problem-Based Learning Conference. Aurora, IL, May 1990.

Bennett, Eric M., and Michael T. Peddle. "Assessment of Alternative Educational Delivery Technologies for Servicing Placebound Students." Report to the Fox Valley Educational Alliance, Center for Governmental Studies, Northern Illinois University, DeKalb, IL, August 1998.

Bils, Jeffrey. "Education Board to Clean Up Its Act." *Chicago Tribune,* March 20, 1997, Section 2, p. 6.

Billings, Jessica C., "Vouchers and Charters and Profits, Oh My!" *The Illinois School Board Journal,* 67 (January–February 1999): 15–18.

Borger, Judith Yates. "Baltimore May Fire Education Alternatives: Company Refuses Budget Cut." *St. Paul Pioneer Press,* November 23, 1995, pp. 1D, 2D.

Boud, David, and Grahame Feletti (eds.). *The Challenge of Problem-Based Learning.* New York: St. Martin's Press, 1991.

Brandon, Jeffrey E., and Basanti Majumdar. "An Introduction and Evaluation of Problem-Based Learning in Health Professions Education." *Community Health,* 20 (April 1997): 1–15.

Bridges, Edwin M. *Problem Based Learning for Administrators.* Eugene, OR: ERIC Clearinghouse on Educational Management, 1992.

Bushweller, Kevin. "Education Ltd.: Wall Street Eyes School Privatization," *The American School Board Journal,* 184 (March 1997): 19–21.

Carnevale, Anthony Patrick. *America and the New Economy: How New Competitive Standards Are Radically Changing the American Workplace.* San Francisco: Jossey-Bass, 1991.

Center on National Education Policy. "Do We Still Need Public Schools?" *School Board News,* April 30, 1996, pp. 5–7.

Charles, R. I., and E. A. Silver (eds.). *The Teaching and Assessing of Mathematical Problem Solving.* Hillsdale, NJ: Lawrence Erlbaum Associates, 1988.

Chen, Desiree. "Charter School Law Keeps Some Guessing: Districts Misread It, Legislator Says." *Chicago Tribune,* January 19, 1997, Section 4 (MetroDuPage), pp. 1–2.

Clotfelter, Charles T., and Helen F. Ladd, "Recognizing and Rewarding Success in Public Schools." In Helen F. Ladd (ed.), *Holding Schools Accountable: Performance-Based Reform in Education,* pp. 23–63. Washington, DC: Brookings Institution Press, 1996.

Cordes, Mark W. "Leapfrogging the Constitution: The Rise of State Takings Legislation." Manuscript, Northern Illinois University College of Law, 1996.

Courant, Paul N., Edward Gramlich, and Susanna Loeb. "A Report on School Finance and Educational Reform in Michigan." In Thomas A. Downes and William A. Testa (eds.), *Midwest Approaches to School Reform,* pp. 5–33. Chicago: Federal Reserve Bank of Chicago, 1995.

Davare, David W. "Courts Take a Narrow View of School Financing." *PA TIMES,* 17 (February 1, 1994): 8.

DeSpain, B. C., and Martha Livingston, "Roads to Reform: Will Charter Schools, Privatization, and Vouchers Lead to Better Schools? Board Presidents and Business Leaders Disagree." *The American School Board Journal,* 183 (July 1996): 17–20.

Downes, Thomas A., and William A. Testa. "Introduction." In Thomas A. Downes and William A. Testa (eds.), *Midwest Approaches to School Reform,* pp. i–x. Chicago: Federal Reserve Bank of Chicago, 1995.

Eisinger, Peter. *The Rise of the Entrepreneurial State.* Madison: University of Wisconsin Press, 1988.

Elmore, Richard F., Charles H. Abelmann, and Susan H. Fuhrman. "The New Accountability in State Education Reform: From Process to Performance." In Helen F. Ladd (ed.), *Holding Schools Accountable: Performance-Based Reform in Education,* pp. 65–98. Washington, DC: Brookings Institution, 1996.

Engstrom, John H., and Leon E. Hay. *Essentials of Accounting for Governmental and Not-for-Profit Organizations,* 5th ed. Boston: Irwin McGraw-Hill, 1999.

Federal Reserve Bank of Atlanta. "School Finance Takes Center Stage in the Southeast." *Regional Update: Federal Reserve Bank of Atlanta,* 7 (July–September 1994): 1–4.

Fennimore, Beatrice S. "Equity Is Not an Option in Public Education." *Educational Leadership,* 54 (October 1996): 53–55.

Ferguson, Janet M., and Paul Nochelski, S. J. "The Power of Letting Go." *The American School Board Journal,* 183 (April 1996): 37–39.

Fischel, William A.,"Does a Shift from Local to State Funding Improve Public Education?" Manuscript, Dartmouth College, December 29, 1997.

Gaebler, Ted. "Building Leadership." Entrepreneurial Government Workshops, Sacramento, CA: Double Vison Productions, 1996.

Gallagher, Shelagh A. "Problem-Based Learning: Where Did It Come From, What Does It Do, and Where Is It Going?" *Journal for Education of the Gifted,* 20 (Summer 1997): 332–62.

Gallagher, Shelagh A., William J. Stepien, and Hilary Rosenthal. "The Effects of Problem-Based Learning on Problem Solving." *Gifted Child Quarterly,* 36 (1992): 195–200.

Gittell, Marilyn, and Laura McKenna, with Victoria Allen, Anthony Hightower, Michelle Ronda, Kirk Vandersall, and Barbara Winfree Louis. "Activist Governors and a New Conservative Direction for Education." Manuscript, Howard Samuels State Management and Policy Center, CUNY, April 1997.

Hanushek, Eric A. et al. *Making Schools Work: Improving Performance and Controlling Costs.* Washington, DC: Brookings Institution, 1994.

Hardy, Lawrence. "Pay to Play: Do Fees for School Sports Undermine the American Promise of Free Public Education?" *The American School Board Journal,* 184 (August 1997): 25–27.

————"A Private Solution," *The American School Board Journal,* 186 (April 1999): 46–48.

Harrington-Lueker, Donna. "The High-Flyer Falls: Cast Out from Baltimore and Hartford, Privatization Pioneer Education Alternatives Inc. is Down But Not Drowned." The *American School Board Journal,* 183 (April 1996): 26–33.

————"The Politics of Reform." *The American School Board Journal,* 183 (August 1996): 30–33.

Haynes, V. Dion. "Oregon Tests School Reform: Teachers Caught in Debate over Grades, Standards," *Chicago Tribune,* September, 4, 1996, Section 1, p. 13.

Henry, Tamara, "Schools Support Some Privatization: But Most Maintain Academic Control," *USA Today,* January 10, 1996, p. D1.

Hickrod, G. Alan, Larry McNeal, Robert Lenz, Paul Minorini, and Linda Grady. "Status of School Finance Constitutional Litigation: The Boxscore." <www.coe.ilstu.edu>, last updated April 1997.

Holder, William W. "Financial Accounting, Reporting, and Auditing," in J. Richard Aronson and Eli Schwartz (eds.), *Management Policies in Local Government Finance* 4th ed. Washington, DC: ICMA, 1996.

Hyman, David N. *Public Finance: A Contemporary Application of Theory to Policy,* 5th ed. Fort Worth: Dryden Press, 1996.

Illinois Association of School Boards. "School Enrollment Hits All-Time High." *School Board News Bulletin,* October 1999, p. 4.

"Innovations 1994: Government at Its Best." *Governing,* October 1994, pp. 36–45.

Jones, Rebecca. "Buyer Beware: Avoiding Privatization's Pitfalls," *The American School Board Journal,* 184 (March 1997): 21–23.

———— "Getting Tough in Chicago." *The American School Board Journal,* 184 (July 1997): 24–26.

Jouzaitis, Carol. "Charter Schools Sprout in Search for Better Way." *Chicago Tribune,* January 23, 1997, Section 1, pp. 1, Back Page.

Kingdon, John. *Agendas, Alternatives, and Public Policies,* 2nd ed. New York: Harper-Collins, 1995.

Kirby, Joseph A. "Hartford Failure Raises Doubts about School Privatization," *Chicago Tribune,* January 28, 1996, Section 1, p. 8.

Kramer, Rita. "Putting Public Schools to the Test." *Wall Street Journal,* February 15, 1995, p. A.

Krugman, Paul. *The Age of Diminished Expectations.* Cambridge, MA: MIT Press, 1994.

Ladd, Helen F. (ed.). *Holding Schools Accountable: Performance-Based Reform in Education.* Washington, DC: Brookings Institution Press, 1996.

Mackey, Scott. "The Property Tax Predicament." *State Legislatures,* August 1994, pp. 23–26.

Mandel, Michael J., Richard A. Melcher, Dori Jones Yang, and Mike McNamee. "Will Schools Ever Get Better?" *Business Week,* April 17, 1995, pp. 64–68.

Mandin, Henry, Allan Jones, Wayne Woloschuk, and Peter Harasym. "Helping Students Learn to Think Like Experts When Solving Clinical Problems." *Academic Medicine,* 72 (March 1997): 173–79.

McConnell, Campbell R., and Stanley L. Brue. *Economics: Principles, Problems, and Policies,* 11th ed. New York: McGraw-Hill, 1990.

McGuire, Therese J. "Issues and Challenges in State and Local Finances." *Policy Forum* (University of Illinois Institute of Government and Public Affairs), 8, no. 3 (1995).

McKinney, Joseph. "Charter Schools: A New Barrier for Children with Disabilities." *Educational Leadership,* 54 (October 1996): 22–25.

Mellish, Xander. "Liberty Bonds for Inner-City Schools." *The Wall Street Journal,* April 8, 1997, p. A22.

Mikesell, John L. *Fiscal Administration: Analysis and Applications for the Public Sector,* 4th ed. Pacific Grove, CA: Brooks/Cole, 1995.

Molnar, Alex. "Charter Schools: The Smiling Face of Disinvestment." *Educational Leadership,* 54 (October 1996): 9–15.

Murnane, Richard J., and Frank Levy. "A Civil Society Demands Education for Good Jobs," *Educational Leadership,* 54 (February 1997): 34–36.

Murphy, Joseph. "Why Privatization Signals a Sea Change in Schooling," *Educational Leadership,* 54 (October 1996): 60–62.

Nathan, Joe. "Chartered Public Schools: A Brief History and Preliminary Lessons." In Thomas A. Downes and William A. Testa (eds.), *Midwest Approaches to School Reform,* pp. 98–109. Chicago: Federal Reserve Bank of Chicago, 1995.

————"Early Lessons of the Charter School Movement." *Educational Leadership,* 54 (October 1996): 16–21.

National Center for Education Statistics. *Digest of Education Statistics, 1997.* Washington, DC: Government Printing Office, 1999.

National Education Association. *Estimates of School Statistics, 1997.* <www.nea.org/publiced/edstats>, accessed April 8, 2000.

Newkirk, Ralph W. *Chaykin CPA Review: Auditing.* Needham Heights, MA: Ginn Press, 1988.

Odden, Allan R. "School Finance and Education Reform: An Overview." In Allan R. Odden (ed.), *Rethinking School Finance: An Agenda for the 1990s,* pp. 1–40. San Francisco: Jossey-Bass, 1992.

Osborne, David, and Ted Gaebler. *Reinventing Government.* Reading, MA: Addison-Wesley, 1992.

Pearson, Rick. "Legislators Get Message, Pass School-Fund Bill." *Chicago Tribune,* December 3, 1997, pp. 1, Back Page.

Peddle, Michael T. "Frustration at the Factory: Employer Perceptions of Workforce Deficiencies and Training Needs." Forthcoming *Journal of Regional Analysis & Policy,* 1999.

Peddle, Michael T., and Eric M. Bennett. "Local Employer Needs Assessment for the Fox Valley Educational Alliance." Research Report, Center for Governmental Studies, Northern Illinois University (DeKalb, IL), December 1997.

Perry, Joellen, and Dan McGraw. "In Cleveland, It's Back-to-School Daze," *U.S. News Online.* <www/usnews.com>, September 6, 1999.

Posavac, Emil J. and Raymond G. Carey. *Program Evaluation: Methods and Case Studies,* 4th ed. Englewood Cliffs, NJ: Prentice-Hall, 1992.

Ravitch, Diane. *National Standards in American Education: A Citizen's Guide.* Washington, D.C.: Brookings Institution Press, 1995.

Reich, Robert B. *Tales of a New America.* New York: Vintage Books, 1987.

——*The Work of Nations.* New York: Vintage Books, 1991.

Reschovsky, Andrew. "Public School Funding and the Two-Thirds Commitment." *The LaFollette Policy Report,* 6 (Fall 1994): 1–4.

Reschovsky, Andrew, and Michael Wiseman. "School Finance Reform: The View from Wisconsin." In Thomas A. Downes and William A. Testa (eds.), *Midwest Approaches to School Reform,* pp. 34–53. Chicago: Federal Reserve Bank of Chicago, 1995.

Ritter, John. "City Head of the Class in School Standards" *USA Today,* April 18, 1997, p. 4A.

Rosen, Harvey S. *Public Finance* 3rd ed. Homewood (IL): Irwin, 1992.

Saks, Judith Brody. "The Voucher Debate: Should Public Money Follow Kids to Private Schools?" *The American School Board Journal,* 184 (March 1997): 24–28.

——. "A Mixed Report Card for Charter Schools." *The American School Board Journal,* 186 (August 1999): 4–8.

Scavo, Carmine, Maurice Simon, and Renata Siemienska. "Perceptions of School/Community Relations: A Cross-National Perspective." Paper presented at Urban Affairs Association Annual Meeting, Louisville, KY, April 1999.

Schrag, Peter. "'F' Is for Fizzle: The Faltering School Privatization Movement," *The American Prospect,* 26 (May–June 1996): 67–71.

Sharp, David. "Your Kids' Education Is At Stake," *USA WEEKEND,* March 14–16, 1997, pp. 46.

Simon, Herbert A. "The Structure of Ill Structured Problems." *Artificial Intelligence,* 4 (1973): 181–201.

Smith, Ron, and Steve Sherrell, "Mileposts on the Road to a Certificate of Initial Mastery." *Educational Leadership,* 54 (December 1996/January 1997): 46–50.

State of Wisconsin, Division of Executive Budget and Finance. "Budget in Very Brief." Madison: State of Wisconsin, February 1997.

Stepien, William J., and Sharon L. Pyke. "Designing Problem-Based Learning Units." *Journal for the Education of the Gifted,* 20 (Summer 1997): 380–400.

Stewart, Felicia Ratliff. "The Urban School Superintendency: A Case Study of Ruth Love in Chicago." Ed.D. dissertation, Department of Leadership and Educational Policy Studies, Northern Illinois University, December 1996.

Stigler, George J. "The Case, If Any, for Economic Literacy." *The Journal of Economic Education,* Summer 1983: 60–66.

"Supreme Court Upholds Wisconsin School Vouchers." *Law Street Journal,* November 10, 1998 <www.lawstreet.com/journal>, accessed October 19, 1999.

Task Force on School Finance. "Report of the Illinois Task Force on School Finance." Springfield, IL: Illinois State Board of Education, January 1993.

"Teachers Are the Key." *The Illinois School Board Journal,* 67 (March–April 1999): 10–12.

Thomas, Robert P. *Economics: Principles & Applications.* Fort Worth: Dryden Press, 1990.

Uline, Cynthia L. "The Privatization of Public Schools: Breaking the Mold in Hartford, Connecticut." *Journal of Research and Development in Education,* 31 (Spring 1998): 176–89.

United States General Accounting Office. "Education Reform: School-Based Management Results in Changes in Instruction and Budgeting." Report to Congressional Committees GAO/HEHS-94-135. Washington, DC: GAO, August 1994.

———. "Regulatory Flexibility in Schools: What Happens When Schools Are Allowed to Change the Rules?" Report to Congressional Committees GAO/HEHS-94-102. Washington, DC: GAO, April 1994.

Varian, Hal R. *Microeconomic Analysis,* 2nd ed. New York: W. W. Norton, 1984.

Voss, James F., Terry R. Greene, Timothy A. Post, and Barbara C. Penner. "Problem Solving Skill in the Social Sciences." In G. H. Bower (ed.), *The Psychology of Learning and Motivation: Advances in Research Theory,* Vol. 17, pp. 165–212. New York: Academic Press, 1983.

"Voucher Plan for Schools Struck Down: Wisconsin Judge Halts Expansion of Program." *Chicago Tribune,* January 15, 1997, p. 8.

Ward, James G., W. Bradley Colwell, and James L. Kestner. "The Committee for Educational Rights v. Edgar: Law or Politics in School Finance Reform?" *Policy Forum* (University of Illinois Institute of Government and Public Affairs), 8, no. 2 (1995).

White, Sammis B. "Baltimore City Public Schools: Experimenting with Private Operation." In Thomas A. Downes and William A. Testa (eds.), *Midwest Approaches to School Reform,* pp.224–38. Chicago: Federal Reserve Bank of Chicago, 1995.

White, Sammis B., Peter Maier, and Christine Cramer, *Fourth-Year Report of the PAVE Scholarship Program.* Milwaukee: Urban Research Center, University of Wisconsin—Milwaukee, 1996.

Williams, Lori C., and Lawrence E. Leak. "School Privatization's First Big Test: EAI in Baltimore." *Educational Leadership,* 54 (October 1996): 56–59.

Witte, John F., and Christopher A. Thorn. "Who Chooses? Voucher and Interdistrict Choice Programs in Milwaukee." In Thomas A. Downes and William A. Testa (eds.), *Midwest Approaches to School Reform,* pp. 127–55. Chicago: Federal Reserve Bank of Chicago, 1995.

Wong, Kenneth K., and Gail L. Sunderman. "Redesigning Accountability at the Systemwide Level: The Politics of School Reform in Chicago." In Thomas A. Downes and William A. Testa (eds.), *Midwest Approaches to School Reform,* pp. 162–87. Chicago: Federal Reserve Bank of Chicago, 1995.

Wood, Robert. (Policy Director for Wisconsin governor Tommy Thompson). Presentation to Rockford, Illinois, Chamber of Commerce, April 28, 1997.

Worthington, Rogers. "Limits on School Aid Are Upheld." *Chicago Tribune,* March 16, 1995, Section 1, p. 3.

Wortley, Jay. "Michigan School Finance Reform." Presentation to Rockford, Illinois Chamber of Commerce. Michigan Senate Fiscal Agency, April 28, 1997.

Young, Jeffrey. *Forbes Greatest Technology Stories.* New York: John Wiley & Sons, 1998.

Youngman, Joan. "State Challenges to Land-Based Local Funding of Public Education," *Landlines* (Lincoln Institute of Land Policy), July 1995, pp. 1–3.

Zinser, Jana. *Reinventing Education,* Denver: National Conference of State Legislatures and Jobs for the Future, 1994.

Index

affirmative action, 216. *See also* discrimination; equal educational opportunity and access

AICPA. *See* American Institute of Certified Public Accountants

Alaska, 122

Alliance for Schools That Work, 46, 47, 56n13, 77
    approach in Baltimore, 47. *See also* Baltimore, Maryland; Education Alternatives, Inc.

allocation mechanisms, 59–61, 69, 71n9, 159, 160
    government-based, 61
    in a mixed economy, 26n1

allocation of education services by private providers, 63, 65, 160. *See also* distributor/allocator role in primary and secondary education

allocator of last resort, 65, 66, 69, 70, 160

allocator role, 59–61, 65, 66, 69, 70, 159, 160. *See also* distributor/allocator role

allocator/distributor role. *See* distributor/allocator role

alternative dispute resolution mechanisms, 32

Alternative Public Schools, Inc. (APS), 45, 54

alternative schools, 65, 72n15, 72n17. *See also* at-risk students; charter schools

Alternative Schools, Inc., 42

American Federation of Teachers (AFT), 47, 97

American Heritage Dictionary, 41

American Institute of Certified Public Accountants, 84, 85

analytical tools, 1. *See also* market role assessment

anticompetitive behavior, 31, 32, 38n8, 44, 45, 56n9. *See also* antitrust laws; government regulation of private behavior

antitrust laws, 31, 32, 38n8. *See also* anticompetitive behavior; government regulation of private behavior

Archdiocese of Indianapolis, 122, 125. *See also* parochial schools; public subsidy of private and parochial schools

Arizona, 122, 206n15

Armey, Dick, 141

art exhibitions in galleries, 20. *See also* classification of goods and services

asymmetric information, 12–14, 17, 32, 87. *See also* market failures

AT&T, 135

at-risk students
    education of, 65, 72n15, 72n17. *See also* charter schools; Peoria Alternative Charter School; privatization of special education and at-risk services

attributes of a good or service. *See* classification of education as an economic good; classification of goods and services

audit and evaluation of educational outcomes, 39n22, 89, 91, 93–96, 102, 157, 210, 216, 217, 222–225. *See also* auditor role in primary and secondary education; evaluator function in primary and secondary education

audit committee, 89, 90, 93, 223

audit function, 83, 90–92, 102
    centrality to school reform, 96, 210, 216, 217
    credibility of, 83, 84, 89, 157. *See also* auditor role

audit policy, 223

audit procedures, 95
    distinguished from auditing standards, 85. *See also* generally accepted auditing standards

audit program, 90, 91

audit provisions
    as part of contracts for services, 90

allocation of local resources under, 201. *See also* Chicago school reform
Chicago White Sox, 191n21
children as education consumers, 32, 34, 36
implications for regulator role, 155
cigarette taxes, 188
circular flow model, 8, 15n5, 73
explained, 15n5, 80n1
citizenship training, 91, 95. *See also* social benefits of education
city managers, 41
as entrepreneurs, 141, 142. *See also* public sector entrepreneurs
civil rights, 36, 39n19, 66, 91, 93. *See also* discrimination; equal educational opportunity and access; equal opportunity; universal educational access and opportunity
class size, 35, 39n22, 55
classification of education as an economic good, 23–26, 112
classification of goods and services, 17–21, 23, 24, 27n16. *See also* classification of education as an economic good
classroom interns, 48
classroom teachers
as producers of education, 75, 76
Cleveland, Ohio, 214
Clinton administration, 88
Clinton, Bill, 193, 195, 196. *See also* Goals 2000
Clotfelter, Charles T., 200
collective bargaining, 32, 34, 97, 100, 177, 184
collective benefits of education. *See* social benefits of education
collective choice decisions, 12, 13, 37n2, 64, 107, 109
collective choice institutions, 64, 107, 109, 117, 120, 121, 139. *See also* collective choice decisions
collective choice mechanisms. *See* collective choice institutions

collusion and predatory behavior, 13, 31, 44. *See also* anticompetitive behavior
Colorado, 52. *See also* Colorado Springs, Colorado
Colorado Springs, Colorado, 42
Colwell, W. Bradley, 111
community "buy in," 67
Committee for Educational Rights v. Edgar (1996), 38n12, 111, 189n1
Committee for Public Education v. Nyquist (1973), 180
comparative advantage
of government administration of education, 55, 159. *See also* administrator role; administrator role in primary and secondary education
compelling public interest, 34
compensation of victims, 38n16
competition for public schools. *See* competition in primary and secondary education
competition in primary and secondary education, 31, 32, 37n4, 37n8, 55, 81n11, 112, 117, 147, 160–162, 166, 167, 184, 189, 203, 215, 218
compliance and outcomes audits
as part of charter renewal for charter schools, 96, 97. *See also* charter schools; compliance audits
compliance audits, 84, 86, 87, 93, 96, 157, 216
Comprehensive Employment and Training Act (CETA), 11, 62
Comprehensive Test of Basic Skills (CTBS), 48
compulsory attendance laws, 34
compulsory collective finance of education, 78, 117–121, 181
controversy over revenue tools used, 119. *See also* compulsory system of collective finance
compulsory collective finance of merit goods, 118, 119

Indiana, 200. *See also* Indianapolis,
  Indiana
Indianapolis, Indiana, 122, 125
individual valuation of a good or service. *See* willingness to pay
Individuals with Disabilities Education
  Act (IDEA), 72n16
indoor concerts, 20. *See also* classification of goods and services
inertia against policy changes
  broken by radical reforms, 212
information
  importance in quality market choices,
    70, 72n24. *See also* asymmetric
    information
information flows
  between producer and consumer,
    159
  self regulation by market mecha-
    nisms, 72n24
information in market for primary and
  secondary education
  template for providing to consumers,
    70
initial endowment of resources, 10
innovation
  fostering of by institutional entrepre-
    neurs, 135, 136
  institutionalization of, 134–136. *See
    also* entrepreneur role
Innovations in American Government
  Awards, 137
Innovations in State and Local Government awards, 137

innovators and innovation, 134, 135.
  See also entrepreneur role
instructional technologies, 68
insurance and tort systems, 32, 38n9
integrated delivery systems, 37n3
integrated learning system software, 48,
  56n13, 57n15. *See also* Tesseract
  Program
integration of public schools, 66
intellectual property
  protection of, 9

intergovernmental fiscal relations, 110,
  111, 114, 123, 125, 141, 194. *See
  also* intergovernmental grants
intergovernmental grants, 61, 111, 125,
  194. *See also* intergovernmental
  fiscal relations
interjurisdictional competition,
  141–144
intermediate reform efforts, 52
internal auditors and audits, 84, 86,
  88–90, 92, 96, 157, 194, 223. *See
  also* internal audits in primary and
  secondary education
internal audits in primary and
  secondary education, 92, 93, 96,
  101, 157, 194, 223. *See also* internal auditors and audits
internal controls, 84, 85, 90–92
internal rate of return, 4
internal reforms, 53
Iowa Tests of Basic Skills, 105n31, 202

Job Training Partnership Act (JTPA), 11
Johnson Controls World Services,
  56n13. *See also* Alliance for
  Schools That Work
Jones, Allan, 3
Jones, Rebecca, 45, 201, 202
Jouzaitis, Carol, 203

Katzenberg, Jeffrey, 137
Kennedy School of Government, 137
Kentucky, 52, 200
Kestner, James L., 111
KinderCare, 76
Kingdon, John, 6n3
Kirby, Joseph A., 50, 51
KPMG, Peat Marwick, 56n13. *See also*
  Alliance for Schools That Work
Kramer, Rita, 88
Krugman, Paul, 11

labor market power of employers, 32
Ladd, Helen F., 194, 200
Lake Oswego, Oregon, 198–200
Leak, Lawrence E., 46, 48, 49